ISLAM AND AUSTRALIA'S FUTURE

Faith, Freedom, and the Challenge of Cultural Incompatibility

ROBERT GRIFFITH

GRACE AND TRUTH PUBLISHING
PO Box 338, Gunnedah NSW 2380 Australia
www.graceandtruthpublishing.com.au

All Bible quotes are from the New International Version (NIV) except where otherwise stated.

NEW INTERNATIONAL VERSION (NIV), Copyright 1973, 1978 and 1984 by international Bible Society. Used by permission of Zondervan Publishing House. All rights reserved.

Other version quotes are from:

AMPLIFIED BIBLE (AMP), Copyright © 1954, 1958, 1962, 1964, 1965, 1987 by The Lockman Foundation. Used by permission.

ENGLISH STANDARD VERSION (ESV), Copyright © 2001 by Crossway Bibles, a division of Good News Publishers. Used by permission. All rights reserved.

NEW AMERICAN STANDARD BIBLE (NASB), Copyright © 1960, 1962, 1963, 1968, 1971, 1972, 1973, 1975, 1977, by The Lockman Foundation. Used by permission.

NEW KING JAMES VERSION (NKJV), Copyright © 1979, 1980, 1982, by Thomas Nelson Inc. Used by permission. All rights reserved.

THE MESSAGE (MSG), by Eugene Peterson, Copyright © 1993, 1994, 1995, 1996, and 2000. Used by permission of NavPress Publishing Group. All rights reserved.

REVISED STANDARD VERSION (RSV), Copyright © 1973, by Thomas Nelson Inc. Used by permission. All rights reserved.

Quotes in square brackets are the author's comment.

ISBN 978-1-7642635-1-1

TABLE OF CONTENTS

1. INTRODUCTION

Australia stands at a cultural and spiritual crossroads. We are a nation blessed with freedom, prosperity, and relative peace. We can pride ourselves for being tolerant, diverse, and welcoming to people from around the world. Our multicultural experiment has, in some ways, enriched our society with food, art, ideas, and talent drawn from every continent. Yet beneath this success story lies a deep tension that cannot be ignored: the growing presence of Islam and the serious challenge it poses to the faith, freedom, and cultural fabric of our nation.

This book is not written to stir up fear or hatred. It is written to tell the truth as honestly as possible, to face the facts with clarity, and to ask hard questions that many in our society would prefer to avoid. Islam is not another religion which is quietly existing alongside many in the public square. It is rather a comprehensive worldview that claims authority over every aspect of human life: spiritual, political, cultural, and legal. Many Australian Muslims live peacefully, integrate successfully, and are making positive contributions to society. But the foundation of Islam remains in sharp conflict with the foundations of Australian life.

At the heart of this conflict lies a serious clash of worldviews. Christianity, which shaped the Western legal and cultural order, proclaims that Jesus Christ is the eternal Son of God, and through His death and resurrection, He has brought salvation by grace to all who believe. Islam denies this, reducing Jesus to a prophet and rejecting the cross as central to redemption.

Where Christianity teaches, *"It is by grace you have been saved, through faith — and this is not from yourselves, it is the gift of God — not by works, so that no one can boast …"* (Ephesians 2:8–9), Islam teaches a religion of works and submission to a legal code that governs every detail of life. These are not small differences; they are absolute contradictions. Both faiths make exclusive claims that can never be reconciled without one surrendering its core truths. But the issue is not simply theological. Australia is also confronted with serious cultural incompatibility.

Our democracy is built upon the separation of church and state, the rule of law, freedom of conscience, and equality before the law. Sharia law, in its traditional form, conflicts with all these principles. It prescribes unequal treatment of men and women, penalties for leaving Islam, and blasphemy laws that silence any dissent. In nations where Islamic communities have grown large enough to press for accommodation, we have seen attempts to establish parallel legal structures, creating a two-tiered system of justice. While Australia has not reached that point (yet), the pressure will increase if the growth in the Muslim population in our country continues at its current rate.

Immigration itself must be a vital part of this whole discussion. Australia has always been a land of newcomers, and yet history shows us that successful integration will require newcomers to embrace the values of the host nation, not seek to replace them. In parts of Europe, we have seen what happens when integration fails: segregation, cultural enclaves, and social unrest. If we are wise, we will learn from these lessons before it is too late.

At the same time, we must also recognise the human dimension. Muslims are not our enemies. They are people created in the image of God, many of whom long for peace, stability, and a better future. As Christians, we are called to love our neighbours, including Muslims, with compassion and humility. Yet love does not mean blindness to truth. The most loving thing we can do is to speak the truth clearly, to defend the freedoms that protect us all, and to hold out the hope of the gospel of Jesus Christ.

This book is therefore written with three aims:

➤ *To expose the theological incompatibility of Islam and Christianity.* These two faiths are not different paths to the same God, but opposing systems with irreconcilable claims about truth, salvation, and the identity of Jesus Christ.

➤ *To examine the cultural clash between Islam and Australian society.* Our freedoms — religious liberty, equality, and democracy — are precious gifts that must not be compromised in the name of tolerance.

➤ *To chart a way forward for Australia.* We must ask what policies, cultural attitudes, and Christian responses are necessary to protect our nation's future while also reaching out to Muslims with love and the life-changing message of Jesus Christ.

The words of Jesus Christ remain as relevant today as when He first spoke them: *"Then you will know the truth, and the truth will set you free."* (John 8:32). Truth must be the foundation of our response — truth about Islam, truth about our culture, and above all, truth about Jesus Christ. Only then will we be equipped to face the challenges ahead with courage, clarity, and hope.

What follows now is a detailed analysis of Islam and its current and future impact on Australia. It is complex , but the key issues at the centre of this whole challenge are not difficult to grasp and you will see them pop up multiple times in almost every chapter of this book. This is not duplication; it is rather an intentional focus on those issues within lots of different contexts. This is really important, and by the end of this book, you will have a firm grasp on the serious problem which our nation is facing as we journey deeper into the 21st century.

The Australia I was born into almost seventy years ago simply does not exist anymore. So much has changed and a lot of that change has occurred in only the past couple of decades. Our nation is under attack – not from guns, bombs and missiles (yet), but from an ideology and a worldview which is diametrically opposed to everything this great southland was built upon.

Australia cannot afford to sleepwalk into its future. We are a young nation in a world that is changing at a breathtaking speed. The choices we make in the coming years will determine whether freedom, truth, and peace endure, or whether they are eroded by the relentless advance of incompatible values. Our foundations are strong, but they are cracking before our eyes.

If you want to stand against the spiritual and cultural tsunami which awaits us, then you should take this book very seriously.

2. THE FOUNDATION OF ISLAM

The life of Muhammad and the birth of Islam

To grasp the foundations of Islam, it is essential to study the life of its founder, Muhammad. Christianity rests upon the life, death, and resurrection of Jesus Christ, who is both Saviour and Lord. Islam, however, is built almost entirely on the revelations and example of Muhammad who is regarded not as divine but as the final prophet, *"the seal of the prophets,"* whose life and teaching provide the authoritative blueprint for every aspect of Muslim existence.

The *Qur'an,* believed by Muslims to be the very word of God, and the *Hadith,* the recorded sayings and actions of Muhammad, remain the twin sources governing all Islamic life. To this day, more than a billion Muslims around the globe seek to emulate Muhammad's example, making his biography essential for those who wish to understand the religion he founded.

Arabia before Islam

The world into which Muhammad was born was fragmented and tribal. Arabia in the sixth century was not a unified nation, but a vast desert peninsula dotted with clans and tribes bound together by kinship and bloodline. These tribes often fought one another in long-standing feuds, but they also established fragile alliances for trade and protection from enemies. Wealth came through commerce, particularly along caravan routes linking Arabia with Syria, Persia, and Yemen.

Religion was equally diverse. Most Arabs then were polytheistic, worshipping a variety of gods and goddesses. Each tribe had its own deities, and idols were housed in local shrines. At the centre of this religious life was Mecca, where the Kaaba — a cube-shaped structure — stood as a sacred site. The Kaaba housed over three hundred idols representing tribal gods, and annual pilgrimages to the shrine brought much prosperity to Mecca. Alongside this polytheism, however, existed Jewish and Christian communities scattered throughout Arabia.

These monotheistic faiths were respected by some Arabs and viewed with suspicion by others. Stories of biblical figures such as Abraham, Moses, and Jesus were known, but often distorted through oral tradition.

This cultural and religious environment provided fertile soil for Muhammad's message. On the one hand, there was significant dissatisfaction with idolatry and tribal corruption; on the other, there was curiosity about the monotheism practiced by Jews and Christians.

It was into this world of competing ideas, violence, and spiritual searching that Muhammad was born around the year 570 AD, a year remembered in Arab tradition as the *"Year of the Elephant,"* when an Ethiopian army attempted unsuccessfully to attack Mecca.

The early life of Muhammad

Muhammad was born into the Quraysh, the most powerful tribe of Mecca, though his immediate family was not wealthy. His father, Abdullah, died before he was born, and his mother, Amina, died when he was only six. Orphaned at such a young age, he came under the care of his grandfather, and later his uncle Abu Talib. Life in the harsh Arabian desert cultivated resilience, and Muhammad grew up aware of both hardship and the importance of tribal loyalty.

As a youth, Muhammad worked as a shepherd and later became involved in the caravan trade. His honesty and reliability earned him the nickname *al-Amin* — *"the trustworthy one."* These qualities helped him gain a reputation in Mecca, which proved vital in the years ahead when he claimed to be a prophet.

At the young age of 25, Muhammad married Khadijah, a wealthy widow who was 15 years older than him. Their marriage was stable and affectionate, producing several children. Khadijah provided financial stability and encouragement, playing a key role when Muhammad later began to receive what he claimed were revelations from God.

The first revelations

When Muhammad was about 40 years old, he developed a habit of retreating to a cave near Mecca to meditate and reflect upon spiritual matters. According to Islamic tradition, it was during one of these retreats that he received his first revelation. The angel Gabriel allegedly appeared to him and commanded him to, *"Recite!"* Terrified, Muhammad fled home, but Khadijah reassured him, convincing him that his experience was genuine.

Over the next 23 years, Muhammad supposedly received many revelations that addressed theology, morality, social order, and law. These revelations were memorised by his followers and later compiled into what became the Qur'an. The early messages proclaimed that there was only one God—Allah—and that idolatry was a very grave sin. Muhammad called his people to abandon their many gods and worship Allah alone, warning of a coming day of judgment when all would be held accountable.

Opposition and persecution

At first, Muhammad shared his message with only a small circle of friends and family. His wife Khadijah, his cousin Ali, and his friend Abu Bakr were among the first converts. However, as he began to preach publicly, resistance grew. The Quraysh, who controlled Mecca's religious life, viewed Muhammad's call to monotheism as a direct threat to their power and to the lucrative trade surrounding the Kaaba.

As more people converted, especially those from lower classes and vulnerable groups, the opposition only intensified. Converts were ridiculed, beaten, and sometimes killed. One of the earliest martyrs, Sumayyah, was executed for refusing to renounce her faith. Muhammad himself was mocked and accused of being a madman or a sorcerer. Yet despite this persecution, he remained resolute. During these years, the Qur'an's revelations focused heavily on the oneness of God, the coming judgment, and moral accountability. They also drew on biblical narratives, though often in altered form, presenting Muhammad as the restorer of the true faith of Abraham.

The Hijrah: migration to Medina

By 622 AD, hostility in Mecca had reached a dangerous level. Muhammad and his followers faced boycotts, many threats, and constant harassment. Eventually, a group from the city of Yathrib (later known as Medina) invited Muhammad to serve as an arbitrator for their disputes. Seeing an opportunity for safety and influence, Muhammad and his followers then migrated to Medina. This event, known as the *Hijrah*, was so significant that it marks the beginning of the Islamic calendar.

In Medina, Muhammad's role expanded dramatically. No longer a persecuted preacher, he now became the leader of a growing community. He established laws, settled disputes, and presided over both religious and political matters. His revelations now began to address governance, social order, and warfare, laying the foundation for Islam as a complete system of life.

Conflict with Mecca

The move to Medina certainly didn't end the conflict with Mecca. Tensions escalated into armed confrontation. The first major battle occurred at Badr in 624 AD. Though heavily outnumbered, Muhammad's forces won a decisive victory. This triumph was interpreted as divine confirmation of Muhammad's mission, boosting morale among his followers.

The following year, however, the Muslims suffered a setback at the Battle of Uhud. Muhammad himself was injured, and many of his followers were killed. Yet his leadership endured, and the community regrouped. In 627 AD, Mecca launched a massive assault on Medina, leading to the so-called *Battle of the Trench*. Muhammad employed defensive tactics, including digging a trench around the city, and successfully repelled the attack.

These conflicts demonstrated Muhammad's shift from prophet to military commander. Warfare became not only a matter of survival but also a means of spreading Islam. The revelations during this period began to address issues of combat, rules of engagement, and the treatment of enemies.

Conquest of Mecca

In 628 AD, Muhammad negotiated a treaty with the Quraysh, allowing Muslims to make pilgrimage to Mecca. However, when the Quraysh violated the terms of the agreement, Muhammad responded with force. In 630 AD, he marched on Mecca with a large army. The city surrendered, and Muhammad entered the Kaaba, destroyed its idols, and rededicated it to the worship of Allah alone.

This event cemented Muhammad's authority all across Arabia. Tribes submitted to him, either through genuine conversion or pragmatic allegiance. Within two years, most of the Arabian Peninsula had embraced Islam.

Final years and death

In 632 AD, Muhammad made his final pilgrimage to Mecca, delivering a long sermon which summarised his teachings and emphasised the unity of the whole Muslim community. Shortly afterward, he fell ill and died in Medina at the age of 62. His death left a leadership vacuum. The community chose Abu Bakr, one of his closest companions, as the first caliph, or successor. This decision set in motion the caliphate system and eventually led to the Sunni-Shia divide over rightful leadership.

Muhammad's legacy

Muhammad's legacy is complex and far-reaching. For Muslims, he is the perfect example of human conduct. Every aspect of his life — from how he prayed to how he governed, fought, and even ate — serves as a model. His actions are preserved in the Hadith, collections of reports about his sayings and his deeds, which alongside the Qur'an form the basis of Sharia law.

For outsiders, however, Muhammad's combination of religious authority and political power raises questions. Unlike Jesus Christ, who declared in John 18:36, *"My kingdom is not of this world,"* Muhammad established a kingdom by conquest and law. This distinction is central to us understanding why Islam has always been as much a political order as a religion.

The importance of context

The world Muhammad lived, in shaped his message profoundly. Arabia's tribalism, its trade routes, and its religious diversity all influenced the whole development of Islam. Muhammad's call to monotheism challenged the dominant polytheism, while his establishment of governance in Medina reflected the need for order in a fragmented society. The fusion of spiritual teaching and political authority that began with Muhammad continues to define Islam today and remains a point of tension with Western societies which separate religion from the state.

The Qur'an and Hadith

If Muhammad's life is the historical foundation of Islam, the Qur'an and Hadith are its textual and doctrinal foundations. Together they form the bedrock of Muslim belief, practice, and law. The Qur'an is regarded by Muslims as the very word of God, uncreated and eternal, delivered verbatim through the angel Gabriel to Muhammad over the course of 23 years.

The Hadith are Muhammad's collected sayings, approvals and actions, preserved through oral transmission and later written compilations. These two sources together govern every sphere of Muslim life—from worship and personal morality to politics, law, and war.

Understanding the Qur'an and Hadith is therefore essential for anyone seeking to grasp the nature of Islam. Not only do they provide spiritual guidance but also establish a worldview that is comprehensive, legalistic, and communal. They explain why Islam has never been merely a private faith but a system that claims to regulate every aspect of life.

The Qur'an: origins and compilation

According to Islamic tradition, the Qur'an was revealed to Muhammad between 610 and 632 AD. The revelations came piecemeal, most often in response to specific events—whether questions posed by followers, challenges from opponents, or circumstances arising in battle and governance.

Some passages are poetic and lyrical, focusing on God's majesty and the coming Day of Judgment. Others are entirely practical, addressing issues of law, warfare, marriage, and inheritance.

During Muhammad's lifetime, the revelations were memorised by his companions and written down on whatever materials that were available — parchment, bones, palm leaves, and stone. Oral recitation was considered to be the most important means of preservation, and many early Muslims committed large portions to memory. The Qur'an itself repeatedly calls on believers to *"recite"* and *"remember,"* reflecting its oral character.

After Muhammad's death in 632 AD, the community faced the urgent need to preserve the Qur'an. Many of those who had memorised it had been killed in battle, and there was fear that portions might be lost.

Abu Bakr, the first caliph, ordered a written compilation. This early collection, according to tradition, was entrusted to Zayd ibn Thabit, one of Muhammad's scribes.

A more decisive step came later under the third caliph, Uthman (r. 644–656). By this time, Islam had expanded rapidly across Arabia and beyond, and variations in recitation began to emerge. To standardise the text, Uthman then commissioned an official version and ordered that all other versions be destroyed. This Uthmanic recension became the foundation of the Qur'an as it is known today.

Muslims believe that the Qur'an we have now is identical to the one that was revealed to Muhammad, preserved perfectly by divine providence. For them, it is not merely inspired but also dictated word-for-word by God.

Unlike the Bible, which was written by multiple authors over centuries and in various literary genres, the Qur'an is viewed as a single, unified revelation, delivered in Arabic and meant to always remain in that language. Translations are considered interpretations rather than true Qur'ans.

Structure and content of the Qur'an

The Qur'an consists of 114 chapters, called surahs, which vary greatly in length. Some are only a few verses long, while others fill dozens of pages. The surahs are not arranged chronologically but roughly by length, with the longer ones placed earlier and the shorter ones later. This arrangement makes it difficult for outsiders to follow any narrative flow, as the text often shifts abruptly between topics.

Thematically, the Qur'an addresses three major concerns:

1. *The Oneness of God (Tawhid):* The Qur'an relentlessly asserts that Allah is one, without partners or equals. Idolatry (shirk) is denounced as the greatest sin.

2. *Prophethood and Revelation:* The Qur'an affirms a line of prophets beginning with Adam and including figures such as Noah, Abraham, Moses, and Jesus. Muhammad is presented as the final prophet, completing and correcting the messages of his predecessors.

3. *Judgment and the Afterlife:* The Qur'an warns repeatedly of the coming Day of Judgment when all people will be held accountable. Paradise and hell are described in vivid detail, motivating obedience through hope and fear.

Alongside these strong theological themes, the Qur'an contains numerous legal and practical instructions. It addresses matters such as marriage, divorce, inheritance, dietary laws, warfare, and punishments for crime. These commands provide the seed for the development of Sharia law.

The doctrine of abrogation

One striking feature of the Qur'an is the doctrine of abrogation (*naskh*). Because revelations were given over time in response to changing circumstances, some later verses supersede earlier ones. For example, early verses revealed in Mecca emphasise patience and peaceful endurance, while later verses revealed in Medina include commands to fight against unbelievers. Muslim scholars developed the principle that the later revelation always abrogates (rescinds) the earlier when contradictions arise.

This principle has profound implications. It means that the more militant verses of the Qur'an, which were revealed in Medina when Muhammad was a political and military leader, carry greater weight than the peaceful verses of the Meccan period. While some Muslims emphasise the earlier verses to portray Islam as peaceful, traditional jurisprudence has often prioritised the later ones, legitimising violence in defence of the faith.

The Qur'an and the Bible

For Christians, one of the most important questions is how the Qur'an relates to the Bible. The Qur'an acknowledges the Torah (given to Moses), the Psalms (given to David), and the Gospel (given to Jesus) as genuine revelations from God. However, it claims that Jews and Christians corrupted all these scriptures, necessitating a final revelation through Muhammad. Thus, while the Qur'an honours biblical figures, it reshapes their stories to fit Islamic theology.

For example, Abraham is presented as a proto-Muslim who also rejected idolatry and was neither a Jew nor a Christian. Jesus is affirmed as a prophet and miracle worker, but His crucifixion is denied. The Qur'an insists that He was not killed but that it only appeared so, rejecting the central truth of the Christian faith. In contrast to the Bible's message of salvation by grace through faith, the Qur'an emphasises submission to Allah and obedience to His commands as the only means to gain divine acceptance.

This radical divergence underscores why the two faiths cannot be reconciled. As Paul writes in Galatians 1:8, *"But even if we or an angel from heaven should preach a gospel other than the one we preached to you, let them be under God's curse!"* For Christians, the Qur'an represents precisely such an alternative gospel, one that distorts the person and work of Jesus Christ.

The Hadith: preserving Muhammad's example

While the Qur'an is considered to be the direct word of God, the Hadith occupy a parallel position of authority because they record the example of Muhammad. Muslims look to Muhammad not only for what he taught but also for how he lived.

The Hadith therefore provide guidance on everything from prayer rituals and dietary rules to warfare, governance, and family life. The Hadith are collections of reports about what Muhammad said, did, or approved of. Each report consists of two parts: the *isnad* (chain of transmission) and the *matn* (content of the report). Islamic scholars developed elaborate methods to evaluate the reliability of Hadith, classifying them as authentic (*sahih*), good (*hasan*), weak (*da'if*), or completely fabricated.

The most influential compilations include those of al-Bukhari, a Muslim whose collections are regarded by Sunni Muslims as the most reliable. Other important collections include those of Abu Dawood, al-Tirmidhi, al-Nasa'i, and Ibn Majah. Together, these six collections form the core of Sunni Hadith literature. Shia Muslims, however, preserve different compilations, reflecting their distinctive theological emphases.

Authority of the Hadith

The Hadith are indispensable to Islam because they clarify and expand the Qur'an. For example, the Qur'an commands all Muslims to pray but does not specify how. The details of the five daily prayers—the number of units, the postures and the recitations—are all found in the Hadith. Similarly, the Qur'an commands *zakat* (almsgiving) but does not prescribe precise amounts; the Hadith provide that information.

Moreover, the Hadith form the basis for vast portions of Sharia law. Rules concerning marriage, divorce, inheritance, criminal penalties, and political leadership are derived not only from the Qur'an but also from the precedents established by Muhammad. In this way, the Hadith have elevated Muhammad's conduct to normative status for all Muslims. As one Hadith clearly and famously declares, *"Whoever obeys the Messenger obeys Allah."*

This elevation of Muhammad's example stands in stark contrast to Christianity. The New Testament records the words and deeds of Jesus, but His authority rests not merely in His example but in His divine identity and redemptive work.

The apostle Paul could say, *"Follow my example, as I follow the example of Christ ..."* (1 Corinthians 11:1), because Christ is the standard. In Islam, however, it is Muhammad's example — down to the smallest detail of his daily life — that becomes binding.

Variations and controversies

The Hadith tradition, however, is not without its controversy. Because they were collected more than a hundred years after Muhammad's death, critics argue that many Hadith reflect later political and theological debates rather than authentic memories. Even within Islam, scholars rejected thousands of Hadith as fabrications. The sheer volume — tens of thousands of reports — makes it difficult to distinguish genuine traditions from invented ones.

The differences between Sunni and Shia Hadith further highlight the role of politics in shaping Islamic tradition. Shia Muslims revere Hadith transmitted through the family of Muhammad, particularly Ali and his descendants, while Sunnis emphasise reports from a much wider community of companions. These differences reinforce the divisions that fractured the Muslim world after Muhammad's death.

Qur'an and Hadith together

Taken together, the Qur'an and Hadith form the dual foundation of Islam. The Qur'an provides the overarching revelation of God's will, while the Hadith supply the practical application through Muhammad's example. Sharia law arises from the interplay between these two sources, interpreted through the consensus of scholars (*ijma*) and reasoning by analogy (*qiyas*).

This symbiosis explains why Islam is not merely a religion in the Western sense of the word. Whereas Christianity distinguishes between the sacred and the secular, Islam does not. The Qur'an and Hadith address not only spiritual devotion but also politics, law, warfare, and family relations, because, for Muslims, religion encompasses the whole of life because Muhammad's example is seen as relevant to every detail of existence.

This comprehensive scope creates challenges in societies like Australia which separate religion from the state. When devout Muslims appeal to Sharia as a divine system, they are never thinking of religion as a private matter of conscience but as a public code meant to govern all of life. The tension between this vision and the Western model of pluralism and democracy will be a recurring theme throughout this book.

The Five Pillars of Islam and the Islamic worldview

If Muhammad's life provides the historical foundation and the Qur'an and Hadith supply the textual foundation, then the *Five Pillars of Islam* constitute the practical foundation of Muslim life. These practices, required of every Muslim who is physically and financially able, are more than mere rituals. They form the daily framework of devotion, establish the rhythm of community life, and create a powerful sense of identity that binds Muslims together across nations and cultures.

To understand the Islamic worldview, one must understand how these pillars shape not only individual piety but also the collective consciousness.

The centrality of the Five Pillars

The Five Pillars are:

1. **Shahada** (Confession of Faith)
2. **Salat** (Prayer)
3. **Zakat** (Almsgiving)
4. **Sawm** (Fasting during Ramadan)
5. **Hajj** (Pilgrimage to Mecca)

Each of these is deeply rooted in the Qur'an and Hadith, and each reflects Muhammad's vision for a community united by worship, discipline, and loyalty to Allah.

The Pillars are not optional extras or cultural customs; they are obligations that define what it means to be a Muslim. Failure to observe them is considered disobedience to God, and in many Muslim societies, neglecting them brings social stigma or even legal consequences.

Whereas Christianity emphasises transformation of the heart by the grace of God through Jesus Christ, Islam will emphasise outward submission through prescribed acts of devotion. These acts reinforce the meaning of the very word *"Islam,"* which simply means *"submission."* The Five Pillars thus express Islam's essence: obedience to Allah's will, demonstrated through ritual practice.

Shahada: *The Confession of Faith*

The first pillar is the *Shahada,* the testimony that *"There is no god but Allah, and Muhammad is his messenger."* This simple statement carries profound implications. To utter the Shahada sincerely is to become a Muslim; it is the gateway into the faith. It is recited daily in prayers, inscribed on flags, and whispered into the ears of newborns.

The Shahada is more than a creed; it is a declaration of allegiance. By affirming Allah as the only God, the believer rejects all other gods, idols, or rivals. By confessing that Muhammad is the messenger of Allah, the believer accepts his authority as final and binding. Together, these two affirmations shape the Muslim worldview: Allah is supreme, and Muhammad's example is the standard.

This stands in stark contrast to Christianity's confession, which centres on Jesus Christ. The apostle Paul wrote, *"If you declare with your mouth, 'Jesus is Lord,' and believe in your heart that God raised him from the dead, you will be saved"*(Romans 10:9). For Christians, salvation rests not on allegiance to a prophet but on the person and work of the Son of God. The Christian confession affirms Jesus' deity and resurrection, truths explicitly denied by the Shahada. Thus, from the very outset, the two faiths proclaim irreconcilable messages.

Salat: *The Discipline of Prayer*

The second pillar, *Salat,* is the practice of praying five times every day at prescribed times: dawn, noon, mid-afternoon, sunset, and night.

Each prayer consists of a sequence of recitations and physical postures — standing, bowing, kneeling, and prostrating — all are performed while facing Mecca. The prayers are announced publicly by the call to prayer (*adhan*), traditionally chanted from a mosque's minaret but now also broadcast electronically.

The discipline of Salat shapes Muslim life in a profound way. It structures the day around acts of devotion, constantly reminding the believer of their submission to Allah. In the Muslim-majority countries, all businesses and schools adjust their schedules to accommodate prayer times. In cities across the world, one can witness Muslims unrolling prayer mats in workplaces, parks, or airports, orienting themselves toward Mecca.

The prayers themselves are largely fixed, consisting of Qur'anic recitations and praises of Allah. While private supplication is permitted, the essence of Salat is strict obedience to a ritual form established by Muhammad himself. This repetition reinforces unity: wherever one travels in the Muslim world, the prayers are the same.

For Christians, this ritualised prayer differs significantly from biblical teaching. Jesus actually warned us against mechanical repetition: *"And when you pray, do not keep on babbling like pagans, for they think they will be heard because of their many words."* (Matthew 6:7). Christian prayer is relational, rooted in intimacy with God as Father, made possible through Christ. While all Muslims bow toward Mecca, Christians are invited to draw near to the throne of grace through Jesus, who intercedes for them. The difference is not merely in its form but also in its theology: one emphasises a pre-prescribed ritual, the other emphasises personal communion.

Zakat: *The Obligation of Almsgiving*

The third pillar, *Zakat*, requires Muslims to give a fixed portion of their wealth — traditionally 2.5% of savings every year — to support the poor, the needy, and the wider community. Unlike voluntary charity, Zakat is considered a religious duty, purifying wealth and demonstrating submission to Allah's command.

The Qur'an frequently emphasises generosity as a sign of one's faithfulness, condemning hoarding and greed. In practice, Zakat often funds welfare, but also religious institutions, mosques, schools, and sometimes political or military causes.

The Hadith expand on who qualifies as recipients, dividing them into categories such as the poor, debtors, and those engaged in jihad. Thus, Zakat is not merely philanthropy; it is a system for sustaining the Islamic community.

This pillar reinforces Islam's communal orientation. Wealth is never seen as personal property but as a trust from Allah to be shared with the *ummah,* which is the global Muslim community. By mandating this financial support, Islam ensures that even personal resources serve the collective.

Christian teaching also emphasises generosity, but with a crucial difference. Giving in Christianity is voluntary and motivated by love, not legal compulsion. Paul wrote, *"Each of you should give what you have decided in your heart to give, not reluctantly or under compulsion, for God loves a cheerful giver."* (2 Corinthians 9:7). Whereas Zakat is a tax-like obligation enforced by religious duty, Christian giving flows from gratitude for God's grace.

Sawm: *Fasting During Ramadan*

The fourth pillar, Sawm, requires Muslims to fast during the month of Ramadan, from dawn to sunset each day. The fast includes abstaining from food, drink, smoking, and sexual relations. Nights are marked by communal meals, prayer, and recitation of the Qur'an. The fast commemorates the month which Muhammad allegedly received his first revelations.

Ramadan is one of the most visible expressions today of Muslim identity. Entire societies adjust their rhythms to accommodate the fast. Restaurants close during daylight hours, workplaces shorten shifts, and evenings come alive with feasting and celebration. For Muslims, the fast fosters self-discipline, empathy for the poor, and solidarity with the community.

The intensity of Ramadan contrasts quite sharply with Christian fasting practices. Jesus assumed His followers would fast but warned against doing so for show: *"When you fast, do not look sombre as the hypocrites do, for they disfigure their faces to show others they are fasting. Truly I tell you, they have received their reward in full."* (Matthew 6:16). Christian fasting is voluntary and focused on humility before God, not adherence to a communal law. Moreover, Christianity emphasises freedom in Christ, where external observances cannot earn righteousness.

Hajj: *Pilgrimage to Mecca*

The fifth pillar, Hajj, requires every Muslim who is physically and financially able to make a pilgrimage to Mecca at least once in their lifetime. During the Hajj, pilgrims wear simple garments that strip away all distinctions of wealth and status, symbolising unity before Allah. The rituals will include circling the Kaaba, walking between the hills of Safa and Marwah, standing in prayer on the plain of Arafat, and performing symbolic acts such as stoning pillars that represent Satan.

The Hajj is a very powerful unifying event, drawing millions of Muslims annually from right across the globe. It reinforces the centrality of Mecca and the Kaaba, binding diverse peoples into one ummah. For many Muslims, the Hajj is the spiritual climax of their whole life, a demonstration of devotion and a source of immense prestige.

For Christians, the concept of pilgrimage takes on a different meaning. The New Testament teaches that believers are pilgrims and strangers on earth, looking forward to a heavenly city (Hebrews 11:13–16).

Worship is not tied to one sacred location but is made possible through Christ, who once told a Samaritan woman, *"A time is coming when you will worship the Father neither on this mountain nor in Jerusalem… true worshipers will worship the Father in the Spirit and in truth."*(John 4:21,23). The exclusivity of Mecca as the centre of devotion highlights again the divergence between the two faiths.

The worldview shaped by the Five Pillars

Together, the Five Pillars shape a distinctly Islamic worldview. They instil a rhythm of life oriented around submission to Allah, reinforce community identity, and ensure loyalty to the ummah above everything else. Each pillar weaves the individual into the collective fabric of Islam, diminishing personal autonomy in favour of communal conformity.

➢ The **Shahada** defines belief and allegiance.
➢ The **Salat** structures the daily routine and reinforces unity.
➢ The **Zakat** redistributes wealth and sustains the community.
➢ The **Sawm** disciplines the body and unites the faithful in shared sacrifice.
➢ The **Hajj** binds Muslims together across nations in a common ritual centre.

These practices function not only as personal devotions but as mechanisms of social cohesion. They remind Muslims that their primary identity is not national or ethnic but religious. A Muslim in Indonesia, Nigeria, or Australia prays in the same way, recites the same Shahada, and aspires to the same pilgrimage. This global uniformity is a source of great strength, enabling Islam to transcend cultural boundaries and maintain cohesion across many centuries. But it is also the source of tension in pluralistic societies like Australia.

Whereas Christianity adapts to many cultural settings without demanding uniform rituals, Islam prescribes specific forms that resist assimilation. The Five Pillars do not easily bend to local customs; they create a culture of their own. This explains why Islamic communities often remain distinct within non-Muslim societies, maintaining parallel structures and resisting full integration.

3. ISLAM AND SOCIETY

The origins of Sharia

The word *Sharia* has entered the vocabulary of modern political debate, yet many misunderstand what it means. In the West it is often reduced to images of harsh punishments, veiled women, or parallel courts in immigrant communities. However, for Muslims, Sharia is far more than a set of laws: it is the divine path revealed by God for human life.

The Arabic term *sharī'a* literally means *"a path to water,"* evoking the image of a life-giving way in the desert. To follow Sharia is to walk the path that leads to God's approval and eternal reward.

From its earliest days, Islam has claimed to be not only a religion of worship but a comprehensive system governing every aspect of life. Sharia is the codification of this claim. It encompasses worship, family relations, commerce, politics, and criminal justice. It is not merely about punishing wrongdoing but about structuring society according to God's will. To understand Islam as it functions historically and today, one must understand the origins of Sharia.

Sharia in the Qur'an

The Qur'an contains the seed of Sharia. While it is often poetic and theological, it also includes numerous legal instructions. These range from rules about marriage, divorce, and inheritance to strict regulations about diet, warfare, and punishments. For example, the Qur'an commands amputations for theft (Surah 5:38), lashes for fornication (Surah 24:2), and retaliation for murder (Surah 2:178). It also gives detailed guidance about fasting, pilgrimage, contracts, and testimony.

Unlike the Bible, which distinguishes between moral law, civil law, and ceremonial law within the covenant with Israel, the Qur'an presents all its commands as direct obligations for the community. There is very little sense of historical context or temporary provision. Because the Qur'an is believed to be God's uncreated word, its legal commands are regarded as timeless.

Yet the Qur'an alone was not sufficient to create a full legal system. Its instructions are scattered and often general. To fill in the details, Muslims therefore turned to the life and sayings of Muhammad, preserved in the Hadith.

The Hadith and legal development

The Hadith became indispensable in shaping Sharia. While the Qur'an commands Muslims to pray, the Hadith explain how many times to pray, the exact words to use, and the physical postures. While the Qur'an commands zakat, the Hadith specify percentages and categories. While the Qur'an commands fasting, the Hadith clarify when to begin and end, what breaks the fast, and how to make up missed days.

Beyond ritual, the Hadith also provide important precedents for governance, commerce, and criminal justice. Because the prophet Muhammad was also the political leader, his actions in Medina became models for the law. If Muhammad approved a business contract, it was deemed permissible. If he punished an adulterer by stoning, that became an acceptable penalty. If he waged war and divided the spoils, his actions established norms for jihad.

By combining Qur'an and Hadith, early Muslims began to build a body of legal precedent. But disputes soon arose. How should contradictory Hadith be reconciled? How should new situations be judged when no explicit text existed? These questions gave rise to the science of jurisprudence (*fiqh*).

The role of the early jurists

After Muhammad's death in 632 AD, the community faced the challenge of applying revelation to new contexts. The caliphs sought guidance from Muhammad's companions, who had witnessed his actions and memorised his sayings.

As Islam expanded beyond Arabia into Persia, Syria, and Egypt, new problems emerged: How should Muslims deal with non-Muslims under their rule? What contracts could they accept from conquered peoples? What taxes were appropriate?

The companions and their successors offered rulings based on their memory of Muhammad's example, their understanding of the Qur'an, and their reasoning.

Over time, centres of legal thought were established in cities like Medina, Kufa, Basra, Damascus, and later Baghdad. Scholars debated, recorded judgments, and began to compile principles.

The jurists developed four primary sources of Sharia:

1. **The Qur'an** – considered the highest authority.
2. **The Sunnah** (example of Muhammad in the Hadith) – second only to the Qur'an.
3. **Ijma** (consensus of scholars) – agreement among qualified jurists carried weight.
4. **Qiyas** (analogical reasoning) – extending principles from known cases to new ones.

These sources allowed the law to expand beyond the text of the Qur'an. For instance, while the Qur'an forbids wine, jurists extended the prohibition to all intoxicants by analogy.

Schools of Islamic law

By the eighth and ninth centuries, distinct schools of law (*madhahib*) emerged within Sunni Islam. Each school developed its own methodology while recognising the legitimacy of the others. Four major schools eventually became dominant:

1. **Hanafi School** – Founded by Abu Hanifa (d. 767) in Kufa, it became known for flexibility and use of reasoning. It spread widely in the Abbasid Empire and remains influential in South Asia, Turkey, and Central Asia.

2. **Maliki School** – Founded by Malik ibn Anas (d. 795) in Medina, it emphasised the practice of the people of Medina as a standard, believing their proximity to Muhammad preserved authentic tradition. It is prominent in North and West Africa.

3. **Shafi'i School** – Founded by al-Shafi'i (d. 820), who systematised the principles of jurisprudence. He gave greater weight to Hadith and developed rigorous methods for evaluating them. The school dominates in East Africa, Southeast Asia, and parts of the Middle East.

4. **Hanbali School** – Founded by Ahmad ibn Hanbal (d. 855), it took the strictest approach, relying heavily on literal interpretations of the Qur'an and Hadith while minimising reasoning. It later influenced Wahhabism in Saudi Arabia.

Shia Islam developed its own legal tradition, centred on the authority of the imams, descendants of Ali. The most prominent Shia school, the Ja'fari school, continues to this day shaping Shia communities in Iran, Iraq, and Lebanon.

Key principles of Sharia

From these schools and sources, Sharia soon developed into a comprehensive system. Several key principles stand out:

- **Divine Origin:** Sharia is considered God's law, not man-made. Human rulers and parliaments cannot alter it fundamentally.

- **Comprehensiveness:** Sharia covers every aspect of life, from worship to contracts to criminal justice. There is no division between sacred and secular.

- **Obligation and duty:** Muslims are judged not only by belief but by obedience to Sharia. Actions are categorised as obligatory, recommended, permissible, disliked, or forbidden.

- **Community and consensus:** The ummah, the Muslim community, is bound together by adherence to Sharia. Consensus among scholars carries authority, reinforcing communal conformity.

- **Adaptability within boundaries:** Through analogy and consensus, jurists could apply principles to new issues. Yet adaptability always remained constrained by the foundational texts.

Sharia as an all-encompassing system

By the time we reached the ninth century, Sharia had crystallised into a comprehensive way of life. It provided Muslims with a sense of certainty: every action could be classified, every dispute adjudicated, and every contract validated. Law was not seen as separate from religion but as an expression of devotion to God. To obey Sharia was to obey Allah; to disobey it was to rebel against Him.

This fusion of law and religion is foreign to Western traditions. Christianity, drawing on Jesus' teaching that His kingdom is not of this world, distinguished between the authority of God and the authority of Caesar. Paul urged believers to obey governing authorities while recognising their ultimate allegiance to Christ. By contrast, Islam never separated the two. Muhammad was both prophet and ruler, and Sharia preserved that integration.

Early implementation in Islamic empires

As Islamic empires expanded across the world, Sharia was implemented alongside customary practices. In those conquered territories, non-Muslims were allowed to maintain their own laws in personal matters but were subject to Sharia in areas of taxation, public order, and restrictions on religious expression. The *dhimmi* system required Jews and Christians to pay a special tax (*jizya*) in exchange for protection, while also accepting social and legal disabilities.

The enforcement of Sharia varied by region and era, but its presence as an authoritative framework was constant. Judges (*qadis*) were appointed to adjudicate cases, issuing rulings based on Qur'an, Hadith, and juristic precedent. Over time, vast legal manuals were compiled, covering topics from ritual purity to international relations.

The functioning of Sharia in Muslim life

Sharia is very often spoken of as though it were simply a list of punishments or a separate legal code competing with Western systems. In reality, it is far broader.

Sharia provides the framework for worship, family life, business, politics, and criminal justice. For devout Muslims, it is the lens through which every aspect of life is meant to be viewed. Unlike Western legal systems that limit themselves to public order and civil rights, Sharia claims jurisdiction over both outward actions and inward intentions. The purpose of Sharia is not merely to regulate society but to cultivate submission to Allah in every imaginable domain.

Sharia in personal and family law

Perhaps the most visible aspect of Sharia in daily life is its strict regulation of family matters. Marriage, divorce, child custody, and inheritance are all governed by detailed rules derived from the Qur'an and Hadith.

Marriage in Sharia is viewed as a contract, not a sacrament. A valid contract requires the consent of the bride's guardian, the presence of witnesses, and the payment of a dowry (*mahr*) by the groom to the bride. Polygamy is permitted, with a man allowed to marry up to four wives, provided he treats them all equally. Women, however, are limited to one husband.

Interfaith marriages are restricted: Muslim men may marry Jewish or Christian women, but Muslim women are generally forbidden from marrying non-Muslim men.

Divorce is also asymmetrical. A man may repudiate his wife by pronouncing *"talaq"* (I divorce you) three times, after which the marriage is dissolved. A woman, by contrast, must seek divorce through the courts and demonstrate grounds such as cruelty, desertion, or failure of provision. Custody laws often favour the father once children reach a certain age, reflecting the patriarchal assumptions of the system.

Inheritance is another area where gender inequality is built into the law. The Qur'an specifies that the male heirs receive twice the share of the female heirs (Surah 4:11). This principle reflects the assumption that men must bear financial responsibility for families, yet in practice it often leaves women disadvantaged.

These family laws are enforced not only in Muslim-majority countries but also informally within all Muslim communities worldwide. In Western nations, some Muslim families apply Sharia rules internally, even if they are not legally recognised by the state. This can create conflicts when community expectations clash with national laws about equality and individual rights.

Sharia in criminal law

When outsiders think of Sharia, what often comes to mind are its harsh criminal penalties. These include punishments such as amputation for theft, stoning for adultery, and flogging for fornication or drinking alcohol. These penalties are known as *hudud* (fixed punishments), considered divinely mandated and therefore immutable.

Hudud crimes include:

➤ *Theft* (punished by amputation of the hand, Surah 5:38).
➤ *Adultery and fornication* (punished by 100 lashes, Surah 24:2; Hadith prescribe stoning for married adulterers).
➤ *False accusation of adultery* (punished by 80 lashes, Surah 24:4).
➤ *Drinking intoxicants* (punished by flogging, based on Hadith).
➤ *Apostasy* (leaving Islam, punished by death, based on Hadith).
➤ *Banditry or armed robbery* (punished by death, crucifixion, or exile, Surah 5:33).

In addition to hudud, Sharia recognises *qisas* (retaliation) for crimes such as murder and bodily harm. The principle of *"an eye for an eye"* applies, though victims' families may choose to accept compensation (*diyya* or blood money) instead. Finally, judges (*qadis*) may impose *ta'zir* punishments at their discretion for offences not covered by hudud or qisas. The severity of hudud penalties shocks many Western observers, but for Muslims they represent divine justice. Because they are rooted in the Qur'an and Hadith, they are seen as unchangeable.

In practice, however, these punishments are not enforced in every situation; evidentiary requirements are strict, and many Muslim governments hesitate to apply them fully due to strong international pressure. Nevertheless, the principle that these penalties remain God's law is deeply ingrained, creating tension with modern notions of human rights.

Sharia in governance and politics

From the earliest days in Medina, Muhammad combined his spiritual leadership with his political rule. This integration of religion and governance became embedded in Islamic tradition. Sharia therefore includes political principles alongside personal and criminal law.

At the heart of Islamic governance is the concept of the *ummah*, the community of believers. The ruler is expected to govern in accordance with Sharia, ensuring justice and obedience to Allah's commands. Unlike Western democracies, sovereignty does not ultimately rest with the people but with God. Human rulers are accountable not to electorates but to divine law.

This principle has some far-reaching implications. It means that Islamic societies have historically struggled to separate religion from politics. Secularism, as developed in the West, is often viewed as alien or even hostile. In classical theory, the caliph served as both the political and the religious leader, uniting the community under Sharia. Even when caliphates fragmented, rulers continued to claim legitimacy by upholding Sharia.

In modern times, Islamist movements have sought to revive this integration. Groups such as the Muslim Brotherhood in Egypt, Jamaat-e-Islami in South Asia, and Hizb ut-Tahrir across many countries, call for governments to implement Sharia fully. For them, democracy is acceptable only if it leads to Sharia, not if it replaces it.

This explains why attempts at secular democracy in many Muslim-majority countries have faced resistance or collapse.

Gender and Sharia

One of the most controversial aspects of Sharia concerns its treatment of women. While some Muslims argue that Sharia elevates women compared to pre-Islamic Arabia, the reality is that it codifies structural inequality.

Women's testimony in court is often valued at half that of a man (Surah 2:282). Inheritance shares are likewise unequal. Dress codes enforce modesty, with varying degrees of compulsion depending on the society. In countries such as Saudi Arabia, Afghanistan, or Iran, strict interpretations require women to cover from head to toe, and violations may be punished by law.

Educational and employment opportunities for women are also shaped by Sharia. While some Muslim nations allow women broad participation, others restrict them to roles within the home. The rationale is often that Sharia defines complementary roles for men and women, with men as protectors and providers. From a Christian perspective, this inequality contradicts the biblical affirmation of equal worth before God.

The apostle Paul wrote in Galatians 3:28, *"There is neither Jew nor Gentile, neither slave nor free, nor is there male and female, for you are all one in Christ Jesus."* While roles may differ, salvation and dignity are equal in Christ. Sharia, by contrast, enshrines male authority as a matter of divine law, limiting women's autonomy.

Apostasy and blasphemy

Perhaps the clearest conflict between Sharia and Western values appears in its treatment of apostasy and blasphemy. The Qur'an itself does not prescribe a worldly penalty for leaving Islam, but the Hadith repeatedly command death for all apostates.

For example, one Hadith records Muhammad saying, *"Whoever changes his religion, kill him."* This tradition has been accepted by classical jurists across the Sunni schools. Blasphemy — defined as insulting Muhammad, the Qur'an, or Islam — is also treated as a capital offence in many interpretations.

In some Muslim-majority countries, such as Pakistan, blasphemy laws are enforced by the state, often resulting in death sentences or mob violence. Even in Muslim minority contexts, accusations of blasphemy can spark outrage, protests, or violence, as seen in the reaction to cartoons depicting Muhammad in Europe.

These provisions reveal a fundamental incompatibility with the Western principles of freedom of religion and freedom of speech. In Sharia, faith is not a just matter of individual choice but of community loyalty. To leave Islam or criticise its foundations is seen not as personal liberty but as treason against the community and rebellion against God.

Sharia as social control

The combined effect of these laws is to create a system of social control that extends beyond individual conscience. Sharia is not content to guide personal spirituality; it demands conformity in public life. Community pressure reinforces this, as honour and shame play a powerful role in enforcing compliance.

This explains why Muslims who migrate to Western societies will very often continue to live under Sharia norms within their communities, even when national law does not require it. Family and community expectations maintain adherence, and informal councils sometimes arbitrate disputes according to Sharia rather than state law. For devout Muslims, this is never optional, it is obligatory: God's law always takes precedence over man's law.

Sharia in the modern world

Sharia is not simply a relic of medieval history. It continues to shape societies, politics, and individual lives across the world today. For some Muslims, Sharia represents a timeless system that must be applied fully, regardless of any cultural or historical changes. For others, it is an ideal that must be adapted to modern realities. The debates within Islam over the role of Sharia are quite fierce, and the outcomes profoundly affect international relations, human rights, and the experience of Muslim minorities in non-Muslim lands.

To understand Islam's challenge to Western societies like Australia, one must examine how Sharia functions today in the contemporary world. The twentieth century witnessed the rise of modern nation-states in the Muslim world; many carved out of the ruins of the Ottoman Empire or European colonialism. These states faced the question: what role should Sharia play in national law? The answers varied widely.

In some countries, Sharia was codified as the basis of legislation. Saudi Arabia, for example, declares the Qur'an and Sunnah as its national constitution. Its legal system relies heavily on Hanbali jurisprudence, enforcing hudud punishments and strict gender segregation. Iran, after the 1979 revolution, instituted a Shia theocracy in which clerics wield ultimate power, and laws derive directly from Ja'fari jurisprudence.

Other countries took a more hybrid approach. Egypt, Pakistan, and Nigeria, for instance, adopted elements of Sharia alongside civil codes inherited from colonial rule. In these systems, Sharia often governs family law — marriage, divorce, and inheritance — while secular courts handle commerce and criminal matters. Yet the boundary between the two is often contested, with Islamist movements pushing hard for fuller implementation.

Other nations attempted secularisation. Turkey under Atatürk abolished the caliphate, banned Sharia courts, and introduced civil law based on European models. Tunisia pursued similar reforms, including banning polygamy. Yet even in these cases, political pressure from Islamic movements often challenged the reforms, revealing the persistent power of Sharia as an ideal.

Reform and resistance

Reformist Muslims in the modern era have sought to reinterpret Sharia in ways compatible with contemporary society. Thinkers such as Muhammad Abduh in Egypt and Fazlur Rahman in Pakistan argued that Sharia should be understood in its historical context, with principles such as justice and welfare guiding reinterpretation.

They emphasised the *maqasid al-sharia* (objectives of the law) —
preservation of life, religion, intellect, lineage, and property —
over literal application of medieval rulings.

Yet these reform efforts often face stiff resistance. Conservative
scholars argue that Sharia is divine and immutable; to reinterpret
it according to modern values is to place human judgment above
God's word.

Some Islamist movements have capitalised on this sentiment,
portraying many reformists as sell-outs to Western influence. As
a result of this, reform remains limited, and many societies
oscillate between partial secularisation and resurgent demands
for stricter Sharia.

Sharia and human rights

The tension between Sharia and international human rights is
one of the most contentious issues of our time. The Universal
Declaration of Human Rights affirms the freedom of expression,
equality of men and women, and freedom of religion. Yet many
provisions of Sharia directly contradict all of these principles.
Apostasy laws deny freedom of religion, gendered inheritance
rules totally undermine equality, and blasphemy laws restrict
free speech.

In response, the Organisation of Islamic Cooperation adopted
the Cairo Declaration on Human Rights in Islam (1990). While it
affirms many rights, it explicitly subjects them to Sharia. In
practice, this means that rights are interpreted through the lens
of Islamic law rather than universal standards. Critics argue that
this renders the declaration totally meaningless as a guarantee of
freedom, since Sharia itself is the standard applied in disputes.

For Christians, this conflict highlights the blatant difference
between Islam's legalism and the freedom found in Christ. As
Paul wrote, *"It is for freedom that Christ has set us free. Stand firm,
then, and do not let yourselves be burdened again by a yoke of
slavery"* (Galatians 5:1). Christianity proclaims the liberty of
conscience under God's grace, while Sharia insists on conformity
to a rigid legal code.

Sharia in minority communities

The spread of Islam through migration has brought Sharia into Western societies. Muslim minorities often establish informal mechanisms for resolving disputes according to Islamic law. These may come from arbitration councils, mosque committees, or community elders. Matters such as marriage, divorce, and inheritance are commonly handled through these structures, even when national law provides some alternative procedures.

In a number of countries, these parallel systems have sparked controversy. In the United Kingdom, Sharia councils have operated for many decades, issuing rulings on family disputes. Supporters argue that they provide culturally sensitive solutions for Muslims. Critics warn that they undermine equality before the law, particularly for women pressured to accept rulings that disadvantage them.

Similar debates have arisen in Canada, where proposals for Sharia-based arbitration in Ontario were eventually rejected after public outcry.

In Australia, while Sharia courts do not yet exist officially, some Muslim communities apply Sharia principles informally, and advocacy groups have occasionally called for legal recognition of Islamic family law. These pressures create challenges for social cohesion, as they encourage the existence of two parallel legal systems.

Sharia and radicalisation

Another dimension of Sharia in the modern world is its role in Islamist radicalisation. Extremist groups such as al-Qaeda, ISIS, and Boko Haram frame their violence as efforts to establish Sharia in its purest form. They denounce Muslim governments that compromise with secular law as apostate regimes and call for jihad to restore God's law.

Their propaganda often highlights hudud punishments, gender segregation, and strict dress codes as symbols of authenticity. For radicalised Muslims in the West, the call to implement Sharia becomes a rallying cry.

Online platforms spread teachings that portray living under secular law as sinful, urging believers to migrate to lands where Sharia is enforced or to work for its implementation locally. This narrative has influenced individuals in Australia, where some have joined jihadist groups overseas or plotted attacks at home.

Implications for Australia

Australia's multicultural society faces many unique challenges in dealing with Sharia. On the one hand, our freedom of religion protects Muslims' right to practice their faith, including personal observances such as prayer, fasting, and dietary laws. On the other hand, pressures to recognise Sharia in family law or finance raise concerns about undermining national unity and equality under the law of our land.

One area of much debate has been Islamic finance, which avoids interest (*riba*) by carefully structuring loans as profit-sharing arrangements. Some Australian institutions have offered Sharia-compliant financial products to Muslim customers. While this may seem harmless, it raises the broader question of whether economic life should be reshaped to accommodate religious law.

Another area is family law. While the Australian legal system already recognises religious marriage ceremonies, it does not enforce religious divorces. Yet within a number of Muslim communities, women who obtain a civil divorce may still be considered married under Sharia unless a religious authority grants an Islamic divorce. This creates pressure on women and raises the possibility of informal parallel systems.

Immigration also magnifies the issue. As the Muslim population grows, so too does the potential for communities to demand accommodation of Sharia practices.

While many Muslims choose to integrate successfully, others view assimilation as betrayal and insist on preserving Islamic norms. The risk is the emergence of cultural enclaves where Sharia is enforced informally, creating tension with surrounding society.

The Christian response

For Christians, the persistence of Sharia highlights the urgency of proclaiming the gospel. Islam's legalism cannot bring the assurance of salvation or the transformation of the heart. The law, Paul teaches, exposes sin but cannot save: *"Therefore no one will be declared righteous in God's sight by the works of the law; rather, through the law we become conscious of our sin."* (Romans 3:20). Sharia binds people under a system of external control, but Christ offers freedom and forgiveness through His death and resurrection.

At the same time, Christians must uphold justice and freedom in society. This means defending equality before the law, resisting the establishment of parallel legal systems, and affirming the principles of democracy that protect liberty for all.

It also means engaging Muslims with compassion, recognising that many live under the heavy burden of Sharia without ever experiencing the joy of God's grace.

4. ISLAM AND CHRISTIANITY: THEOLOGICAL INCOMPATIBILITY

Jesus in Islam and Jesus in Christianity

At the centre of the Christian faith stands the person of Jesus Christ. The gospel is not merely a set of teachings or laws but the good news of what God has done in and through His Son. For Christians, Jesus is the eternal Word made flesh, fully God and fully man, who through His life, death and resurrection has reconciled sinners to God. The entire New Testament bears witness to His identity as the Son of God and to His work as the Saviour of the world.

Islam, however, honours *Isa ibn Maryam* (Jesus, son of Mary) — as one of the greatest prophets, born miraculously of the Virgin Mary, performing miracles by God's permission, and serving as a messenger to the children of Israel. Yet Islam emphatically denies the central claims of Christianity: that Jesus is the Son of God, that He died on the cross for the sins of the world, and that He rose again in glory. These denials strike at the very heart of the gospel.

To compare the two portrayals of Jesus is to see why Christianity and Islam cannot be reconciled as two versions of the same truth. They're not complementary, they're contradictory, proclaiming fundamentally different messages about the identity of Jesus and the way of salvation.

Jesus in the Qur'an

The Qur'an refers to Jesus more than 90 times, often with respect. He is called Messiah (*al-Masih*), prophet (*nabi*), servant of Allah, and word from God (*kalimatullah*). His virgin birth is affirmed in Surah 19, where Mary is visited by the angel and conceives by God's command.

The Qur'an also attributes miracles to Jesus: healing the blind and the leper, raising the dead, and even creating a bird from clay and breathing life into it by God's permission.

Yet for all this honour, the Qur'an is equally clear in its rejection of Christian claims. Surah 4:171 declares: *"The Messiah, Jesus son of Mary, was only a messenger of Allah, and His word which He conveyed to Mary, and a spirit from Him. So believe in Allah and His messengers, and do not say 'Three.' Cease! It is better for you. Allah is only one God. Far is it removed from His transcendent majesty that He should have a son."*

This passage captures the Islamic perspective: Jesus is a prophet and Messiah, but not divine; he is honoured but not worshipped. The doctrines of the Trinity and the Sonship of Jesus are rejected as blasphemy.

The Christian confession of Jesus

The New Testament presents a radically different picture. From the opening of John's Gospel, Jesus is identified as divine: *"In the beginning was the Word, and the Word was with God, and the Word was God... The Word became flesh and made his dwelling among us. We have seen his glory, the glory of the one and only Son, who came from the Father, full of grace and truth."* (John 1:1, 14).

Jesus is not merely a prophet pointing to God; He is God the Son come into the world. He forgives sins, receives worship, calms storms, and raises the dead by His own authority. When Thomas confessed, *"My Lord and my God!"* (John 20:28), Jesus accepted this worship. Paul affirms that *"in Christ all the fullness of the Deity lives in bodily form"* (Colossians 2:9).

For Christianity, the incarnation is non-negotiable. If Jesus is not God, He cannot save. If He is only a prophet, then His death has zero redemptive power. The gospel rests on the reality that the eternal Son took on human flesh to reconcile humanity to the Father.

The crucifixion: denial and affirmation

The gulf between Christianity and Islam is clearest at the cross. The Qur'an emphatically denies the crucifixion: *"They said, 'We killed the Messiah, Jesus son of Mary, the messenger of Allah.' But they did not kill him, nor did they crucify him, though it was made to appear so to them... Rather, Allah raised him up to Himself."* (Surah 4:157–158)

Muslim interpreters have offered various explanations: that someone else was crucified in Jesus' place, that it only appeared so to the bystanders, or that the account was corrupted. The consistent point is that Jesus did not die on the cross.

Christianity, however, proclaims the crucifixion as the central event of salvation. All four Gospels testify to it, as do the earliest Christian creeds. Paul writes, *"For what I received I passed on to you as of first importance: that Christ died for our sins according to the Scriptures, that he was buried, that he was raised on the third day according to the Scriptures."*(1 Corinthians 15:3–4). Without the cross, there is no forgiveness of sins, no reconciliation with God, no gospel.

This denial is not a secondary difference but a total contradiction. Islam removes the very heart of Christianity. It reduces Jesus from Saviour to messenger, from Redeemer to teacher. It leaves humanity still trapped in sin, without the atonement that the Bible proclaims.

The resurrection: hope vs. absence

The Qur'an never mentions the resurrection of Jesus. Instead, it teaches that Allah raised Him to Himself, preserving Him from death and humiliation. Islamic tradition often portrays Jesus as alive in heaven, awaiting a future return at the end of time, when he will defeat the Antichrist, break the cross, kill the pigs, and establish justice before dying a natural death.

By contrast, the New Testament proclaims the resurrection as the vindication of Jesus' identity and the guarantee of believers' hope. *"God has raised this Jesus to life, and we are all witnesses of it."* (Acts 2:32). Paul declares, *"If Christ has not been raised, your faith is futile; you are still in your sins."* (1 Corinthians 15:17). The resurrection is not an optional doctrine but the foundation of the Christian faith. Christian hope is not merely that Jesus lives in heaven but that He conquered death itself.

His resurrection is the first fruits of the new creation, the promise that those who belong to Him will also be raised. By denying the crucifixion, Islam also denies the resurrection, leaving no victory over sin or death.

The role of Jesus at the end of time

Both Islam and Christianity assign a role to Jesus in the end times, but the visions are incompatible. In Islamic eschatology, Jesus returns as a just ruler who will restore Sharia, destroy the cross as a symbol of falsehood, and lead people to Islam. His mission is not to reign as the risen Son of God but to confirm Muhammad's message and correct Christian error.

In Christian eschatology, by contrast, Jesus returns in glory as the King of kings and Lord of lords. He comes not to abolish the cross but to consummate the salvation He accomplished there. Revelation 5:9-12 describes Him as the Lamb who was slain, now exalted and worshipped by every tribe and nation. His return brings the final judgment and the renewal of all creation. The difference could not be starker. For Islam, Jesus' second coming confirms Islam. For Christianity, it vindicates the gospel. Both cannot be true.

Prophet vs. Son of God

Underlying all these contrasts is the fundamental question of Jesus' identity. Islam insists He is a prophet—great, but only human. Christianity confesses Him as the eternal Son of God, equal with the Father, worthy of worship.

The Qur'an strongly rejects divine sonship repeatedly. Surah 112 declares: *"Say, He is Allah, One. Allah, the Eternal Refuge. He neither begets nor is born, nor is there to Him any equivalent."* To Muslims, the idea that God could have a son is blasphemous, suggesting weakness or division in God's nature.

Yet the Bible presents sonship not as biological generation but as eternal relationship within the Trinity. Jesus is the beloved Son who reveals the Father: *"No one has ever seen God, but the one and only Son, who is himself God and is in closest relationship with the Father, has made him known."* (John 1:18). His sonship is the very foundation of Christian faith and the source of eternal life. This divide cannot be bridged by dialogue that seeks to minimise differences.

To say that Jesus is only a prophet is to strip Him of His divinity, deny His saving work, and reject the heart of the gospel. To confess Him as Son of God is to deny Islam's central claim of absolute monotheism.

Implications for dialogue

Because Islam and Christianity make contradictory claims about Jesus Christ, efforts at theological reconciliation inevitably fail. Interfaith dialogue can promote some mutual understanding and peaceful coexistence, but it cannot produce a common creed. At most, participants may affirm shared values such as justice, compassion, and the dignity of all human beings. But on the question of Jesus, the two faiths stand diametrically opposed.

This has profound implications for Christian witness to Muslims. Evangelism cannot assume a shared foundation. A Muslim may respect Jesus as a prophet, but until he confesses Jesus as Lord and believes in His death and resurrection, he has not embraced the gospel. The task is to present Jesus as He truly is, trusting the Holy Spirit to open eyes to the glory of Christ.

Salvation in Islam and salvation in Christianity

The question of salvation is the most urgent question in human life. How can a sinful person be reconciled to a holy God? How can guilt be removed, judgment averted, and eternal life gained? Every religion offers an answer, but the answers vary radically.

In Christianity, salvation is by grace alone, through faith alone, in Christ alone. In Islam, salvation depends on submission, obedience, and the weighing of deeds on the Day of Judgment. These two systems are not complementary. They are mutually exclusive, leading to profoundly different experiences of faith.

Salvation in Islam: submission and deeds

Islam derives its very name from the word "submission." To be a Muslim is to be one who submits to Allah's will. The path of salvation is framed as obedience to God's commands, revealed in the Qur'an and demonstrated by Muhammad.

The Five Pillars—confession, prayer, almsgiving, fasting, and pilgrimage—are central duties, and obedience to Sharia law is essential. The Qur'an portrays the Day of Judgment as the weighing of deeds.

Surah 101:6–9 declares: *"Then those whose scales are heavy [with good deeds] – it is they who will be successful. But those whose scales are light – their refuge will be the Abyss."* The imagery is that of a cosmic scale, balancing good and evil. One's fate depends on the outcome.

This creates a religion of uncertainty. A Muslim can strive to obey, but he can never be sure his good deeds will outweigh his sins. Even the great Muhammad himself is depicted as seeking forgiveness for his faults (Surah 47:19). Ultimately, salvation in Islam depends on both human effort and God's mercy, which is sovereign and unpredictable.

Surah 3:129 affirms: *"To Allah belongs whatever is in the heavens and whatever is in the earth. He forgives whom He wills, and punishes whom He wills. And Allah is Forgiving and Merciful."* There's no guarantee, only hope.

The role of the Five Pillars

The Five Pillars function as visible markers of faith, but they also serve as the basis for judgment. The Shahada affirms allegiance, but allegiance must be proven by works. The five daily prayers structure life around obedience but missing them is a sin to be accounted for. Almsgiving purifies wealth, but failure to give properly is recorded against us. Fasting during Ramadan can demonstrate devotion, but infractions must be made up. The pilgrimage to Mecca, if neglected without valid reason, leaves an obligation unmet.

Beyond these pillars, countless other requirements exist within Sharia. Dietary restrictions, dress codes, ritual purity, and financial transactions are all matters of obedience. The devout Muslim must constantly strive to fulfil duties while avoiding prohibitions. Islam's legalism extends to every detail of life, making salvation an ongoing project of conformity.

The absence of atonement

One of the most striking features of Islam is the absence of atonement. The Bible teaches that *"without the shedding of blood there is no forgiveness."* (Hebrews 9:22). From the sacrifices of the Old Testament to the cross of Christ, atonement is central to God's plan of redemption. In Islam, by contrast, there is no sacrifice for sin. Repentance, good works, and divine mercy are the only means of forgiveness.

This is why the Qur'an denies the crucifixion of Jesus. If He did not die, there is no atonement, no substitutionary sacrifice, no reconciliation with God through the blood of the Lamb. Islam strips the cross of all its power and leaves sinners without a Redeemer. It teaches that God forgives directly, without any mediation, but this forgiveness is arbitrary, not grounded in justice. Sin is not paid for; it is merely overlooked or punished.

Assurance in Islam: elusive and uncertain

The inevitable consequence of this system is uncertainty. No Muslim can be sure of salvation. Even the most devout live in fear that their deeds may not be sufficient. The Hadith record Muhammad himself saying, *"By Allah, though I am the Apostle of Allah, yet I do not know what Allah will do to me."* If even the prophet of Islam had no assurance, how can his followers?

The only exceptions in Islamic tradition are those who die in jihad, who are promised immediate entry into paradise. This is why radical groups exalt martyrdom: it provides the only guarantee in an otherwise very uncertain religion. For ordinary Muslims, salvation remains a matter of anxious striving, never of settled peace.

Salvation in Christianity: grace and faith

The gospel proclaims a radically different message. Salvation is not earned by works but given as a gift of grace through faith in Jesus Christ. Paul writes, *"For it is by grace you have been saved, through faith – and this is not from yourselves, it is the gift of God – not by works, so that no one can boast."* (Ephesians 2:8–9).

This is the heart of the good news: what humans could never achieve by their efforts; God has accomplished in Christ. On the cross, Jesus bore the penalty of sin, satisfying divine justice and reconciling sinners to God. 2 Corinthians 5:21 says, *"God made him who had no sin to be sin for us, so that in him we might become the righteousness of God."* Salvation is not a matter of scales but of substitution. Christ took our place so that we might receive His righteousness.

Faith is the means by which this gift is embraced. To trust in Jesus Christ is to rely not on one's own works but on His finished work. This faith is not mere intellectual assent but personal trust in Jesus as Lord and Saviour. The believer rests in the promise of God, confident that Christ's sacrifice is sufficient.

The assurance of salvation

Because salvation in Christianity rests on God's grace rather than human effort, believers can have assurance. *"Therefore, since we have been justified through faith, we have peace with God through our Lord Jesus Christ."* (Romans 5:1). This peace is not presumption but confidence in God's promise. The Holy Spirit testifies to the believer's adoption, thereby assuring them of their inheritance (Romans 8:15–17).

This assurance produces joy and freedom. The Christian obeys not out of fear of judgment but out of gratitude for grace. Good works are the fruit of salvation, not the condition for it. As Paul explains in Ephesians 2:10, *"For we are God's handiwork, created in Christ Jesus to do good works, which God prepared in advance for us to do."* Works are evidence of faith, not its foundation.

Law and the gospel

The contrast between Islam and Christianity can also be seen in the role of law. In Islam, law is central to salvation; whereas in Christianity, the law exposes sin but points us towards Christ. Paul writes, *"Therefore no one will be declared righteous in God's sight by the works of the law; rather, through the law we become conscious of our sin."* (Romans 3:20). The law shows God's holiness and our failure, driving us to the Saviour.

Once in Christ, believers are no longer under the law as a system of salvation. They live by the Spirit, who writes God's commands on their hearts. This does not mean lawlessness but a new obedience flowing from love. The Christian life is not a treadmill of legalistic striving but a walk in the Spirit, marked by freedom and transformation.

The fruit of each system

The practical fruit of these two systems is vastly different. In Islam, the constant weighing of deeds only fosters anxiety and legalism. Obedience is motivated by fear of judgment and hope of reward. The community polices conformity, and failure brings shame. Even devout Muslims may live with a gnawing sense of inadequacy. In Christianity, the fruit is peace and joy. Believers know their sins are forgiven and their future secure. Obedience flows from love, not fear. The church becomes a community of grace, bearing one another's burdens and encouraging faith. Where Islam offers uncertainty, Christianity offers assurance; where Islam demands submission, Christianity always proclaims freedom.

Exclusivity of the gospel

Because the systems are so different, they cannot both be true. If salvation is by works, grace is unnecessary. If salvation is by grace, works cannot earn it. The apostle Paul warned against false gospels that distort the message of Christ: *"I am astonished that you are so quickly deserting the one who called you to live in the grace of Christ and are turning to a different gospel – which is really no gospel at all."* (Galatians 1:6–7). Islam is precisely such a different gospel: it denies the cross, replaces grace with law, and leaves sinners without assurance.

This incompatibility has immense implications. It means that efforts to blend Islam and Christianity into a single path are doomed to failure. The *"Chrismal"* movement, which claims the two faiths are complementary, simply ignores the fundamental contradiction at the heart of salvation. One says, *"Do this and you might be saved;"* the other says, *"It is finished."* (John 19:30).

Scripture and authority

The question of authority is a big one. How does one know what God has said? Where does ultimate truth actually come from? For Muslims, the answer is the Qur'an, which is supplemented by the Hadith and interpreted through centuries of Islamic scholarship. For Christians, the answer is the Bible—i.e. the Old and New Testaments—as the inspired and authoritative Word of God, pointing to Jesus Christ as the final revelation. Because these authorities differ radically, Islam and Christianity proclaim not just different doctrines but different foundations of truth.

The Qur'an's claim

The Qur'an presents itself as the final, uncorrupted revelation of God. Surah 2:2 declares, *"This is the Book about which there is no doubt, a guidance for those conscious of Allah."* Surah 15:9 affirms, *"Indeed, it is We who sent down the Qur'an and indeed, We will be its guardian."* Muslims therefore believe the Qur'an is perfect, preserved word-for-word from the time of Muhammad, unchanging and eternal.

The Qur'an also positions itself as a corrective to previous scriptures. It affirms that God gave the Torah to Moses, the Psalms to David, and the Gospel to Jesus. Yet it claims that Jews and Christians distorted or corrupted all these texts. Surah 2:75 laments that some of the people of the Book *"used to hear the words of Allah then distort it after they had understood it."* Surah 3:78 warns of those who *"twist their tongues with the Book so that you may think it is from the Book, but it is not from the Book."* Thus, the Qur'an acknowledges earlier revelation but denies its current reliability. It insists that the final message given to Muhammad supersedes all that came before. To accept Islam is to affirm the Qur'an as supreme authority.

The Bible's witness

The Bible, by contrast, bears consistent witness to itself as the Word of God. Paul writes in 2 Timothy 3:16, *"All Scripture is God-breathed and is useful for teaching, rebuking, correcting and training in righteousness."*

Peter affirms, *"Prophecy never had its origin in the human will, but prophets, though human, spoke from God as they were carried along by the Holy Spirit."* (2 Peter 1:21). Jesus Himself affirmed the authority of the Old Testament, declaring, *"Scripture cannot be set aside."* (John 10:35).

The New Testament continues this thought, presenting itself as apostolic testimony to Christ. Paul's letters were recognised early as Scripture (2 Peter 3:16), and the Gospels were written by eyewitnesses or those closely associated with them. The canon developed not by arbitrary decision but by recognition of what was already authoritative in the churches.

For Christians, the Bible is not only authoritative, it is also sufficient. It reveals God's character, exposes human sin, and proclaims salvation through Christ. To add or subtract from it is to distort the gospel. Revelation 22:18–19 warns against altering the words of Scripture, underscoring its finality.

Transmission and reliability

Muslims often claim that the Bible has been corrupted, pointing to differences in manuscripts or variations in translations. Yet historical evidence shows that the Bible has been transmitted with remarkable accuracy. Thousands of manuscripts of the New Testament, some dating to the second century, allow scholars to reconstruct the text with great confidence. The Dead Sea Scrolls confirm the reliability of the Old Testament as we have it now, demonstrating continuity over centuries.

By contrast, the Qur'an's transmission is not as straightforward as Muslims claim. Early Islamic sources record that multiple versions of the Qur'an existed before Uthman standardised the text. Reports mention that some companions preserved different readings, and entire surahs were said to be lost.

The decision to burn alternative copies indicates that variations did exist. Modern discoveries of early Qur'anic manuscripts, such as those in Sana'a, Yemen, reveal textual differences that challenge the claim of perfect preservation.

While Muslims insist that God has miraculously preserved the Qur'an, the historical evidence suggests a more complex process. The belief in perfection rests on faith, not on verifiable history. In contrast, the Bible makes no such claim of word-for-word preservation but has a demonstrably reliable transmission record supported by abundant manuscripts.

Different approaches to revelation

The Qur'an and the Bible also differ in their very nature. The Qur'an is believed to be a direct dictation from God Himself to Muhammad, with Muhammad merely being the recipient. Its style is often oracular, presenting commands, warnings, and affirmations. It is not a narrative; it is actually a collection of pronouncements.

The Bible, however, is a collection of diverse writings over centuries—history, poetry, prophecy, letters—through which God spoke by His Spirit through human authors. It presents a coherent story of creation, fall, redemption, and restoration, culminating in Christ. The incarnation of Jesus reflects this incarnational pattern of revelation: God works through human history to reveal Himself.

This difference leads to contrasting views of God. In Islam, revelation is primarily about law—rules to follow, obligations to meet. With the Christian faith, revelation is primarily about relationship, God revealing Himself in Christ so He can reconcile sinners. The Bible reveals a God who enters history and speaks in human words; the Qur'an presents a God who dictates commands but remains distant.

Authority in practice

Because of these differences, authority functions differently. In the religion of Islam, ultimate authority lies in the Qur'an, but because it is often vague or general, the Hadith and Sharia fill in all the details. The authority structure is therefore text plus tradition, mediated through scholars. Ordinary Muslims depend heavily on clerics to interpret rulings.

In the Christian faith, ultimate authority lies in Scripture alone. Tradition and church teaching have a role, but they are both subordinate to the Word of God. The Reformation crystallised this principle in the doctrine of *sola Scriptura*. Believers are now encouraged to read the Bible for themselves, trusting the Spirit to illuminate its meaning. Authority is decentralised because the Word itself is accessible.

This explains why the Christian faith has proved more adaptable across cultures. Because Scripture reveals principles rather than a rigid legal code, it can be applied in diverse settings without demanding uniformity of ritual. Islam, by contrast, insists on conformity only to Sharia, leading to tensions in multicultural societies.

The clash of exclusivity

At the deepest level, the Qur'an and the Bible make mutually exclusive claims. The Qur'an denies the Sonship of Jesus, the Trinity, and the cross — truths that are central to the Bible. The Bible proclaims Jesus as the only way to God: *"Salvation is found in no one else, for there is no other name under heaven given to mankind by which we must be saved."*(Acts 4:12).

The Qur'an, by contrast, insists that Islam is the final and only acceptable religion: *"The only religion in the sight of Allah is Islam."* (Surah 3:19).

Both cannot be right. To accept one is to reject the other. This is why any attempt to harmonise Islam and Christianity inevitably distorts one or both. The foundation of authority is irreconcilably different.

Implications for faith and witness

For Christians, recognising this incompatibility is really crucial for faithful witness. Dialogue with Muslims must be honest, not papering over differences. The question of authority should be addressed directly: why trust the Qur'an over the Bible, or vice versa? Historical evidence, internal consistency, and the witness of the Holy Spirit all confirm the reliability of Scripture.

At the same time, Christians must avoid arrogance. The goal is not to win arguments but to point people to Christ. The authority of the Bible is not a mere intellectual claim but a living reality, as God speaks to us all through His Word to convict, comfort, and transform.

As Hebrews 4:12 declares, *"For the word of God is alive and active. Sharper than any double-edged sword, it penetrates even to dividing soul and spirit, joints and marrow; it judges the thoughts and attitudes of the heart."*

5. AUSTRALIA'S CULTURAL FOUNDATIONS

Australia's Christian heritage and Western foundations

Every nation is built upon foundations deeper than just laws or borders. Beneath the surface of any society, you will find values, traditions, and convictions that shape its character. In Australia, those solid foundations are unmistakably Western and, more specifically, they are profoundly Christian. Even though modern Australia is often described as secular, the soil in which it grew was tilled by biblical truth, watered by Christian morality, and shaped by the institutions of Western civilisation.

If Australians are to understand the cultural challenges posed by Islam, they must first grasp the cultural framework that has defined their own society. The contrasts are glaring. Whereas Australia inherited principles of liberty, equality, and democracy rooted in Christianity, Islam rests on Sharia law, communal conformity, and submission to an all-encompassing religious-political order.

The arrival of Christianity in Australia

When the First Fleet landed at Sydney Cove in 1788, it carried more than convicts and soldiers. It carried the worldview of a nation shaped by centuries of Christian influence. Alongside tools and weapons, the settlers brought Bibles and prayer books. The Reverend Richard Johnson was appointed chaplain to the colony, and he preached the first Christian sermon in Australia from Psalm 116:12–13: *"What shall I return to the LORD for all his goodness to me? I will lift up the cup of salvation and call on the name of the LORD."*

Though the colony's beginnings were often brutal, the presence of Christianity shaped its moral trajectory. Johnson tirelessly cared for convicts, ministered to the sick, and established the first Christian school. He believed education was inseparable from faith, teaching children to read using the Bible. This was typical of British colonies: Christianity was not an optional accessory but a central pillar of public life.

Churches quickly became the anchors of this new society. They offered not only worship but also moral instruction, literacy, charity, and stability. While convicts and settlers were far from universally devout, the institutional influence of Christianity was woven into the fabric of daily life.

English Common Law: A Christian legacy

Australia's legal system, inherited from Britain, was built on English common law. Common law was certainly not created in a vacuum; it grew out of centuries of Christian thought about justice, morality, and human dignity.

The Magna Carta of 1215 laid early foundations, declaring that even the king was subject to the law. It began with the clear acknowledgment of God and the church. Later developments, such as the English Bill of Rights in 1689, enshrined liberties rooted in biblical convictions: the presumption of innocence, trial by jury, limits on arbitrary power, and protections for property.

These principles flowed from Christian theology. The biblical teaching that all people are made in God's image (Genesis 1:27) affirmed human dignity. The recognition of sin tempered power with checks and balances. Justice was grounded not in the whim of rulers but in the character of God, who is just and impartial.

When Britain exported its institutions to Australia in 1788, it also exported this moral vision. Courts, legislatures, and parliaments operated with an inherited conviction that law should be applied impartially, that rulers are accountable, and that individuals possess rights. Such ideas contrast profoundly with Islamic jurisprudence, where law is not an evolving system of justice but a fixed divine code — Sharia — interpreted by clerics and enforced by rulers.

The Christian roots of democracy

Democracy in Australia also reflects Christian heritage. Ancient Greece provided early democratic ideas, but it was Christianity that supplied the moral soil in which representative government flourished.

The Protestant Reformation (1517-1648) had a strong emphasis on the authority of Scripture over both church and state. It taught the priesthood of all believers, affirming that ordinary people had a direct relationship with God. This encouraged literacy, personal responsibility, and participation in civic life. Reformers like John Calvin emphasised covenantal governance — leaders were accountable to God and the people, not absolute in their own power.

John Locke, influenced by biblical principles, articulated natural rights, religious liberty, and government by consent. These ideas profoundly shaped the English tradition and, by extension, the colonies. Australia inherited the Westminster-style government, a constitutional monarchy, and parliamentary democracy — all systems designed to limit tyranny and protect liberty.

When Australians later pioneered reforms such as the secret ballot and women's suffrage, they did so within a framework already steeped in Christian morality. The assumption that every person deserves a voice, that rulers should be accountable, and that freedom is a good to be protected, all flowed from a biblical vision of human dignity and justice.

The value of the individual

One of the distinctive contributions of Christianity to Australian society is the emphasis on the individual. Ancient empires valued the collective — the tribe, the city-state, the ruler — too often at the expense of the individual. Islam likewise elevates the community (*ummah*) above personal autonomy, demanding conformity for the sake of group honour.

Christianity, however, proclaims that each person is precious to God. Jesus told parables of a lost sheep, a lost coin, and a lost son, emphasising heaven's joy over one sinner who repents (Luke 15). Paul declared that in Christ *"there is neither Jew nor Gentile, neither slave nor free, nor is there male and female, for you are all one in Christ Jesus"* (Galatians 3:28). This emphasis on individual dignity shaped Western civilisation. Laws were then written to protect personal rights.

Hospitals and schools were founded to care for individuals, not merely preserve communities. Charity was extended to the poor not because they served the state but because they bore God's image. In Australia, this translated into institutions that valued equality before the law and fairness in society.

Churches as builders of society

Churches played a crucial role in establishing Australia's social fabric. They founded schools, hospitals, orphanages, and many charitable organisations. The first hospitals were all staffed by Christians who viewed caring for the sick as an expression of Christ's love. Mission societies reached out to the Indigenous Australians, seeking (albeit imperfectly) to share the gospel and provide education.

Even when our church attendance waned in later centuries, the influence of Christianity endured. Public morality continued to draw on biblical principles. The idea of giving everyone "a fair go" reflects the Golden Rule taught by Jesus: *"Do to others what you would have them do to you."* (Matthew 7:12). Compassion for the underdog, suspicion of unchecked authority, and the belief in equality all echo Christian themes.

Australian holidays reflect this heritage as well. Christmas and Easter, tied to the life of Jesus Christ, remain central national celebrations. Parliament still opens with prayer. These practices are not cultural accidents but reminders of the nation's roots.

The Enlightenment and its limits

Australia was also shaped by Enlightenment ideals—reason, science, and secular governance. Yet even these developments were indebted to Christianity. The scientific revolution arose from the conviction that the world is ordered by a rational Creator. Enlightenment thinkers who emphasised rights and liberty built on the strong biblical foundations, even when they downplayed them. Australia's secular institutions thus do not erase its Christian heritage; they presuppose it. Rights, freedoms, and equality are sustained only when grounded in the belief that humans have inherent worth given by God.

As the theologian G.K. Chesterton observed, the modern world is full of Christian ideals gone mad—separated from their roots, they lose coherence.

Contrasting with Islamic foundations

When these foundations are compared with those of Islam, the differences are striking. Islam is not rooted in common law or constitutionalism but in Sharia Law, a rigid system of divine commands. It does not exalt the individual but the community, enforcing conformity at the expense of personal liberty. It does not embrace democracy as a natural outgrowth of human dignity but regards divine sovereignty as incompatible with human consent.

In Islamic jurisprudence, rulers are guardians of divine law, not servants of the people. Rights are distributed unequally—men over women, Muslims over non-Muslims. Freedom of religion and speech are alien concepts, as apostasy and blasphemy are punishable by death. Where Christianity fostered voluntary faith and liberty of conscience, Islam enforces submission and will punish dissent.

Thus, when Muslim communities seek to transplant Islamic norms into Western societies, they inevitably clash with the Christian foundations of those societies. The tension is not accidental but structural: two worldviews with incompatible roots cannot produce identical fruit.

Preserving the foundations

Recognising Australia's Christian and Western heritage is not a matter of nostalgia but of necessity. If Australians forget these foundations, they risk undermining the very freedoms they cherish. Multiculturalism, if pursued without discernment, can erode the values that sustain democracy.

Not all cultures are equally compatible with liberty. Not all religions affirm equality or individual rights. To preserve our freedom, Australians must be honest about their heritage.

They must remember that liberty, justice, and equality were not inventions of secular modernity, they are precious gifts nurtured by Christianity. They must also recognise that ideologies like Islam, which deny these principles, will not integrate seamlessly into the national fabric.

Australian culture and identity

If Australia's political and legal systems rest upon Christian and Western foundations, its cultural identity has grown from those roots in unique ways. Every society develops its own distinctive ethos, the spirit that characterises its people. For Australians, this ethos has been shaped by our geography, history, and inherited values. Four features will stand out in particular: egalitarianism, mateship, secularism, and multiculturalism. These four features, celebrated as hallmarks of the Australian way of life, reveal both the strengths of the nation and its potential points of cultural vulnerability.

The spirit of egalitarianism

Few traits are more associated with our Australian culture than egalitarianism — the conviction that all people deserve *"a fair go."* This spirit runs deep, shaping everything from politics to sport to workplace relations. It reflects deep suspicion of elitism and hierarchy, favouring informality and equality.

The roots of Australian egalitarianism lie partly in its convict past. The early colony was not composed of aristocrats but of ordinary men and women, many transported for petty crimes. Though brutal in conditions, the shared hardships fostered a sense of rough equality. Titles and class distinctions carried less weight in the colonies than in Britain. Later waves of free settlers reinforced this ethos, building a society where opportunity seemed open to all.

The bush experience also contributed. Settlers facing the harsh realities of the land learned to depend on each other rather than on distant authorities. This bred self-reliance but also solidarity: one's neighbour was a fellow struggler, not a rival.

From this context emerged the belief that everyone should be treated with fairness, without regard to birth or privilege.

Christianity amplified this spirit by affirming the equal dignity of every person before God. The gospel proclaimed that all are sinners in need of grace and that all are equal at the foot of the cross. Paul's declaration that in Christ *there is neither Jew nor Gentile, slave nor free, male nor female* (Galatians 3:28) resonated with the conviction that no one should be excluded from justice or opportunity.

In modern Australia, egalitarianism manifests in our everyday interactions. Australians tend to be informal, using first names rather than titles. They are wary of pretension and quick to cut down "tall poppies" — those who appear to exalt themselves. Politically, egalitarianism has encouraged universal suffrage, labour rights, and social welfare systems. Culturally, it has fostered a sense that everyone deserves respect and a chance to succeed.

Yet egalitarianism also faces serious challenges. It can slip into mediocrity, which can then resent excellence or achievement. It can downplay legitimate authority and undermine respect for leaders. And when confronted with cultures that do not share its assumptions — such as Islamic cultures that emphasise hierarchy, gender inequality, and communal honour — egalitarianism may struggle to respond. Its very openness can leave it vulnerable to ideologies that reject equality as a principle.

The ideal of mateship

Closely linked to egalitarianism is the ideal of mateship. More than simple friendship, mateship conveys loyalty, solidarity, and mutual support. It is the belief that in times of hardship or danger, one's mates can be relied upon. Mateship emerged from the convict era and the struggles of rural life. Settlers working in the bush relied on one another to survive. The gold rushes of the nineteenth century, with their rough camps and their shifting populations, further reinforced the need for trust among mates.

But it was in war, particularly the ANZAC experience of World War I, that mateship became enshrined as a deep national virtue. Soldiers enduring the horrors of Gallipoli and the Western Front found solace in their mates, whose loyalty very often meant the difference between life and death.

Today, mateship continues to shape our Australian identity. It is celebrated in literature, film, and political rhetoric. Politicians invoke it to describe national solidarity; sporting teams embody it in their camaraderie; communities express it in times of crisis, such as bushfires or floods. To be called *'a good mate'* is one of the highest compliments an Australian can receive.

Mateship aligns very closely with Christian teaching. Jesus told His disciples, *"Greater love has no one than this: to lay down one's life for one's friends."* (John 15:13). The loyalty and self-sacrifice of mateship reflect, however faintly, the love of Christ Who gave Himself for His people. The church, too, models a community bound by love and mutual support.

Yet mateship also has its limitations. It can become exclusive, favouring the insiders over the outsiders. At times it has been male-dominated, marginalising women. It may prioritise loyalty to friends over adherence to principle. And when applied to multicultural society, mateship may be strained.

Does the Muslim newcomer, with different values and loyalties, become a mate in the same sense? Or does mateship falter when cultural barriers are high?

The rise of secularism

While Christianity profoundly shaped Australia's heritage, the nation has also been marked by a growing secularism. From the nineteenth century onward, Enlightenment principles of reason, science, and progress gained a lot of influence. As immigration diversified and urbanisation spread rapidly, church attendance declined. In recent decades, census results show a growing proportion of Australians identifying as having *"no religion."*

Secularism in Australia, however, has a distinctive flavour. It is not militant atheism but pragmatic indifference. Religion is often regarded as a private matter, not to intrude into public life. Australians are more likely to respect faith than to attack it, but they are also likely to dismiss it as irrelevant. The phrase *"live and let live"* captures this attitude. This secular ethos has some advantages. It allows for pluralism, enabling people of different beliefs to coexist peacefully. It prevents any one denomination from dominating public life. It reflects the Christian principle of liberty of conscience, even if detached from its theological roots.

But secularism also creates weaknesses. By relegating religion to the private sphere, it forgets the Christian foundations upon which our freedom rests. It assumes that values like equality and human rights can persist without their biblical grounding. In reality, these values are fragile when cut off from their source.

Furthermore, secularism may be naïve when confronted with Islam. Because secular Australians too often treat religion as optional, they struggle to grasp this faith that demands total submission in every sphere of life. They may assume Islam can be privatised in the same way Christianity has been. Yet Islam resists privatisation, insisting on shaping law, politics, and culture. Secularism's blind spot is its failure to recognise that not all religions function alike.

The experiment of multiculturalism

Perhaps the most distinctive feature of our modern Australian identity is multiculturalism. From its beginnings as a British colony, Australia has become home to waves of immigrants from Europe, Asia, and beyond. After World War II, immigration programs welcomed millions of newcomers. In the late twentieth century, policies of multiculturalism encouraged not merely assimilation but the celebration of cultural diversity.

Multiculturalism has brought many blessings. It has enriched Australian cuisine, art, music, and commerce. It has broadened perspectives, fostering tolerance and inclusion. It has allowed Australia to thrive as a globalised nation, drawing talent and energy from around the world.

Yet multiculturalism also poses dilemmas. At its best, it balances cultural diversity with shared values and national unity. At its worst, it fragments society into enclaves which have competing loyalties. The key question is whether all cultures are equally compatible with Australian foundations. While Italian, Greek, Vietnamese, and Indian communities have generally integrated while preserving traditions, Islamic communities present unique challenges.

This is because Islam is not merely a culture but a comprehensive religious-political system. For many Muslims, preserving Sharia is not optional but essential. Thus, when multiculturalism seeks to affirm every culture as equally valid, it then risks endorsing practices that contradict our Australian values—such as gender inequality, restrictions on free speech, or parallel legal systems.

The interplay of these traits

Taken all together, egalitarianism, mateship, secularism, and multiculturalism form a complex picture of Australian identity. They reflect the nation's rich history of hardship, solidarity, openness, and pragmatism. They provide resilience in crises and foster an inclusive society. Yet they also carry vulnerabilities.

➤ *Egalitarianism* may struggle to confront cultures that reject equality.

➤ *Mateship* may exclude those who do not share the same loyalties.

➤ *Secularism* may underestimate religions that refuse privatisation.

➤ *Multiculturalism* may embrace diversity without discernment, undermining national unity.

The challenge for Australia is to preserve the strengths of its culture while guarding against its weaknesses. This requires honesty about the foundations of the nation and clarity about the values that cannot be compromised. This biblical view shaped Western liberty.

Freedom was never absolute but ordered toward the good. Laws restricted harm while allowing wide scope for personal choice. Liberty of conscience encouraged responsibility to God and to our neighbour.

By contrast, Islamic law subordinates individual responsibility to communal conformity. Freedom is not understood as a moral good but as a potential threat to unity. Individual rights are sacrificed for the collective. This explains why Muslim societies have struggled to embrace democratic freedoms: they clash with the underlying assumption that obedience to Sharia is always paramount.

Freedom under pressure in Australia

In recent decades, Australia has seen increasing pressure on its freedoms. Laws against *"hate speech"* and *"offensive expression"* have increasingly been used to silence legitimate debate about Islam. Public figures who criticise Islamic doctrines risk being labelled intolerant. Universities often suppress dissenting views in the name of inclusion.

At the same time, Islamic communities have been pressing for recognition of Sharia in matters such as family law and finance. While official attempts have been resisted, informal parallel systems operate within communities. Women, in particular, may face pressure to submit to Sharia norms even when Australian law provides greater equality.

If Australians really value their freedoms, they must resist these encroachments. Liberty requires courage—the courage to speak truth, to defend rights, and to hold fast to principles even when unpopular.

The Christian foundation of liberty

Ultimately, the freedoms Australians cherish won't be sustained without their Christian foundation. Secular society assumes liberty as a given, but it was Christianity that provided its moral basis.

The belief that every person is made in God's image grounds equality. The conviction that conscience is accountable to God grounds religious freedom. The example of the prophets and apostles speaking truth to power grounds free speech.

Without these key foundations, freedom risks collapsing into relativism or being surrendered to authoritarian systems. Islam can never offer an alternative foundation for liberty; its system undermines precisely those freedoms Australians hold dear. If Australia forgets its Christian roots, it will lack the strength to resist Islam's encroachments.

If you think this is all theoretical, then I caution you to wait until you read the next chapter and discover the incredible growth of the Muslim population in Australia. Not all of these Muslims bring a deep commitment to the ideals and worldview of Islam, but we can assume the vast majority of them will.

As you read those numbers, I encourage you to then ponder the Australia of tomorrow when all those Muslims vote for our governments and when a growing number of them are elected to local, State and Federal leadership positions. It will not take very long for our whole nation to be directed down a path from which there will be no return. I don't wish to be alarmist, I just need to tell it like it is, in the hope that someone is listening.

6. THE CHALLENGE OF ISLAM IN AUSTRALIA

The growth of Islam in Australia

The presence of Islam in Australia is not new. Muslim contact with the continent predates European settlement, yet only in recent decades has it become a significant and visible part of the national landscape. Understanding this growth is essential for grasping the cultural challenges it poses. Islam has expanded through immigration, natural increase, and the establishment of communities and institutions. The scale and character of this growth raises profound questions about integration, cultural compatibility, and the future of Australian society.

Early Muslim contact with Australia

Long before the First Fleet arrived in 1788, Muslim traders from what is now Indonesia had contact with northern Australia. The Makassans from Sulawesi sailed to Arnhem Land to harvest trepang (sea cucumber), trading with Indigenous peoples. These visits left traces in language, art, and even DNA. A number of Indigenous Australians adopted words from Malay languages, and oral traditions recall contact with seafarers who prayed to their God facing west.

Yet these early interactions were seasonal and temporary. They did not result in any permanent settlements or lasting Islamic influence. It was only with European colonisation and the later waves of global migration that Islam established a foothold in Australia.

Nineteenth-century Muslim presence

The first significant Muslim communities arrived in Australia in the nineteenth century, primarily from Afghanistan and British India. These *"Afghan cameleers,"* as they were known, played a vital role in opening up Australia's interior. They transported goods across the desert, assisted explorers, and provided critical services in regions much too harsh for horses or bullocks. The cameleers established small communities around outback towns, building makeshift mosques out of corrugated iron or mudbrick.

Some married local women, though most eventually returned home or assimilated. While their contribution was significant, their numbers remained very small, and they left little enduring institutional presence.

By the early twentieth century, restrictive immigration laws such as the White Australia Policy curtailed further immigration of Muslims. As a result, Islam remained a marginal presence in Australian society for decades.

Post-World War II migration

The transformation began after World War II, when Australia shifted from restrictive immigration policies to mass migration programs. Seeking to boost our population and labour force, the government encouraged immigration first from Europe and later from Asia and the Middle East.

Muslims arrived in larger numbers, particularly from Lebanon and Turkey. The Lebanese Civil War (1975–1990) drove many thousands of refugees to Australia, most of them settling in Sydney and Melbourne. Turkish immigrants also arrived under labour agreements, forming communities also in urban centres. These groups quickly established mosques, cultural associations, and businesses, thereby laying the groundwork for the visible Muslim communities we see today.

From the 1970s onward, the immigration of Muslims diversified further, as they soon came from Bosnia, Indonesia, Pakistan, Bangladesh, Somalia, Iraq, Afghanistan, and more recently from Syria. Today, Australia's Muslim population now reflects this diversity, representing dozens of nationalities and cultures.

Demographic growth

The growth of Islam in Australia is striking. Census data reveals a steady increase in Muslim numbers over the past half-century. In 1971, there were fewer than 23,000 Muslims in the country. By 1981, the number had grown to 77,000. By 2001, it had more than tripled to 281,000.

The 2016 census recorded over 600,000 Muslims, making Islam the second-largest religion after Christianity. Current estimates suggest the figure is now well over 800,000, or about 3.5% of the population. So, the number of Muslims in Australia has grown by over 3,300% since 1971.

This growth is driven by three key factors: immigration, higher fertility rates, and community consolidation. Muslim families tend to have a lot more children than non-Muslim Australians, contributing to natural increase. Migration continues to add tens of thousands each year, particularly through humanitarian and family reunion programs. The establishment of mosques and schools has reinforced community identity for Muslims, which reduces assimilation and ensures continuity.

Geographic concentration

Muslims in Australia are certainly not evenly distributed. They are concentrated in major urban centres, particularly Sydney and Melbourne. In Sydney, suburbs such as Lakemba, Auburn, and Bankstown host large Muslim populations, with mosques, halal shops, and Islamic schools defining the cultural landscape. In Melbourne, we have suburbs like Broadmeadows, Coburg, and Dandenong playing a similar role.

This geographic concentration creates distinct cultural enclaves. While multiculturalism celebrates diversity, such concentration can foster segregation rather than integration. In some suburbs, English is seldom heard on the streets today, and Sharia-based practices influence social life. These enclaves serve as hubs for Islamic identity but also raise concerns about parallel societies forming within the nation.

Institutions of Islam in Australia

Alongside demographic growth has come the establishment of Islamic institutions. Mosques, once rare, now number over 200 across the country. They range from small community prayer halls to very large centres with schools, libraries, and cultural facilities.

Prominent mosques, such as the Lakemba Mosque in Sydney, serve not only as places of worship but also as community hubs and political platforms.

Islamic schools have proliferated, with dozens now educating tens of thousands of students. These schools provide instruction not only in standard curricula but also in Islamic theology, Arabic, and Sharia-based values. While some may emphasise integration with Australian society, others reinforce separation, raising serious concerns about the messages conveyed to young Muslims about identity and loyalty.

Islamic organisations, from charities to advocacy groups, have become influential. They provide social services, they lobby governments, and they shape public debate. Groups such as the Australian Federation of Islamic Councils (AFIC) now claim to represent Muslim interests across the nation. Some promote moderation and coexistence; others push for greater recognition of Sharia and resist assimilation into broader society.

The role of immigration policy

Immigration policy has been a major driver of Islam's growth. Australia's humanitarian intake has welcomed refugees from Muslim-majority nations such as Afghanistan, Iraq, and Syria. Family reunion programs have expanded communities, while skilled migration has attracted professionals from countries like Pakistan and Malaysia.

Critics will argue that immigration policy has not adequately considered the cultural compatibility. While diversity enriches society, importing large numbers from cultures shaped by Sharia creates tensions with Australia's foundations. The assumption that all groups will integrate equally ignores the distinctive challenges posed by Islam's comprehensive worldview.

Supporters of the current policies will emphasise humanitarian responsibility and economic contribution. They point to Muslim doctors, engineers, and business owners as evidence of positive integration.

Yet the statistics reveal some ongoing disparities in employment, education, and social cohesion, with Muslim communities often experiencing a higher unemployment and a lower participation rate than the average across Australia.

Political and cultural influence

As Muslim numbers grow rapidly, so too does their political influence. Muslim candidates have been elected to local councils, state parliaments, and even the federal parliament.

Advocacy groups lobby for recognition of Islamic holidays, halal certification, and accommodation of Sharia practices in areas such as finance and family law. Public debates over issues such as headscarves, prayer rooms, and religious education illustrate the cultural impact of Islam.

While some demands are quite reasonable accommodations of religious practice, others push the boundaries of compatibility with our Australian values. The tension lies in distinguishing between legitimate religious freedom and creeping Islamisation. Halal certification provides a telling example. What began as a simple accommodation for Muslim consumers has now grown into a multi-million-dollar industry, raising many questions about transparency, funding, and indirect support for Islamic organisations. Critics argue that such systems normalise Sharia requirements in the broader economy, subtly reshaping society.

Intergenerational dynamics

The growth of Islam in Australia is not only numerical but also generational. The children and grandchildren of immigrants face the challenge of identity. Are they Australians who happen to be Muslim, or Muslims who happen to live in Australia? The answer varies widely.

Some embrace integration, thriving in education, business, and civic life. They see no contradiction between their faith and their citizenship. Whereas others retreat into insular communities, emphasising separation and resisting any assimilation.

Islamic schools, satellite television, and many online networks reinforce global Muslim identity, often at the expense of national belonging. This generational struggle mirrors that of other migrant groups but with a key difference: Islam is not merely a private faith but a comprehensive system. For many, preserving Islamic identity means preserving Sharia, which cannot be fully reconciled with Australian values. This makes the question of integration more complex than for other communities.

The visibility of Islam

Unlike earlier waves of migration, Islam is highly visible. The distinctive dress of Muslim women, the sound of the call to prayer, the construction of mosques, and the availability of halal food all make Islam a prominent feature of urban life. Visibility in itself is not negative, but it accentuates differences.

When those differences challenge core values — such as gender equality or freedom of speech — they become sources of tension. The visibility of Islam also fuels public debate. Media coverage of terrorism, radicalisation, or cultural clashes often focuses attention on Muslim communities. This can create a climate of suspicion, sometimes unfairly, but it also reflects legitimate concerns about integration and cultural compatibility.

A defining challenge

The growth of Islam in Australia is not simply a demographic fact but a defining cultural challenge. It forces Australians to ask hard questions about identity, values, and the future. Can a society built on Christian, Western foundations accommodate large communities shaped by Sharia? Can those foundational Australian values like egalitarianism, mateship, secularism, and multiculturalism withstand the pressure of a worldview that demands submission rather than freedom?

These questions will become more pressing as Muslim numbers continue to rise. Immigration trends suggest that Islam will remain one of the fastest-growing religions in Australia. How the nation responds will shape its future.

Cultural and social challenges

The rapid growth of Islam in Australia has not only demographic significance but also profound cultural and social implications. Immigration is never a neutral process; newcomers bring with them languages, traditions, and beliefs that interact with the host society. When these elements harmonise, they can enrich the national fabric. When they clash, they can generate friction, confusion, and sometimes conflict. In the case of Islam, the challenges are especially acute, because it is not simply a private religion but a comprehensive worldview with serious social, political, and legal dimensions.

Integration or segregation?

One of the central questions raised by Islam in Australia is whether Muslim communities integrate into broader society or form segregated enclaves. Integration must involve adopting national values while preserving certain cultural traditions.

Segregation involves maintaining distinct communities with limited engagement in wider society. Evidence suggests that both trends are now present. Some Muslims have integrated successfully, contributing to business, education, and politics. Others, however, cluster in concentrated suburbs where Islamic identity dominates.

In areas such as Lakemba in Sydney and Broadmeadows in Melbourne, Islamic institutions, signage, and dress create cultural enclaves. Residents may live their daily lives with little interaction beyond their community.

This segregation is reinforced by several factors:

➢ *Language barriers* among first-generation migrants.
➢ *Islamic schools* that educate children primarily within Muslim frameworks.
➢ *Social pressures* to preserve honour and avoid assimilation.
➢ *Religious imperatives* that discourage close association with non-Muslims.

Such patterns challenge the multicultural model. Rather than blending into a shared Australian identity, these segregated communities risk forming *"parallel societies."* This creates friction with neighbours, strains on social services, and questions about long-term unity.

The influence of Sharia

At the heart of these cultural challenges lies the influence of Sharia. For devout Muslims, Sharia is not optional; it is the divine law governing all of life. In Muslim-majority nations, Sharia shapes legal codes and social norms. In Australia, where national law prevails, Sharia will often manifest in community practices, arbitration councils, and advocacy for accommodation.

Sharia affects family life through marriage and divorce practices. Islamic marriage contracts, polygamous unions, and gender-based inheritance norms sometimes operate informally even when not recognised by Australian law. Women seeking divorce may feel trapped if their community refuses to grant a religious dissolution. Some Islamic councils have attempted to arbitrate disputes, raising concerns about unequal treatment of women and the undermining of national law.

Sharia also influences economic practices. Islamic finance, which avoids interest, has grown in popularity, with banks offering Sharia-compliant products. While framed as consumer choice, these systems subtly embed Sharia into the financial sector. Advocacy for a much broader recognition of Sharia occasionally surfaces. Some Muslim leaders have called for partial legal recognition in family matters, arguing for cultural sensitivity. Yet such recognition would fracture the principle of equality before the law, establishing separate standards for different communities.

Gender issues

Gender is arguably one of the most contested areas of cultural clash. Australian society is built on the principle of equality between men and women, enshrined in law and reinforced by decades of social progress.

Islam often encodes gender inequality into its practices. In Islamic law, a woman's testimony is worth half that of a man's. Inheritance rules grant daughters half the share of sons. Men may marry multiple wives; women may not marry multiple husbands. Divorce is a lot easier for men than for women. Such principles, while not always enforced in Australia yet, influence attitudes within Muslim communities.

The wearing of the hijab, niqab, or burqa illustrates the tension. Some women freely choose to wear these garments as an expression of faith. Others face family or community pressure. For broader Australian society, the face veil raises questions about social cohesion, security, and gender equality.

Debates over whether to ban the burqa in certain settings reveal the clash between cultural accommodation and national values. Reports of honour-based violence and forced marriages further expose tensions.

While not representative of all Muslims, such cases highlight the dangers of importing any cultural practice incompatible with Australian law. Women caught between loyalty to their families and the protections of national law face difficult choices.

Education and identity

Schools are also battlegrounds for cultural formation. Australian public schools are designed to foster our shared civic values, teaching history, literature, and ethics within a framework of national identity. Islamic schools, however, prioritise religious identity. They all teach Arabic, Qur'anic recitation, and Islamic studies alongside standard subjects.

Some Islamic schools will emphasise integration, encouraging students to engage confidently with the wider society. Others, however, foster separation, warning against Western values and promoting Sharia norms. Investigations have revealed instances where radical preachers were invited to speak, or where curricula presented Australia as morally corrupt compared to Islamic ideals.

Even in public schools, cultural clashes occur. Muslim students may demand prayer rooms, halal food, or an exemption from certain activities. While accommodation of religious needs is reasonable, constant demands for special treatment will risk undermining the principle of shared schooling. Schools may become sites of tension rather than unity.

This challenge is particularly acute for those second-generation Muslims. Raised in Australia yet tied to Islamic identity; they often wrestle with the question of belonging. Do they see themselves primarily as Australians, or as members of the global ummah? This identity struggle shapes their attitudes toward integration or isolation.

Security concerns and radicalisation

The cultural challenge of Islam cannot be separated from the security concerns. Radicalisation has emerged as a persistent issue in Australia, with a minority of Muslims embracing extremist ideologies.

These individuals often come from marginalised backgrounds, struggling with their identity and community pressures. Online propaganda and radical preachers exploit these vulnerabilities. Cases such as the 2014 Sydney siege, in which a self-styled Islamic cleric took hostages at the Lindt Café, shocked the nation. Subsequent plots and attacks, though smaller in scale, kept the threat alive. Intelligence agencies devote significant resources to monitoring potential extremists, many of whom cite loyalty to Sharia and hostility to Western society.

The link between theology and radicalisation is often denied in public discourse, with commentators attributing extremism to poverty or alienation. Yet the doctrinal roots are clear. The call to jihad, the glorification of martyrdom, and the promise of paradise for fighters are embedded in Islamic texts. While most Muslims reject violence, the presence of these teachings within the tradition cannot be ignored. Security concerns exacerbate cultural tensions. They can make neighbours suspicious, fuel political debates, and test the limits of multicultural tolerance.

They also raise hard questions: can a society truly integrate communities where even a small fraction embrace ideologies hostile to its values?

The role of public discourse

Debates about Islam in Australia play out in the public square, where freedom of speech collides with demands for sensitivity. Advocates of multiculturalism insist that criticism of Islam fuels division and prejudice. Critics argue that honest, open debate is essential for democracy.

Media coverage often shapes perceptions. Incidents of terrorism receive widespread attention, while stories of ordinary Muslims living peacefully will often go unnoticed. Conversely, fear of stigmatising communities can lead to a self-censorship, with journalists avoiding critical coverage.

Universities and public institutions have also become arenas of contention. Islamic student associations campaign for prayer facilities and recognition of Islamic holidays. Guest speakers promoting radical ideologies sometimes gain platforms under the banner of diversity. Efforts to challenge these trends are often met with accusations of Islamophobia.

This climate of sensitivity can really hamper robust discussion. Australians now risk losing the ability to distinguish between criticism of Islam as an ideology and prejudice against Muslims as individuals. Yet the distinction is vital. A democratic society must be free to critique ideas, including religious doctrines, while upholding the dignity of all people.

The burden of multiculturalism

Underlying these challenges is the issue of multiculturalism. Australia's multicultural policy celebrates diversity, whilst also encouraging migrants to maintain cultural traditions while participating in national life. In many cases, this model has succeeded, enriching society with cuisine, art, and innovation. But Islam presents a unique test.

Because Islam is not merely a culture but a comprehensive system, accommodating it fully seriously risks undermining core Australian values. When multiculturalism treats all cultures as equally valid, it may fail to discern practices that contradict democracy, equality, and freedom.

The burden of multiculturalism is that it often places the onus on the host society to adapt rather than on migrants to integrate. Demands for halal certification, separate legal arbitration, or exemptions from some laws, are examples of this pressure. Each concession may seem minor, but together they shift the cultural balance.

Australians must therefore ask whether multiculturalism should have limits. Should cultural practices that violate human rights or undermine social cohesion ever be accommodated? Or must integration take precedence over diversity when values collide?

Christianity's contrast

The serious challenges posed by Islam highlight by contrast the strengths of Australia's Christian heritage. Christianity affirms freedom of conscience, equality before God, and the dignity of women and men alike. It encourages believers to live as good citizens, obeying the law while honouring God. Paul instructed Christians in 1 Thessalonians 4:11, to *"make it your ambition to lead a quiet life: you should mind your own business and work with your hands."*

When Christians immigrated to Australia — from Great Britain, Europe, or elsewhere — they brought values compatible with democracy and liberty. They built schools, hospitals, and many charities that served the whole community. They always sought integration, not isolation, even while preserving their faith.

This notable contrast underscores why Islam presents unique difficulties. It does not integrate naturally with Western values but often resists them. The challenge is therefore not simply one of diversity but of fundamental incompatibility.

Looking ahead

Australia faces hard choices in addressing these cultural and social challenges. Pretending that Islam is identical to other migrant faiths ignores reality. Equally, demonising all Muslims fails to distinguish between individuals and ideologies. The path forward requires clarity: affirming the dignity of Muslims as people while resisting ideologies that undermine Australia's foundations.

Integration must be the expectation, not segregation. Sharia-based practices that directly contradict national law cannot be accommodated. Gender equality and freedom of speech must be non-negotiable. Multiculturalism must be balanced by unity around our shared values. Only with such clarity can Australia even begin to navigate the challenges posed by Islam's growth.

Future implications

The story of Islam in Australia is not merely about the past or present; it must be about the future. The demographic, cultural, and political trends visible today will shape the whole nation for generations. Australia now faces some pressing questions: What trajectory will Muslim communities now follow? How will their growth influence politics, law, and culture? What tensions may emerge between Islam and our Australian identity? And, most crucially, what is at stake for the freedoms and values that define the nation?

Demographic projections

As the saying goes: demography is destiny. Numbers will shape influence, and population growth will carry long-term cultural consequences. Australia's Muslim population, though currently a minority, is arguably the fastest-growing religious group. Fertility rates among Muslims remain higher than the national average, and immigration from those Muslim-majority nations continues through humanitarian, family reunion, and skilled migration streams. If current trends continue, then the Muslim population could double within a generation, reaching well over 1.5 million by 2040.

In certain suburbs of Sydney and Melbourne, Muslims may form local majorities already. This concentration magnifies influence: when numbers are high in particular areas, they can shift local politics, schools, businesses, and cultural life.

Demographic growth also fuels confidence within communities. A small, dispersed minority often seeks quiet coexistence. A larger, concentrated minority may press for accommodation, recognition, and influence. The trajectory suggests that questions of Sharia recognition, cultural accommodation, and political representation will intensify rather than diminish.

Political influence

As numbers grow, so does political influence. Muslims already hold seats in local councils, state parliaments, and the federal parliament. Advocacy groups lobby for recognition of Islamic holidays, opposition to *'Islamophobia,'* and accommodation of religious practices.

In democratic systems, numbers translate into votes. Political parties seeking support in key electorates with large Muslim populations may tailor policies accordingly. Already, debates over asylum seekers, foreign policy in the Middle East, and anti-terrorism laws are influenced by Muslim lobbying.

The long-term question is whether Islamic political influence will align with Australian foundations or seek to reshape them. Will Muslim politicians defend freedom of speech even when Islam is criticised, or will they push for blasphemy-style restrictions? Will they uphold gender equality, or press for accommodations to Sharia family law? The answers will profoundly affect the trajectory of Australian democracy.

Interfaith tensions

Islam's growth also raises the prospect of interfaith tensions. Australia has prided itself on religious pluralism, where Christians, Jews, Buddhists, Hindus, and secular citizens coexist peacefully. But Islam's exclusivist claims, and its communal assertiveness create serious challenges.

Muslims are taught that Islam is the final and true religion, that Muhammad is the last prophet, and that those who reject Islam are in error. While Christianity also makes exclusive claims, its integration into Australian life has historically promoted liberty and respect for others' conscience. Islam's exclusivism, however, is coupled with a legal framework — Sharia — that does not easily tolerate pluralism.

Already, various disputes have arisen over planning approvals for mosques, calls to prayer, and the operation of Islamic schools. Local residents often resist such developments, citing concerns about traffic or noise, but underlying tensions about cultural change are evident. Media coverage amplifies these disputes, fuelling suspicion on both sides. Future interfaith relations will depend on whether Muslim communities embrace the principles of Australian pluralism or push for privileges that undermine equality. The more assertive Islam becomes, the more tension is likely to rise.

Education and the next generation

The long-term influence of Islam in Australia will depend a lot on the next generation. Communities, schools and families, are shaping young Muslims' identities. If they are raised to see themselves primarily as members of the global ummah, loyalty to Australia will invariably weaken. If they are taught to embrace Australian values while practising personal faith, integration may still be possible.

Islamic schools play a decisive role here. Those that emphasise coexistence and civic responsibility can nurture constructive citizens. Those that stress separation and suspicion of Western values always risk producing alienation and radicalisation. The curriculum choices made today will echo for decades to come. Universities are another major battleground. Muslim student associations can advocate strongly for Islamic causes, sometimes promoting radical speakers. As educated young Muslims rise into leadership positions, their outlook will shape our politics, media, and business. Whether they champion integration or confrontation will determine the cultural climate.

The question of Sharia

Perhaps the most contentious future issue is the role of Sharia. While full implementation is highly unlikely in Australia, the pressure for accommodation in specific areas will certainly persist. Family law is one such area. Muslim women already face dilemmas when civil divorce is not recognised within their communities. Advocacy for Sharia arbitration will certainly grow, presented as a matter of religious freedom.

Islamic finance is another domain. Sharia-compliant products are expanding, and as demand grows, financial institutions may increasingly adapt. While not inherently threatening, such adaptations normalise Sharia principles in public life.

The danger is incrementalism. Each concession appears minor, but collectively they shift the legal and cultural framework. Once Sharia principles gain recognition in one domain, they may spread to others. The long-term trajectory here could erode the principle of one law for all, replacing it with parallel systems based on religion.

The stakes for Australian identity

All these trends converge on a central question: what is at stake for Australia's identity? If Islam continues to grow numerically, politically, and culturally, will the nation retain its Christian and Western foundations? Or will it drift toward accommodation of incompatible values?

Australian identity has always been dynamic, shaped by waves of migration. Italians, Greeks, Vietnamese, and others enriched the culture without undermining its foundations. By contrast, Islam, presents not simply a culture but a competing system. If allowed to reshape law and public life, it could erode the very freedoms that enable multiculturalism to flourish.

Freedom of speech could be curtailed by demands to criminalise criticism of Islam. Freedom of religion could be weakened by privileging Islam while silencing evangelism. Gender equality could be undermined by tolerating Sharia-based practices.

At stake is nothing less than the character of the nation. Will Australia remain a free, open, and democratic society rooted in Christian values? Or will it compromise those values in the name of diversity, only to lose them in the process?

The Christian response

For Christians, these challenges are both sobering and urgent. The rise of Islam highlights the need to reaffirm and proclaim the gospel. Only Christ offers true reconciliation with God, freedom of conscience, and assurance of salvation. The church must not retreat into fear but engage with Muslims in love, offering the hope of Jesus Christ while defending the freedoms that make such a witness possible.

Christians must also remind their fellow citizens of the nation's foundations. Liberty, justice, and equality are not just secular inventions but fruits of Christianity. If Australia abandons its roots, it will lack the strength to resist Islam's encroachments. The church has a prophetic role: to call the nation back to its foundations and to defend freedom for all.

7. SHARIA: THE QUESTION OF COMPATIBILITY

The nature of Sharia

Few words generate as much controversy in our contemporary discussions of Islam as the word *Sharia*. For some, it evokes images of harsh punishments and authoritarian rule; for others, it represents a divine path of true guidance. To understand the challenge it poses to Australia, one must grasp what Sharia actually is. Sharia is not simply a set of religious rituals, it is a comprehensive system governing law, morality, and society. Sharia is the very heartbeat of Islam, shaping everything from personal devotion to criminal justice, from family life through to international relations. Its scope is complete, and its claims are absolute. So let's examine Sharia more closely now.

The meaning of Sharia

The word *Sharia* comes from an Arabic root meaning *"path"* or *"way."* In Islamic thought, it signifies the divinely ordained path by which Muslims must all live. It is not limited to religious observance but encompasses every dimension of life—personal, social, economic, political, and judicial. For Muslims, Sharia is not human legislation but God's eternal law, revealed through the Qur'an and exemplified in the life of Muhammad. To follow Sharia is to submit to God's will. To reject it is to rebel against divine authority. This absolutist claim is what makes Sharia fundamentally different from our secular legal systems, which derive authority from human consensus or social contract.

The sources of Sharia

Sharia is derived from four main sources, though their authority and interpretation vary across Islamic traditions:

1. **The Qur'an** – Islam's foundational text, believed to be the literal word of God dictated to Muhammad. While the Qur'an addresses theology and morality, it also contains many legal prescriptions. Verses outline rules for inheritance, marriage, divorce, contracts, punishment, and warfare. Though only a portion of the Qur'an is explicitly legal, Muslims regard its principles as binding.

2. **The Sunnah (Hadith)** – The recorded sayings and actions of Muhammad. Because the Qur'an is often vague, the Sunnah provides practical detail. For example, while the Qur'an commands prayer, it is the Hadith that specify how to perform it. The Hadith collections also contain rulings on punishment, governance, and social conduct. Together, Qur'an and Sunnah form the dual foundation of Sharia.

3. **Ijma (Consensus)** – When the Qur'an and Sunnah leave issues unresolved, Muslim scholars appeal to consensus among jurists. The principle of ijma gives authority to the collective judgment of the community's main scholars. Over many centuries, this consensus shaped much of Sharia's interpretation.

4. **Qiyas (Analogy)** – Reasoning by analogy allows scholars to apply established rulings to new situations. For example, the Qur'an forbids wine; but by analogy, jurists extended the prohibition to all intoxicants.

These sources are interpreted in schools of Islamic jurisprudence (*fiqh*), which systematised Sharia into detailed codes.

The Schools of Law

In Sunni Islam, four major schools of law (*madhahib*) emerged:

➤ *Hanafi* – The most widespread, known for its flexibility and reasoning.

➤ *Maliki* – Rooted in the practices of Medina, often conservative.

➤ *Shafi'i* – Systematic in methodology, emphasising Hadith.

➤ *Hanbali* – The strictest, literalist, and most influential in modern Wahhabi and Salafi movements.

In Shia Islam, the Ja'fari school dominates, with its particular jurisprudential traditions. These schools developed between the eighth and tenth centuries, codifying rulings on virtually every aspect of life. Though they differ in detail, they share the conviction that Sharia governs all domains.

The scope of Sharia

Sharia is not confined to criminal law, as often portrayed in Western media. Its scope is vast, and it includes:

➤ *Ritual law* – Rules for prayer, fasting, pilgrimage, dietary laws, and ritual purity.
➤ *Family law* – Regulations on marriage, divorce, polygamy, inheritance, guardianship, and custody.
➤ *Commercial law* – Contracts, loans, trade, property, taxation, and prohibitions of interest (*riba*).
➤ *Criminal law* – Punishments for theft, adultery, apostasy, blasphemy, and other offences.
➤ *Political law* – Duties of rulers, conduct of war (*jihad*), treatment of non-Muslims, and governance.
➤ *Social law* – Dress codes, gender relations, modesty, and public morality.

In Islamic thought, there is no sacred-secular divide. Religion and politics, worship and law, personal piety and public order are all one. Sharia seeks to order the entirety of society under divine will.

Categories of human action

A distinctive feature of Sharia is its classification of all human actions into five categories:

1. *Obligatory (fard/wajib)* – Acts required by God, such as prayer, fasting, and paying alms. Neglecting these is sinful.
2. *Recommended (mustahabb)* – Acts encouraged but not required, such as extra prayers or charitable deeds.
3. *Permissible (mubah)* – Neutral actions that are neither commanded nor forbidden.
4. *Disliked (makruh)* – Acts discouraged but not sinful, such as divorce (though permitted, it is often considered disliked).
5. *Forbidden (haram)* – Acts strictly prohibited, such as adultery, theft, interest, and consuming pork or alcohol.

This categorisation demonstrates the totalising nature of Sharia: everything humans do, falls into a divine moral framework. Nothing is religiously neutral.

Hudud punishments

Among the most controversial aspects of Sharia are the *hudud* punishments, considered fixed by God. They include:

➤ *Theft* – Punishable by amputation of the hand.

➤ *Adultery* – Punishable by stoning to death for married offenders or 100 lashes for unmarried offenders.

➤ *Apostasy* – Leaving Islam is punishable by death, according to many jurists.

➤ *Blasphemy* – Insulting God, Muhammad, or the Qur'an, are often punishable by death.

➤ *Drinking alcohol* – Punishable by 40–80 lashes.

While not all Muslim-majority nations will enforce these various punishments today, they remain part of classical Sharia. Their presence highlights the profound divergence from Western legal principles, which emphasise human rights and proportional justice.

Dhimmi status and non-Muslims

Sharia also regulates the status of non-Muslims. Jews and Christians, known as *"People of the Book,"* were historically granted protection under Islamic rule as *dhimmis*. In return, they paid a special tax (*jizya*), accepted restrictions on worship and public expression, and acknowledged Muslim dominance.

While dhimmi status offered limited tolerance compared to outright persecution, it enshrined second-class citizenship. Non-Muslims were excluded from equal participation in society. Conversion to Islam was encouraged, while conversion from Islam was forbidden. This system, though varying in severity, reveals how Sharia envisions relations between Muslims and others: not as equals under a common law, but as hierarchically ordered communities.

Historical application

Throughout history, Sharia has shaped Islamic civilisation. From the Abbasid Caliphate to the Ottoman Empire, rulers enforced Sharia to varying degrees. Courts presided over by *qadis* (judges) adjudicated disputes, applying rulings from the schools of law. Scholars held immense power as interpreters of Sharia, often more influential than political rulers.

Sharia governed not only all the religious rituals but also trade, taxation, and warfare. It really regulated everything from the construction of wells to the division of spoils after battles. The integration of religion and law produced societies where Islam permeated every sphere.

Yet Sharia was never static. Local customs always influenced its application. Some rulers enforced it strictly; others used it selectively. But its central claim remained: God's law covers all of life, and no human authority can overrule it.

Sharia and modern misunderstandings

In the West, Sharia is often misunderstood. Some imagine it only in terms of punishments, ignoring its broader scope. Others minimise Sharia as merely personal devotion, comparable to Christian piety. Both views are incomplete.

For Muslims, Sharia is holistic. It is prayer and fasting but also contracts and courts. It is personal morality, but also political authority. To suggest that Muslims can practise Islam while ignoring Sharia is to misunderstand its essence. While some Muslims reinterpret or downplay aspects of Sharia in modern contexts, the ideal of comprehensive divine law remains central.

The theological weight of Sharia

At its core, Sharia is inseparable from Islam's doctrine of God. Allah is absolutely sovereign, and His will is revealed in law. Obedience to Sharia is obedience to God. This contrasts sharply with Christianity, where salvation rests not on law but on grace through Christ.

Paul wrote, *"Therefore no one will be declared righteous in God's sight by the works of the law; rather, through the law we become conscious of our sin."* (Romans 3:20). For Christians, law exposes sin and points us to Christ, but it cannot save. In Islam, by contrast, law is the means of submission. Sharia is not a signpost to grace, but the very path of obedience required for divine approval.

This theological weight explains why Sharia cannot be easily reformed or abandoned. To dilute Sharia is, for many Muslims, to dilute Islam itself.

Implications for compatibility

Understanding the nature of Sharia is crucial for evaluating its compatibility with Australian society. It cannot be overstated: Sharia is not merely a set of private rituals; it is a comprehensive system claiming authority over law, politics, and culture. It envisions a society ordered not by democratic consent but by divine command.

The scope of Sharia — its regulation of family, commerce, crime, and governance — means it cannot simply coexist with secular legal systems. Where Sharia prevails, alternative systems are subordinate. This absolutist claim makes accommodation in pluralistic societies deeply problematic, if not impossible.

Sharia in the modern world

To understand the challenge Sharia poses for Australia, one must look not only at its historical origins but also at how it operates in the modern world.

Sharia is not a relic of the past but a living system that continues to shape nations, communities, and individuals. Its application varies widely: in some countries, it is enforced rigidly; in others, it coexists uneasily with other secular codes. In the West, Sharia emerges in more subtle ways, through cultural demands, legal accommodations, and community practices. Examining these contemporary realities reveals both the resilience of Sharia and the obvious difficulties it presents for societies built on different foundations.

Sharia in Muslim-majority States

Across the Muslim world, Sharia retains a powerful role in shaping law and governance. The degree of enforcement varies, but the principle of divine law remains central.

Saudi Arabia offers the most rigid model. There, Sharia is the law of the land, interpreted through the Hanbali school of jurisprudence and enforced by the religious police. Hudud punishments such as amputations and public beheadings are carried out. Women's rights remain heavily restricted, though recent reforms have loosened some constraints. Political dissent is treated as rebellion against God's order.

Iran provides another model, combining Sharia with theocratic rule. After the 1979 Islamic Revolution, Iran adopted a system of *velayat-e faqih* (guardianship of the jurist), where clerics hold ultimate authority. Laws reflect Ja'fari jurisprudence, with very strict codes on dress, family, and blasphemy. Apostasy and proselytism are punished harshly, and freedom of speech is limited.

Pakistan has a hybrid system. While retaining some secular legal frameworks from its colonial past, it has progressively Islamised many of its laws. Blasphemy laws impose severe penalties, often exploited to persecute minorities. Hudud ordinances introduced in the 1970s prescribe serious punishments such as stoning and whipping, though enforcement varies.

Sudan, Nigeria, and Afghanistan illustrate further variations. Northern Nigeria has implemented Sharia in criminal law, leading to stonings and amputations. Sudan under Islamist rule enforced hudud punishments, though recent political changes have softened enforcement.

Afghanistan under the Taliban represents perhaps the starkest example: girls excluded from education, women confined to the home, public executions conducted in stadiums, and rigid enforcement of every aspect of Sharia.

Even in nations where Sharia is not the sole legal system, it often dominates family law. In Egypt, Jordan, and also in Malaysia, inheritance, marriage, and divorce are all governed by Sharia principles, with unequal treatment of men and women. Non-Muslims are subjected to these codes in certain areas, reinforcing inequality.

Reform attempts

Throughout modern history, Muslim thinkers have debated how Sharia should be applied. Some have sought reform, arguing that traditional jurisprudence must adapt to new realities. Others have insisted on strict enforcement, seeing all compromise as betrayal.

Modernists such as Muhammad Abduh in Egypt (nineteenth century) argued for reinterpretation (*ijtihad*) of the sources, emphasising Sharia's spirit rather than its literal rulings. They sought to harmonise Islam with modern science, education, and governance.

Islamists, by contrast, rejected reform. Thinkers like Sayyid Qutb in Egypt and Abul A'la Maududi in South Asia argued that Islam demands total submission to Sharia in all areas. For them, secular law is idolatry (*jahiliyya*), and only full enforcement of divine law brings true justice. Their ideas inspired movements such as the Muslim Brotherhood, Jamaat-e-Islami, and later radical groups including al-Qaeda.

Reformist governments have attempted compromise. Turkey, under Atatürk in the early twentieth century, abolished Sharia courts and adopted secular codes, though Islamic revival has since regained much ground. Tunisia has pursued relatively progressive reforms, including banning polygamy. Indonesia combines Islamic law in family matters with a broader pluralist framework. Yet reform faces limits. Because Sharia is seen as divine, altering it is viewed by many as heresy. Attempts to reinterpret it, often meet fierce opposition from clerics and traditionalists. Even where reforms occur, core inequalities — such as women's inferior status in inheritance — usually remain.

The persistence of Sharia

What is striking is not how often Sharia has been reformed but how persistently it reasserts itself. Movements for Islamic revival across the twentieth and twenty-first centuries demonstrate the enduring appeal of Sharia. From the Iranian Revolution to the rise of the Taliban, from Boko Haram in Nigeria to ISIS in Iraq and Syria, the cry has been consistent: *"Return to Sharia."*

Even when Muslims migrate to the West, Sharia retains its pull. Community leaders often frame their identity around preserving Islamic law and resisting assimilation. The belief that Sharia is timeless and universal makes compromise very difficult. While individuals may adapt, many communities frequently strive to maintain Sharia norms in dress, diet, marriage, and all dispute resolution.

Sharia in western societies

In the West, Sharia cannot (yet) be imposed as state law, but its influence is clearly visible. Muslim communities establish Sharia councils or arbitration bodies to resolve family disputes. Islamic schools teach Sharia-based curricula. Advocacy groups lobby for accommodation of religious practices.

The United Kingdom provides a notable example. Dozens of Sharia councils operate, handling issues of marriage, divorce, and inheritance. While technically voluntary, women often feel pressured to submit to these councils rather than pursue their rights in civil courts. Critics argue that this creates parallel legal systems, undermining equality before the law.

In the United States, Islamic finance has now expanded, offering Sharia-compliant loans and investments. Halal certification is influencing food industries. While these may seem minor, they represent the embedding of Sharia norms into public life.

In Australia, as earlier chapters noted, similar trends are visible. Mosques and schools promote Sharia values. Advocacy for recognition of Islamic family arbitration has surfaced.

Halal certification has grown into a multimillion-dollar industry. While not formal law, these practices import Sharia principles into the Australian context.

Cultural pressures

Beyond legal accommodations, Sharia exerts cultural pressure. Dress codes such as the hijab, niqab, and burqa each symbolise submission to Sharia norms. Campaigns for separate swimming times, prayer facilities, and exemptions from school activities illustrate the demand for public recognition. Each concession normalises Sharia expectations in broader society.

The most contentious issue is undoubtedly blasphemy. While all Western societies strongly uphold freedom of speech, Muslim communities often demand restrictions on any criticism of Islam. Protests against cartoons of Muhammad, calls to criminalise *"Islamophobia,"* and threats against critics, reveal the collision between Sharia's prohibition of blasphemy and Western free expression.

This cultural pressure often succeeds because Western societies prize tolerance. Left unchecked, this risks eroding foundational freedoms. What begins as respect for diversity can slide into acceptance of censorship, inequality, and segregation.

The dilemma of multiculturalism

Multiculturalism only intensifies this challenge. By affirming all cultures as equally valid, it leaves little room to question Sharia's compatibility. Critics are dismissed as intolerant, even when raising legitimate concerns. The result is a climate where Sharia advances quietly, shielded from scrutiny.

Yet multiculturalism faces a paradox. It depends on the shared freedoms — speech, religion, law — that Sharia undermines! By protecting Sharia practices in the name of diversity, societies risk undermining the very framework that enables diversity to exist. Australia must grapple with this paradox honestly, recognising that not all cultural practices will be equally compatible with democracy.

Reform or resistance?

What, then, is the future of Sharia in the modern world? Two paths are visible. One is reform: Muslims reinterpreting Sharia to align with universal human rights, equality, and pluralism. The other is resistance: Muslims insisting on traditional Sharia, rejecting compromise.

Reform is championed by a number of intellectuals, activists, and politicians. They argue that Sharia's core is justice and mercy, not literal punishments, so they call for contextual interpretation, emphasising principles rather than rigid codes. Some will point to Qur'anic verses like Surah 2:256, *"There is no compulsion in religion"* to support freedom of conscience.

Resistance, however, remains powerful. For many, abandoning Sharia is abandoning Islam. The rise of Islamism in the twentieth century shows the strength of this conviction. Groups from the Muslim Brotherhood to ISIS insist that Sharia is central and non-negotiable.

This clash between reform and resistance will shape Islam's trajectory globally and in Australia. Which path prevails will determine whether Islam integrates peacefully or remains in conflict with Western societies.

Lessons for Australia

Australia must pay close attention to these global dynamics. If Sharia continues to shape Muslim-majority nations with rigidity and inequality, importing communities so deeply attached to Sharia poses many challenges. If reform movements succeed, integration may be easier. But history suggests caution: attempts at reform often falter, while calls for strict Sharia persist.

In the current Australian context, vigilance is essential. Respect for Muslims as individuals must not blind our society to the ideological claims of Sharia. Legal pluralism — separate systems for different groups — must be rejected. Equality before the law, freedom of speech, and liberty of conscience are non-negotiable.

Sharia in the modern world is not a static code but a dynamic force. It shapes nations, inspires movements, and challenges Western societies. Its persistence reveals its centrality to Islam, while reform efforts expose the difficulties of adaptation. For Australia, the lesson is very clear: Sharia is not merely a private religious practice but a comprehensive system with many public implications. To preserve our national foundations, Australians must understand Sharia's global realities and resist pressures to accommodate what is incompatible with freedom.

The question of compatibility

The debate over Islam in Australia ultimately centres on one crucial question: can Sharia coexist with Australian democracy, human rights, and the rule of law? At first glance, some argue yes. They point to many Muslims who live peacefully in Western societies, participating in politics, working in business, and contributing to civic life. They note that not all Muslims seek to impose Sharia, and many interpret their faith in flexible ways.

Yet the issue is not what some Muslims practise privately but what Sharia claims publicly. Once its full scope is examined, the question of compatibility becomes unavoidable. Sharia is not merely a set of devotional practices but a comprehensive system that competes directly with the very foundations of Australia's cultural and political order.

Sharia and democracy

Democracy rests on the principle that sovereignty belongs to the people, who elect representatives to govern the land. Laws can be debated, amended, or repealed according to the will of the people. At its heart lies the belief that human beings possess the authority to legislate for themselves within the framework of justice.

Sharia, by contrast, declares that sovereignty belongs only to Allah. Human beings have no authority to create laws contrary to Allah's revelation. The Qur'an and Sunnah provide eternal guidance, which jurists interpret but cannot override.

This principle renders democracy, in its pure form, incompatible with Sharia. Islamist thinkers such as Sayyid Qutb and Maududi made this explicit. For them, democracy is a form of idolatry (*shirk*), because it elevates human authority above divine law. In their vision, true justice will come only through implementing Sharia in every sphere of life.

Even moderate Muslims will struggle with this tension. Some attempt to reconcile Sharia and democracy by redefining terms: democracy becomes consultation (*shura*), elections become a means of choosing leaders who will enforce Sharia, and freedom is reinterpreted as obedience to God's will.

Yet this is not democracy in the Western sense; it is theocracy by another name. Australia's democratic institutions cannot coexist with a system that denies their legitimacy.

If Sharia were given legal recognition, even in limited areas, it would establish the principle that Islamic divine law outranks democratic law. This precedent would erode the very foundation of popular sovereignty.

Sharia and human hights

Modern human rights frameworks, such as the Universal Declaration of Human Rights, affirm equality of all people regardless of gender, religion, or belief. They protect freedoms of speech, conscience, and religion.

These principles, though often seen as secular, are deeply rooted in Christianity's affirmation of human dignity. Sharia, however, will systematically undermines these rights.

➤ *Freedom of religion:* Apostasy from Islam is punishable by death in classical Sharia. Evangelism by non-Muslims is forbidden. Religious liberty is thus denied.

➤ *Freedom of speech:* Blasphemy laws criminalise criticism of Islam, Muhammad, or the Qur'an. Even in Muslim-minority contexts, pressure is exerted to silence critique.

➤ *Gender equality:* Women receive half the inheritance of men, face unequal divorce rights, and are restricted in leadership. Their testimony is worth half that of men in some legal contexts.

➤ *Equality before the law:* Non-Muslims historically lived as *dhimmis*, tolerated but inferior, paying extra taxes and excluded from full participation.

Attempts to reconcile Sharia with human rights have been very limited. The Cairo Declaration on Human Rights in Islam (1990), drafted by the Organisation of Islamic Cooperation, affirmed rights only insofar as they also conformed to Sharia. This demonstrates the incompatibility: where Sharia rules, rights are conditional, not universal.

Sharia and Australian law

Australia's legal system rests firmly on English common law, parliamentary sovereignty, and equality before the law. Its principles include presumption of innocence, trial by jury, and uniform application of justice. Sharia challenges all of these.

In family law, Sharia permits polygamy, unequal inheritance, and male-dominated divorce. In criminal law, it prescribes punishments such as amputation and stoning. In civil law, it forbids interest, altering financial systems.

To recognise Sharia in any official capacity would fracture the unity of law and Australians would no longer live under one standard but under parallel systems determined by religion.

Already, informal Sharia councils are operating within Muslim communities in Western nations. While presented as voluntary, social pressure often compels compliance, particularly among women.

If Australian authorities were to legitimise such councils, even in arbitration, they would sanction inequality and undermine national law.

The problem of incrementalism

As mentioned earlier, the real danger here lies in incrementalism. Muslim communities rarely demand full Sharia immediately. Instead, they seek gradual accommodations: recognition of halal certification, exemptions from dress codes, provision of prayer facilities, acknowledgment of Islamic holidays, and eventually arbitration in family disputes. Each step seems minor, but together they establish the principle of Sharia's legitimacy. Once embedded, Sharia norms expand. What begins as a cultural accommodation becomes a legal precedent. Western societies, committed to tolerance, are struggling to draw lines, fearing accusations of discrimination. Incrementalism thus advances Sharia without confrontation, eroding freedoms over time.

Can 'Private Sharia' be harmless?

Some argue that Sharia is harmless if confined to personal life — dietary rules, prayer, fasting, modest dress. Indeed, Muslims should be free to practise these under Australia's commitment to religious liberty. But the difficulty lies in the indivisibility of Sharia. For those devout Muslims, it is neither optional nor compartmentalised. Personal devotion flows naturally into public law. So, to accept 'private Sharia' as harmless without acknowledging its claim to totality is just naïve. Even personal practices can shape public space.

When halal certification dominates food industries, when veiling becomes widespread, when schools restructure for Islamic prayer, Sharia influences the broader society. What begins as private devotion can become cultural expectation, then legal demand.

Case studies of incompatibility

Historical and contemporary examples prove the incompatibility of Sharia with Western systems.

➤ **Nigeria**: In northern states where Sharia was introduced alongside national law, tensions erupted. Christians faced discrimination, and hudud punishments clashed with constitutional protections.

- ➤ **United Kingdom**: Sharia councils operate unofficially, but investigations reveal women are pressured into unequal settlements. Parallel systems erode equality before the law.

- ➤ **France**: Efforts to restrict Islamic dress have led to clashes over freedom and identity, highlighting the difficulty of accommodating Sharia norms in secular systems.

- ➤ **Australia**: Though Sharia is not legally recognised, demands for accommodation continue — family arbitration, prayer in schools, halal certification. Each debate illustrates the friction between Sharia claims and Australian principles.

These cases demonstrate that even partial recognition of Sharia destabilises national law and unity.

Theological incompatibility

Beyond legal and political incompatibility lies great theological tension. Christianity proclaims salvation by grace, liberty of conscience, and the lordship of Jesus Christ over creation. Islam proclaims submission to law, coercion of conscience, and the supremacy of Sharia.

Paul warned the Galatians against returning to legalism: *"It is for freedom that Christ has set us free. Stand firm, then, and do not let yourselves be burdened again by a yoke of slavery."* (Galatians 5:1).

For Christians, Sharia represents that yoke: a system of works that cannot save and that enslaves societies. The incompatibility is not only cultural but spiritual. Where the Spirit of the Lord is, there is freedom (2 Corinthians 3:17). Where Sharia rules, there is control. The two can never be reconciled.

What is at stake for Australia

The question of Sharia's compatibility is not just theoretical. If Australians accept even partial recognition of Sharia, they risk undermining the principles that safeguard their freedom.

- ➤ *Freedom of speech* could be curtailed by blasphemy-style restrictions.
- ➤ *Freedom of religion* could be compromised by privileging Islam and silencing evangelism.
- ➤ *Equality before the law* could fracture if family or financial matters were governed separately.
- ➤ *Democratic sovereignty* could erode if divine law were placed above the will of the people.

What is at stake is the character of the nation itself. Australia must decide whether it will preserve its Christian and Western foundations or compromise them for the sake of multicultural accommodation.

A path forward

The path forward requires clarity. Australians must:

- ➤ Affirm the freedom of Muslims to practise personal devotion within the bounds of national law.
- ➤ Reject all attempts to recognise or accommodate Sharia as a parallel legal system.
- ➤ Defend freedom of speech, ensuring criticism of Islam is protected as legitimate discourse.
- ➤ Reaffirm Christian foundations, recognising that liberty, equality, and dignity flow from the gospel.

Only by standing firm on these principles can Australia resist the encroachment of Sharia and preserve the freedoms that define its identity.

8. IMMIGRATION AND THE FUTURE OF AUSTRALIA

Immigration has always been central to the story of Australia. From its beginnings as a British colony to its emergence as a modern multicultural society, this nation has been shaped by successive waves of newcomers. Each of these waves brought opportunities and tensions, enriching the culture while testing the fabric of national unity. To understand the challenge of Islamic immigration today, one must first understand the wider story of how immigration has worked in Australia's history.

The colonial foundations

When Britain established its penal colony in 1788, immigration to Australia was initially involuntary. Convicts transported from Britain and Ireland formed the bulk of the early population. Yet even in this penal context, immigration was nation-building. Free settlers followed, drawn by land grants and opportunity.

Throughout the nineteenth century, immigration expanded. The discovery of gold in the 1850s brought thousands from Britain, Ireland, and beyond. Chinese migrants arrived in significant numbers, sparking racial tensions and restrictive legislation. Despite these tensions, the overwhelming cultural character of the colonies remained British and Christian. The legal system, language, institutions, and values all reflected this heritage.

Muslims were present in fairly small numbers from the mid-nineteenth century. Afghan cameleers and Indian hawkers contributed to transport and trade, especially in the outback. They built the first mosques, such as the Adelaide mosque (1888), but their numbers were too small to shape national culture. The dominant ethos remained firmly Western and Christian.

The White Australia Policy

At Federation in 1901, immigration became a defining national issue. The new Commonwealth government introduced the Immigration Restriction Act, which was better known as the *White Australia Policy.*

Its aim was clear: preserve Australia as a nation with European, predominantly British, heritage. The infamous dictation test allowed authorities to exclude unwanted migrants, particularly from Asia. The White Australia Policy reflected both racial prejudice and cultural concern. Leaders feared that large-scale Asian or non-European immigration would undermine wages, social cohesion, and national identity. While harsh by today's standards, the policy was seen as essential then for preserving Australia's Western character.

For many decades, immigration was tightly controlled. Most newcomers were British, with smaller numbers from Europe. Muslims, along with some other non-Europeans, were largely excluded. As a result, Islam remained virtually invisible in early twentieth-century Australia.

Post-War immigration and the end of white Australia

World War II changed everything. With a population of seven million and fears of invasion fresh in our memory, Australia embarked on a massive immigration program. The slogan was *"populate or perish."* Over the next decades, millions arrived, first from Britain and later from continental Europe. Italians, Greeks, Dutch, and Germans joined the Australian story, contributing to industry, agriculture, and urban growth.

This wave reshaped Australian society. Ethnic neighbourhoods sprang up, European cuisines enriched the culture, and Catholic and Orthodox communities grew. Yet the newcomers, while diverse, shared a broad cultural compatibility. They came from Christian backgrounds, valued work and family, and integrated into democratic institutions.

By the 1960s and 1970s, pressure had mounted to dismantle the White Australia Policy. Changing attitudes, decolonisation, and the civil rights movement made racially based immigration untenable. The policy was gradually abolished, replaced by a points-based system that assessed migrants by skills, not race. This shift opened the door to non-European immigration.

Migrants from Asia, the Middle East, and Africa began arriving in significant numbers. Australia's identity began to move from a British outpost to a multicultural nation.

The rise of multiculturalism

The 1970s and 1980s saw the official rise of multiculturalism. Governments promoted the idea that cultural diversity was not a threat but a strength. Migrants were encouraged to maintain their traditions while participating in Australian society. Ethnic media, cultural festivals, and community grants flourished.

Multiculturalism brought benefits. Vietnamese refugees, by way of example, rebuilt their lives after the war, contributing to commerce and culture. Indian and Chinese migrants excelled in the education and business fields. Australia's global connections expanded, and its cuisine, arts, and workforce were all enriched.

Yet multiculturalism also created some dilemmas. How much diversity could be accommodated without it eroding our shared values? Should cultural practices that conflicted with equality or freedom be tolerated? These questions became sharper as Islamic immigration grew.

Islamic immigration in the modern era

The 1970s saw the beginning of significant Islamic immigration. Two groups in particular transformed the landscape: Lebanese and Turkish migrants.

Lebanese Muslims arrived in large numbers during their civil war of the 1970s and 1980s. Many settled in Sydney's western suburbs, particularly in areas such as Lakemba, Auburn, and Bankstown. They established mosques, schools, and businesses, creating visible Islamic communities.

Turkish migrants also arrived under bilateral labour agreements. Concentrated in Melbourne and Sydney, they founded cultural associations and mosques, maintaining very strong ties to their homeland.

In the decades which followed, Islamic immigration diversified further. Bosnian Muslims arrived during the Balkan conflicts of the 1990s. Afghan, Iraqi, and Somali refugees came, fleeing war and persecution. More recently, Syrian refugees have now joined them. Each group added to the mosaic of Australia's Muslim population. As outlined in chapter 6, the Muslim population in Australia has grown from 23,000 in 1979, to over 800,000 today. That is striking in itself, however, as we discuss in this book, the visibility of Islam in Australia is far greater than the numbers alone would suggest.

Contrasts with earlier immigration

Islamic immigration differs from the earlier waves in several respects.

> *Cultural distance:* European migrants, though linguistically and religiously diverse, shared broad cultural compatibility. Islam, by contrast, embodies a worldview fundamentally different from Western liberal democracy.

> *Religious claims:* Christianity and secularism accept a separation of religion and state. Islam insists on integration of law, politics, and faith.

> *Integration patterns:* Many European migrants dispersed and assimilated within a generation. Muslim migrants often cluster in enclaves, preserving distinct identities.

> *Demographic growth:* Higher fertility rates among Muslims accelerate their growth relative to other groups.

These contrasts explain why Islamic immigration raises sharper questions about cultural compatibility than previous waves.

Multiculturalism meets Islam

Multiculturalism assumed that all cultures could coexist under one set of shared democratic values. But Islam severely tests this assumption. Practices such as gender segregation, polygamy, forced marriage, and restrictions on free speech conflict with Australian law. Demands for recognition of Sharia in family matters highlight the tension.

When multiculturalism treats all cultures as equally valid, it struggles to resist those that contradict foundational values. The result will be either cultural relativism—accepting incompatible practices—or conflict as values collide. Australia now faces this dilemma with Islamic immigration.

Public perceptions and the media

The growth of Islam has provoked intense public debate. Media coverage of terrorism, radicalisation, and cultural clashes has heightened anxiety. Incidents such as the Sydney siege (2014) or reports of honour-based violence fuel suspicion. At the same time, advocates emphasise Muslim contributions, highlighting professionals, entrepreneurs, and community leaders.

Public opinion remains divided. Some Australians will embrace multiculturalism wholeheartedly, viewing Islam as one more faith among many. Others fear cultural erosion and security risks. The divide often reflects deeper questions about national identity: Is Australia defined by Western and Christian values, or is it a neutral multicultural space where all cultures are equal?

The lessons of history

Australia's immigration history offers lessons. Earlier waves enriched the nation without undermining its cultural or spiritual foundations because they were broadly compatible with its core values. Italian and Greek migrants, for example, brought distinct traditions but shared Christian heritage and commitment to work and family. Vietnamese refugees arrived with different religions but embraced education, entrepreneurship, and civic participation.

Islamic immigration, however, presents some unique challenges because of Sharia's comprehensive claims. Unlike other faiths, Islam does not easily separate private devotion from public law. The risk is that Islamic enclaves develop parallel systems that resist assimilation. The history of immigration shows that integration is possible—but only when newcomers embrace the nation's foundations. If communities demand exceptions or recognition of practices which are incompatible, the foundations themselves are threatened.

A defining moment in history

Australia now faces a defining moment in our history as a nation. Immigration will obviously continue; the question is whether it will strengthen or weaken the nation.

If Islamic immigration followed the pattern of earlier waves, that is, embracing Australian values while still preserving personal traditions, the challenge may be manageable. But if Islamic communities insist on Sharia, resist assimilation, and grow in demographic and political influence, the future will look very different.

Immigration has always been a difficult balancing act — between openness and preservation, compassion and caution. In the case of Islam, that balance requires unusual clarity. Australia must recognise both the dignity of Muslims as individuals and the dangers of accommodating a system incompatible with freedom.

The pressures of Islamic immigration today

Immigration has always shaped Australia, but in the twenty-first century, it has become one of the most contested issues in public life. For so many Australians, immigration is associated with new opportunities, economic growth, and cultural diversity. For others, it raises concerns about security, cohesion, and identity.

No stream of immigration is more controversial than that from Muslim-majority nations. The growth of Islamic communities has presented Australia with new pressures — social, economic, political, and cultural — that test the nation's capacity to balance openness with preservation.

Humanitarian and refugee intakes

A major source of Islamic immigration in recent decades has been Australia's humanitarian program. Wars and instability in the Middle East, Central Asia, and Africa have driven millions from their homes, and Australia has played its part in resettling refugees. Afghan, Iraqi, Syrian, Somali, and Sudanese refugees have found new lives in Australian cities. This large intake reflects Australia's humanitarian commitments.

Refugee programs are framed as moral obligations, rooted in compassion for the vulnerable. Churches and charities often support these efforts, reflecting biblical commands to care for the stranger and the oppressed (Deut. 10:18–19; Matthew 25:35). Yet humanitarian intakes also create real challenges. Refugees often arrive with little education, limited English, and deep trauma. Integration can be slow and costly.

Muslim refugees face particular obstacles. Many come from societies where Sharia dominates, where women are secluded, and where distrust of the West is deeply ingrained. Adjusting to Australia's freedoms can be very disorienting. Some embrace opportunity; others retreat into enclaves, preserving cultural norms incompatible with their new context.

Chain migration and family reunion

Beyond humanitarian intake, much Islamic immigration occurs through family reunions. Once a refugee or a migrant is established, they can sponsor relatives. This process, known as chain migration, expands communities rapidly. A single family may bring dozens over time, concentrating settlement in specific suburbs.

Chain migration reinforces cultural continuity. Unlike skilled migration, which prioritises individuals with education and language ability, family reunion brings people who may lack such skills. They arrive and join ready-made communities where English is seldom spoken and Islamic practices are preserved. This pattern only intensifies segregation. Rather than dispersing across the nation, migrants will cluster with relatives and co-religionists. Suburbs become dominated by particular cultural groups, with their own mosques, schools, and businesses. While this provides comfort for newcomers, it hinders integration and fosters parallel societies.

Settlement patterns and enclaves

The geographic concentration of Muslims in Australia is striking. In Sydney, suburbs such as Lakemba, Auburn, Bankstown, and Punchbowl have large Muslim populations.

In Melbourne, Broadmeadows, Coburg, and Dandenong play similar roles. These suburbs are marked by mosques, halal shops, Islamic schools, and Arabic signage.

While concentration is not unique to Muslims — many ethnic groups cluster initially — it becomes problematic when it persists across generations. Italians, Greeks, and Vietnamese initially formed enclaves but gradually dispersed. Muslims, however, often remain concentrated, preserving distinct identities. This persistence is then fuelled by strong religious institutions that reinforce separation.

The visibility of these Islamic enclaves generates both pride and tension. For Muslims, it provides a real sense of belonging and continuity. For other Australians, it raises serious concerns about integration and national unity. Enclaves risk becoming "states within a state," where Sharia norms overshadow Australian law.

Economic contributions vs. welfare dependence

Immigration is often justified on economic grounds, with claims that migrants boost the workforce and drive innovation. Many Muslims contribute significantly. Doctors, engineers, business owners, and professionals from Muslim backgrounds enrich the economy. Their success stories certainly highlight the potential of integration. Yet statistics also reveal many challenges. Muslim Australians, particularly from refugee backgrounds, experience higher unemployment and lower labour-force participation than the national average.

Language barriers, limited education, and discrimination all play a role. But cultural factors also matter. Traditional gender roles may limit women's participation, and reliance on their community networks may reduce engagement with society. Welfare dependence is higher among some Muslim groups, particularly recent arrivals. This strains public services and fuels resentment among other Australians, who perceive newcomers as beneficiaries rather than contributors. While many overcome these barriers over time, the persistence of economic disparities highlights integration difficulties.

Education and assimilation

Education is central to integration. For Muslim Australians, the outcomes will vary widely. Some excel, particularly second-generation students who embrace new opportunities. Others lag behind, struggling with language and cultural adjustment.

Islamic schools play a decisive role. Dozens now operate across the country, educating tens of thousands of children. Some balance Islamic instruction with civic education, preparing students for integration. Others, however, foster separation, emphasising Sharia values over any kind of Australian identity. Investigations have revealed schools misusing funds or inviting radical speakers, raising concerns about what is being taught.

Public schools also face serious challenges. Muslim students may demand prayer rooms, halal food, or exemptions from certain activities. While accommodation of faith is reasonable, persistent demands risk undermining the principle of shared schooling. Schools then become sites of cultural negotiation rather than integration.

Assimilation is further complicated by global Islamic identity. Social media, satellite television, and online networks connect young Muslims to the wider ummah. Events in Palestine, Syria, or Afghanistan resonate deeply, shaping identity more than local context. For some, loyalty to global Islam outweighs loyalty to Australia.

Gender and family pressures

Gender dynamics have certainly highlighted the pressures of Islamic immigration. Australian law enshrines equality between men and women, yet Islamic traditions often impose inequality. Polygamy, while illegal, occurs informally. Women may face pressure to marry within the community, wear hijab, or avoid employment. Divorce is more difficult for women than men under Sharia norms, leaving some trapped in abusive situations. Cases of forced marriage and honour-based violence, though not widespread, have been documented.

These practices clash directly with our Australian values. They illustrate how cultural norms from Islamic societies can persist within migrant communities, challenging the principle of gender equality. Support services struggle to respond. Women torn between community loyalty and personal freedom often face isolation. Advocacy groups highlight these issues, but cultural sensitivities make intervention difficult.

Security concerns

Perhaps the most serious pressure associated with Islamic immigration is security. A small but significant minority of Muslims in Australia have embraced radical ideologies. Dozens have travelled overseas to join jihadist groups. Others have plotted attacks at home.

The Sydney siege in 2014, where hostages were taken in the Lindt Café, shocked the nation. Other incidents, though smaller in scale, have kept fears alive. Counter-terrorism agencies monitor potential extremists constantly. The cost of these efforts — in money, manpower, and public anxiety — is high. Radicalisation often occurs among second-generation Muslims who often feel alienated from both their parents' culture and Australian society. Online propaganda exploits these tensions, offering belonging and purpose in jihad. While most Muslims reject extremism, the presence of radicalisation within their communities intensifies scrutiny and suspicion.

Public debate and political pressure

Islamic immigration has become a flashpoint in public debate. Advocates will emphasise compassion, diversity, and economic contribution. Critics will highlight serious security risks, welfare dependence, and obvious cultural incompatibility. Politicians walk a tightrope every day, balancing multicultural ideals with public concerns. Advocacy groups lobby for accommodation of Islamic practices — recognition of Islamic holidays, provision of prayer rooms, halal certification, and even consideration of Sharia arbitration. Each demand raises questions about how far this accommodation should go. At what point does tolerance become compromise?

Public discourse is all too often polarised. Critics of Islamic immigration are accused of Islamophobia, while defenders are accused of naivety. The debate reflects deeper tensions about national identity. Is Australia defined by Western values, or is it a neutral multicultural space? The answer shapes immigration policy and cultural expectations.

Assimilation vs. multiculturalism

At the heart of the debate lies the question: should immigrants assimilate into Australian culture, or should Australia adapt to them? Assimilation emphasises a shared national identity rooted in Western values. Multiculturalism emphasises diversity and coexistence.

With earlier immigrant groups, assimilation largely prevailed. Italians, Greeks, and Vietnamese gradually integrated while preserving traditions. With Islam, assimilation is harder. Sharia claims to govern all of life, resisting compartmentalisation. Multiculturalism, by treating all cultures as equal, struggles to confront this incompatibility. The result is great tension. Some Muslims integrate fully, balancing faith with citizenship. Others retreat into enclaves, preserving their separation. The national conversation oscillates between celebration of diversity and anxiety about cohesion.

The Christian perspective

For Christians, the pressures of Islamic immigration highlight the need for compassion and clarity. Scripture calls believers to welcome the stranger (Leviticus 19:34) but also to guard against false teaching (Galatians 1:8). Compassion must not mean compromise. Australia should extend kindness to Muslims as people while resisting ideologies that undermine freedom. The gospel offers the hope of transformation.

Many Muslims in Australia have encountered Christ through the witness of churches, discovering grace and freedom. Yet this mission depends on preserving freedoms of speech and religion. If Sharia gains ground, those freedoms will be eroded.

Islamic immigration places Australia at a pressure point. The nation must decide whether it will uphold assimilation into its Western foundations or accommodate practices incompatible with them. The stakes are very high: cultural cohesion, gender equality, national security, and freedom itself. The pressures of today foreshadow the challenges of tomorrow. Unless addressed with clarity, compassion, and conviction, these pressures may fracture the very fabric of Australian society.

Future trajectories

Immigration is never only about the present. Its deepest impact is generational. Policies adopted today shape communities for decades, altering demographics, politics, and culture. With Islamic immigration, this long-term perspective is essential. The numbers may appear modest now, but the trends point toward significantly more influence in the future. Whether this influence strengthens or undermines Australia will depend on decisions made in the coming years.

Demographic momentum

One of the most important concepts in immigration studies is demographic momentum. Even if migration were reduced tomorrow, existing communities continue to grow through natural increase. Muslim families in Australia have on average, more children than non-Muslims. This higher fertility rate, combined with continued migration, ensures that the Muslim share of the population will rise. Projections suggest that by 2040, Muslims could number up to 2 million, which is about 7% of the whole population. While still only a minority, concentrated settlement always magnifies influence. In parts of Sydney and Melbourne, Muslims could easily form local majorities. These demographic shifts will shape schools, local councils, and cultural life.

Demographic momentum also affects our confidence. Small minorities often seek quiet coexistence; larger minorities press hard for recognition. As the numbers grow, so do the demands for accommodation — Islamic holidays, halal certification, prayer facilities, and even Sharia arbitration — are all likely to increase.

Political influence

Numbers translate into political weight. In democratic systems, voting blocs matter. Already, Muslim candidates hold positions at the local, state, and federal levels. Advocacy groups lobby politicians, using the language of diversity and human rights to press for recognition.

Future political influence will likely expand. Electorates with large Muslim populations have become swing seats. Political parties, eager for votes, may tailor policies accordingly. We have already seen debates over asylum seekers, anti-terrorism laws, and hate-speech legislation influenced by Muslim advocacy.

The key question here is direction. Will Muslim politicians and activists champion Australian values, defending free speech and gender equality even when Islam is criticised? Or will they push for restrictions, privileging Islam in law and culture? The answer will shape Australia's political climate.

Cultural influence

Beyond politics, cultural influence is already visible and will grow. Halal certification dominates the food industry. Islamic dress is increasingly common in public life. Mosques and schools are shaping whole neighbourhoods. Media outlets provide platforms for Muslim voices, and universities host Islamic associations.

As communities grow, so will cultural assertiveness. Demands for recognition of Islamic identity will only expand. Campaigns against *"Islamophobia"* will pressure our institutions to censor criticism. Artistic and academic expressions deemed offensive may be silenced. The whole cultural climate could shift toward accommodation rather than open debate. The trajectory depends on whether Australian society maintains confidence in its own values. If it forgets its Christian and Western foundations, it will lack the conviction to resist pressures. Cultural influence does not require majority status; it requires persistence, assertiveness, and the willingness of others to yield ground.

Risks of parallel societies

Perhaps the greatest risk is the emergence of parallel societies. When immigrant groups remain concentrated, preserve their own norms, and resist assimilation, they create cultural enclaves. Over time, these enclaves can function as societies within a society, governed informally by their own rules.

In Europe, such enclaves are already evident. Neighbourhoods in Paris, London, and Brussels are dominated by Islamic identity, where police fear to enter and Sharia norms hold sway. Australia is not at that point, but the risk is real. In Sydney's western suburbs and parts of Melbourne, Islamic enclaves already shape local culture distinct from broader Australian society.

Parallel societies erode our national unity. They create suspicion, strain public services, and help foster radicalisation. They also undermine the basic principle of equality before the law. When different groups live by different standards, cohesion is lost.

Australia must ask whether it will allow parallel societies to develop or insist on integration into one national culture. The answer will determine its future stability.

Security concerns

Security remains a pressing issue in future trajectories. While only a small minority of Muslims embrace extremism, the consequences are severe. Radicalisation among youth, inspired by global jihadist movements, remains a huge risk. The internet ensures that extremist propaganda circulates freely every day.

Even without large-scale attacks, the mere threat of terrorism shapes public life. Governments devote billions to security, surveillance, and counter-terrorism. Communities feel fear and suspicion. Social trust is eroded.

Future immigration from unstable Muslim-majority nations will likely bring further security challenges. Screening cannot catch every risk. Even second-generation migrants may radicalise, caught between cultures and drawn to extremist ideologies.

Economic impact

The economic impact of Islamic immigration is mixed and will continue to shape future trajectories. Skilled migrants from Muslim backgrounds contribute positively, working as doctors, engineers, and entrepreneurs. Refugees and family reunion migrants, however, often struggle, leading to higher welfare dependence.

If current patterns persist, economic disparities between Muslim communities and the wider population may grow. This risks creating cycles of disadvantage, resentment, and alienation — fertile ground for radicalisation. It also burdens public services, fuelling political backlash. The long-term question is whether Muslim communities will integrate economically, as earlier migrant groups did, or remain concentrated in lower socio-economic strata. Education and employment outcomes will be decisive.

The challenge of multiculturalism

Australia's official embrace of multiculturalism complicates future trajectories. By celebrating diversity, it often avoids difficult questions about cultural compatibility.

Critics of Islamic immigration are branded intolerant, while advocates downplay challenges. But multiculturalism depends on shared foundations: equality, freedom, and democracy. If these are compromised, multiculturalism collapses. The more Australia accommodates incompatible practices, the more it undermines its own framework.

Future debates will hinge on whether multiculturalism has limits. Should practices such as polygamy, gender segregation, or blasphemy restrictions be tolerated? Or must integration into Australian values take precedence?

The answer will determine whether diversity strengthens or fractures the nation. I will dig deeper into the Multicultural challenge in a future chapter.

Policy choices for the future

Australia faces critical policy choices in shaping its immigration future:

➤ *Immigration levels and sources* – Should intake from Muslim-majority nations be limited, redirected, or maintained? Balancing humanitarian obligations with cultural compatibility is essential.

➤ *Integration vs. accommodation* – Will policies insist on assimilation into Australian values, or will they allow parallel legal and cultural systems?

➤ *Education* – Will Islamic schools be held accountable to teach civic values and equality, or allowed to foster separation?

➤ *Security* – How will authorities balance protection from radicalisation with freedom of religion and speech?

➤ *Public discourse* – Will Australians defend the right to critique Islam without fear of censorship, or will political correctness stifle debate?

Each choice carries some long-term consequences. The future of Australian freedom, our identity, and our unity hangs on these decisions.

The stakes for national identity

At stake in these trajectories is nothing less than our national identity. Will Australia remain a Western, democratic, Christian-influenced society, or will it drift toward cultural relativism and eventual Islamisation?

History shows that nations can change dramatically through immigration. The character of cities, institutions, and laws shifts with demographics and cultural pressure. If Australia forgets its foundations, it may find itself accommodating practices once unthinkable: Sharia arbitration, restrictions on speech, and gender inequality. The challenge is not merely managing diversity but preserving identity. Diversity without unity is only fragmentation.

Unity without values is coercion. Australia can only navigate the pressures of Islamic immigration by reaffirming its Christian and Western heritage.

The Christian response

For Christians, these trajectories call for vigilance and mission. Vigilance, to defend freedoms which will allow the gospel to be preached. Mission, to reach Muslims with the good news of Christ. The church must model both conviction and compassion, refusing to compromise truth while extending love.

The gospel provides what Sharia cannot: forgiveness of sins, assurance of salvation, and freedom of conscience. Paul's words remain urgent: *"It is for freedom that Christ has set us free. Stand firm, then, and do not let yourselves be burdened again by a yoke of slavery"* (Galatians 5:1). Only the freedom of the gospel can preserve Australia's liberty in the face of Sharia's claims.

9. CULTURAL INCOMPATIBILITY: ISLAM AND AUSTRALIAN VALUES

The core values of Australian society are under threat

Nations are not defined merely by borders or governments but by shared values — the principles that shape their institutions, culture, and identity. For Australia, certain values have long been central: freedom, equality, mateship, democracy, and the rule of law. These values emerged from Western civilisation, were nurtured by Christianity, and were tested by history. They remain the foundation upon which Australian society rests.

The question before us is whether these values are compatible with Islam. Many Australians assume that all cultures share some basic commitments to freedom and fairness. Yet a closer examination reveals profound differences. Sharia law and Islamic culture, rooted in very different assumptions, challenge each of Australia's core values.

Freedom

Freedom is one of the most cherished values in Australian. Those who call Australia home, pride themselves on their ability to speak their minds, practise their faith, and live without excessive interference. Freedom of speech, religion, and association are taken for granted, even if they are not always enshrined explicitly in the Constitution.

This love of freedom is deeply Christian in origin. The Bible affirms liberty of conscience: *"Now the Lord is the Spirit, and where the Spirit of the Lord is, there is freedom."* (2 Corinthians 3:17). Jesus invited, but never coerced, faith. The early church grew not by force but by persuasion. Over centuries, this conviction shaped Western notions of freedom.

Islam, however, views freedom very differently. Sharia does not protect freedom of conscience in the same way. Apostasy — leaving Islam — is punishable by death in many interpretations.

Blasphemy—criticising Muhammad or the Qur'an—will incur severe penalties. Freedom of speech is curtailed when it conflicts with Islamic sensibilities. Freedom of religion is tolerated only within strict limits.

Even in Muslim-minority contexts, Islamic advocacy will press for restrictions on freedom. A growing number of campaigns against *"Islamophobia"* frequently blur the line between prejudice against Muslims as people and criticism of Islam as an ideology. The effect is chilling: public discourse is constrained, not by law alone but by fear of offence or retaliation. The Australian instinct to *"live and let live"* collides with an Islamic system that insists some freedoms must be curtailed to protect religion. This is not merely a minor cultural difference but a fundamental clash of worldviews.

Equality

Equality is another defining Australian value. The idea of *"a fair go"* resonates deeply in the national psyche. Australians expect that people will be treated without favouritism, regardless of wealth, status, or background. This egalitarian ethos is visible in the informality of social life, where titles carry little weight and everyone calls each other by their first name.

Again, Christianity undergirds this value. The gospel proclaims that all are created in God's image, and all stand equal at the foot of the cross. Paul declared, *"There is neither Jew nor Gentile, neither slave nor free, nor is there male and female, for you are all one in Christ Jesus."* (Galatians 3:28). This deep theological conviction helped dismantle slavery and inspire movements for human rights.

Sharia, however, institutionalises inequality. It treats men and women differently in inheritance, testimony, and divorce. Men may marry multiple wives; women may not marry multiple husbands. Non-Muslims are tolerated as *dhimmis* but subjected to extra taxes and restrictions. Even within Islam, different sects face unequal treatment. These inequalities are not accidental but systemic. They reflect the very structure of Islamic law, which divides humanity into categories of privilege and restriction.

To import Sharia into Australia would be to abandon the principle of equality. The Australian value of *"a fair go"* cannot coexist with a system that declares some inherently worth half as much as others.

Mateship

As discussed in chapter 5, mateship is uniquely Australian. More than simple friendship, mateship embodies loyalty, solidarity, and mutual support. It was forged in hardship—among convicts, in the bush, and on the battlefield. To be a mate is to stand by someone regardless of circumstance, to share burdens and risks. Mateship has Christian echoes. In John 15:13, Jesus told His disciples, *"Greater love has no one than this: to lay down one's life for one's friends."* The gospel community is called to bear one another's burdens and love as Christ loved.

Islam complicates this concept of mateship. Sharia encourages loyalty first to the *ummah*—the global community of Muslims. Brotherhood is defined by faith, not shared citizenship. While Muslims may show kindness to non-Muslims, the deepest bonds of loyalty are reserved for fellow believers.

This creates tension in multicultural societies. Can Muslims truly embrace mateship with non-Muslims when Sharia frames outsiders as *kuffar* (unbelievers)? Some Muslims do, of course, form genuine friendships across cultural lines.

But the theological underpinning of Islam prioritises separation. Loyalty to the global *ummah* often overrides loyalty to the nation. Australia's ethos of inclusive mateship collides with an ideology that divides the world into believers and unbelievers.

Democracy

Democracy is central to Australia's political life. The principle that citizens elect their leaders, that laws can be debated and changed, and that power rests with the people, defines the nation's governance. Australians accept democracy not as perfect but as the best available system of government.

Christianity influenced this development quite profoundly. The biblical idea that rulers are accountable to God and people, the Protestant emphasis on the individual's conscience, and the separation of church and state all paved the way for democratic institutions.

Islam, however, does not embrace democracy in the same way. Sovereignty belongs to Allah, not to the people. Sharia is divine law, not subject to human amendment. While Islamic thinkers sometimes use democratic mechanisms, such as elections, these are often reframed as tools for selecting leaders who will enforce Sharia.

This is not democracy in the Western sense. It is theocracy by another name. Islamist movements make this explicit: for them, democracy that contradicts Sharia is illegitimate. Sayyid Qutb declared democracy to be idolatry, because it elevates human will above divine command.

In practice, attempts to combine Sharia with democracy result in parochial systems where rights are conditional and dissent is suppressed. For Australia, whose institutions rest firmly on parliamentary sovereignty, importing Sharia would result in undermining democracy itself.

The rule of law

The rule of law underpins Australian society. It means that laws apply equally to all, rulers and citizens alike. It ensures justice is impartial, rights are protected, and disputes are resolved by evidence rather than power. Australians trust that courts, however imperfect, will adjudicate fairly.

This principle has biblical roots. When King David sinned, he was held accountable by the prophet Nathan (2 Samuel 12). No one, not even the king, could stand above God's law. Western civilisation developed this into the principle that even rulers must obey the law. The Magna Carta, the English Bill of Rights, and the Westminster tradition reinforced this conviction.

Sharia redefines the rule of law. It is not impartial justice but divine decree. Men and women are treated differently. Muslims and non-Muslims face very different rules. Apostates and blasphemers are punished severely, not for harming others, but for offending religion. Rulers are not accountable to the people in the same way but serve as guardians of Sharia.

This is a fundamentally different concept of law. It undermines equality, erodes rights, and replaces civic justice with religious conformity. To allow Sharia a foothold in Australia would be to fracture the unity of the law. Australians would no longer live under one standard but under parallel systems.

Why these values matter

Some argue that values are flexible, that societies evolve, and that cultural differences can be managed. But Australia's core values are not arbitrary. They are the foundation of its freedoms and its institutions. Without democracy, equality, mateship, the rule of law and freedom, Australia would not be the nation it is.

These values are not merely secular ideals but fruits of Christian heritage. They emerged from the gospel's influence on Western civilisation. They are sustained by remembering that influence. If forgotten, they can erode. Islam challenges each of these values at its root. Sharia restricts freedom, institutionalises inequality, redefines loyalty, denies democracy, and fractures the rule of law. The clash is not superficial but fundamental.

The stakes are high

Australia must recognise the stakes. To accommodate Sharia in the name of tolerance or multiculturalism is to compromise its very identity. Each concession erodes our core values. Each accommodation shifts the cultural balance.

The question is not whether Muslims are able to live peacefully in Australia – many do. The question is whether the system of Sharia can coexist with Australian values. The answer, once the principles are understood, is clear: it cannot.

The task for Australians is to reaffirm their values, defend their foundations, and resist pressures to compromise. Only then can the nation preserve the freedom and fairness that define it.

Specific areas of incompatibility

Abstract principles become concrete in daily life. Values such as freedom, equality, and democracy are not only debated in our parliaments and universities; they will shape our marriages, schools, workplaces and communities. When cultures interact, incompatibility is most visible in these ordinary areas of life. Between Islam and Australian society, the clash emerges clearly in gender relations, family structures, education, speech, and the treatment of minorities.

Gender relations

Perhaps the most obvious area of incompatibility lies in gender relations. Australian society, shaped by Christianity and later by waves of social reform, affirms equality between men and women. Women vote, work, and lead alongside men. While inequality might persist in practice, the principle of equality is enshrined in law and widely accepted in culture.

Islamic tradition, by contrast, encodes gender inequality. Sharia grants men authority over women in marriage, inheritance, and testimony. A man's word in court may outweigh a woman's. Sons inherit twice the share of daughters. Husbands may divorce unilaterally, while wives face greater obstacles.

Polygamy illustrates the divide. While illegal in Australia, it is permitted under Sharia. Even some Muslim men in Australia maintain multiple wives informally, supported by religious authorities but outside civil law. This undermines the principle of one law for all and raises questions of justice for the women involved.

Dress codes further highlight tension. The hijab, niqab, and burqa are defended by some as symbols of faith or modesty. Others see them as instruments of control.

In contexts where women face pressure or coercion to veil, freedom of choice is compromised. Australian society, which values both gender equality and individual liberty, struggles to reconcile this with communal enforcement of modesty.

Cases of forced marriage and honour-based violence, though not representative of all Muslims, reveal the darker side of cultural incompatibility, demonstrating how deeply embedded notions of family honour and female obedience can clash with Australian commitments to individual rights and protection from abuse.

Family life

Family is central to both Islam and Australia, but the two models diverge significantly. Australian law recognises marriage as a partnership of two equals, with protections for children and recognition of individual rights. Divorce, while regrettable, is legally accessible. Custody decisions prioritise the welfare of the children.

In Islamic law, family is governed by Sharia principles. Marriage is a contract between a man and a woman, but the man is often granted greater authority. Polygamy is allowed, and divorce laws privilege men. Custody rules often favour fathers or male relatives once children reach a certain age.

These differences become more acute in multicultural contexts. Muslim families may observe Sharia-based practices informally, creating direct conflicts with Australian law. Women may find themselves divorced religiously but not civilly, or vice versa. Children may be pressured to follow Islamic norms even when broader society offers alternatives.

The principle of endogamy—marriage within the community— also affects integration. Muslim families often discourage marriage to non-Muslims, especially for women. This limits social mixing and reinforces separation.

By contrast, earlier waves of immigrants integrated thereby blending cultures. The persistence of endogamy only slows assimilation and sustains incompatibility.

Education

Schools are crucibles of culture. They transmit values, they shape identity, and they prepare the next generation for citizenship. The differences between the Islamic and Australian approaches to education reveal profound incompatibility.

In Australian public schools, the aim is to foster civic equality, critical thinking, and a shared identity. While imperfect, the system seeks to prepare every student for participation in a democratic society. Religious instruction is optional.

Islamic schools, however, prioritise religious identity. Dozens of these schools now operate across Australia, funded partly by government, educating tens of thousands of students. While some provide balanced education, others emphasise separation. Curricula often include Arabic, Qur'an memorisation, and Sharia principles. In some cases, radical preachers have been invited, or textbooks have portrayed Western society as corrupt.

Even in public schools, tensions arise. Muslim students request prayer rooms, halal food, or exemptions from sport and music. While accommodation of faith is reasonable, persistent demands risk fragmenting the shared experience of schooling. Schools become sites of cultural negotiation rather than integration.

The impact on identity is quite significant. Second-generation Muslims, raised in Islamic schools or within strong religious communities, often struggle to reconcile Australian and Islamic identities. For some, loyalty to the global *ummah* outweighs loyalty to the nation. Education, therefore, rather than fostering integration, can reinforce incompatibility.

Free speech

Freedom of speech is a pillar of Australian society. Australians value the ability to criticise leaders, debate policies, and express opinions without fear. This freedom underpins democracy, media independence, and open debate. Islam, however, places strict limits on speech.

Blasphemy — criticising Muhammad, the Qur'an, or Islamic law — is prohibited, often with very severe penalties. Apostasy is likewise firmly punished. Even in the Western contexts, Muslim communities often demand restrictions on criticism of Islam, framing it as hate speech or Islamophobia.

The clash is really evident in controversies over cartoons of Muhammad, debates about halal certification, or public criticism of Sharia. While Australians view such discussions as legitimate free expression, Muslims often see them as intolerable insults. The result is pressure to curtail speech, either through legal restrictions or cultural intimidation. This tension has practical consequences. Politicians, journalists, and academics may self-censor for fear of backlash. Universities may cancel speakers critical of Islam. Ordinary Australians may hesitate to voice concerns. The chilling effect undermines open debate.

Free speech cannot survive if one ideology is exempt from criticism. Yet this is precisely what Sharia must demand. The incompatibility is stark indeed: Australia prizes open debate, while Islam insists on protecting religious sensitivities.

Treatment of minorities

How societies treat minorities reveals much about their values. Australia, despite failures, has sought to protect minority rights. Indigenous Australians, though historically marginalised, are now formally recognised and supported. Religious minorities practise freely. Anti-discrimination laws protect vulnerable groups.

In Islamic societies, minorities often fare poorly. Jews and Christians may be tolerated as *dhimmis*, second-class citizens paying special taxes and facing restrictions. Atheists and converts from Islam face persecution. Blasphemy and apostasy laws punish dissent. In some nations, such as Saudi Arabia, churches are banned altogether. This pattern matters for Australia because it highlights the values Muslim migrants bring with them. If raised where minorities were suppressed, will they embrace Australia's commitment to pluralism?

Some do, gratefully. Others, however, replicate attitudes of intolerance, resisting interfaith friendships or pressuring those converts from Islam. The incompatibility is not only theoretical. Reports of hostility toward ex-Muslims in Australia, or of antisemitism within many Muslim communities, illustrate how imported attitudes clash with national values.

Everyday incompatibilities

Beyond these broad categories, incompatibility is visible in daily life. Workplace norms may clash with religious dress or prayer schedules. Sporting clubs may face demands for segregation. Local councils may debate mosque construction and Islamic festivals. Each issue may only seem small, but collectively they highlight the serious challenge of reconciling divergent cultural expectations.

Australians are generally tolerant and pragmatic, willing to accommodate diversity. But tolerance has some limits. When accommodations undermine equality, freedom, or cohesion, incompatibility becomes undeniable. The cumulative effect of countless small clashes is cultural strain.

Why integration is difficult

Why, then, has integration been more difficult for Islamic communities than for others? Several factors stand out:

1. *Totalising worldview* – Islam is not merely a religion but a comprehensive system, leaving little room for compartmentalisation.
2. *Global identity* – Loyalty to the *ummah* often outweighs national loyalty, hindering assimilation.
3. *Strong institutions* – Mosques, schools, and community groups reinforce separation rather than blending.
4. *Demographic confidence* – Higher fertility rates encourage cultural preservation rather than adaptation.
5. *Theological rigidity* – Because Sharia is viewed as divine, reform or compromise is difficult.

These factors combine to create resilience against assimilation. While individuals may integrate, communities often resist, maintaining practices incompatible with Australian values.

The Christian contrast

The incompatibilities between Islam and the Australian society highlight the unique contribution of Christianity. Christian immigrants brought with them values that harmonised with democracy and freedom. They built schools, hospitals, and charities that served the whole community. They integrated while preserving their faith.

This is not accidental. Christianity, unlike Islam, distinguishes between God's kingdom and earthly kingdoms. Jesus said, *"Give back to Caesar what is Caesar's, and to God what is God's."* This distinction allows Christians to live faithfully under diverse governments, freely contributing to society without demanding a theocratic order.

The contrast is quite instructive. It shows why Islamic cultural practices create incompatibility where other faiths do not. It also highlights the importance of preserving Australia's Christian foundations as the basis for freedom and equality.

What's at stake for Australia?

These areas of incompatibility are not minor cultural quirks. They strike at the heart of Australian identity. Gender equality, family law, education, free speech, and minority rights are cornerstones of the nation. If compromised, Australia ceases to be itself.

Each accommodation of incompatible practices erodes national cohesion. Each concession shifts the balance. The question is not whether Muslims can live peacefully in Australia—many do—but whether Islamic culture, if unchecked, will undermine the values that make such peace possible. The stakes are high: the preservation of our Australian identity, freedom, and unity. Recognising incompatibility is the first step toward removing it.

Australia is more than a geographical space. It is a community bound by values that have been tested, refined, and cherished across generations. Freedom, equality, mateship, democracy, and the rule of law are not simply abstract concepts but the living foundation of the nation. They shape how Australians govern themselves, treat one another, and imagine their future. The pressing question is whether these values can withstand the cultural pressures posed by Islam. Can Australia continue to thrive as a free, democratic, egalitarian society if it overlooks practices and principles drawn from Sharia?

The fragility of values

Values are not self-sustaining. They must be defended, taught, and lived out, or they erode. History provides ample examples. Nations that once prized liberty have slid into authoritarianism. Societies that once cherished equality have later succumbed to hierarchy and privilege. Freedom is always only one generation away from extinction.

Australia's values, though deeply rooted in its strong Christian heritage, are fragile in a secular age. Younger generations, often unaware of the biblical foundations of freedom and equality, treat these values as given, assuming they require no defence. Yet when challenged by incompatible systems, complacency can be fatal.

Islam does not share Australia's values in the same way. Sharia does not protect freedom of conscience, gender equality, or the rule of law as Australians understand them. If Islamic cultural influence grows unchecked, it will challenge the resilience of Australian values.

The risk of accommodation

The danger is not that Sharia will suddenly replace Australian law. The greater risk is incremental accommodation. Small concessions, made in the name of tolerance, accumulate into significant change. Prayer rooms in schools, halal certification, recognition of Islamic holidays, and family arbitration all seem minor in isolation. Together, they normalise Sharia expectations.

Australians may not notice until the cultural balance has shifted dramatically. What was once just unthinkable—parallel legal systems, restricted speech, widespread gender inequality—may become accepted as normal. Accommodation, rather than open confrontation, is the means by which incompatible values gain ground.

Learning from Europe

Europe provides some sobering lessons. Nations such as France, Britain, and Sweden embraced multiculturalism, assuming all cultures could coexist equally. Instead, they now face parallel societies, cultural clashes, and persistent security concerns. No-go zones in certain cities, pressure for Sharia recognition, and rising antisemitism confirm the inevitable trajectory.

Australia has the opportunity to learn from Europe's mistakes. It can affirm diversity while setting some firm boundaries. It can welcome migrants while insisting on integration. It can defend freedoms unapologetically rather than sacrificing them to appease sensitivities. But this requires courage and clarity.

The role of the Church

Christians have a unique responsibility in defending Australian values. These values, after all, are not secular achievements but fruits of the gospel. Freedom of conscience flows from Christ's respect for voluntary faith.

Equality flows from the truth that all are made in God's image. Democracy flows from the conviction that rulers are accountable to God and people. The rule of law flows from the biblical idea that no one, not even kings, is above God's standard.

If Australia forgets these roots, it will lack the conviction to defend its values. The church must remind the nation where its freedoms come from. More than that, it must embody these values in its life together. When Christians practise love, justice, and freedom, they strengthen the cultural fabric. The church also has a mission to Muslims.

Many who migrate to Australia encounter, for the first time, genuine freedom to hear the gospel. If Christians retreat in fear, that opportunity is lost. But if they engage with compassion and courage, many Muslims may discover the grace of Christ, which offers what Sharia cannot — peace with God through forgiveness.

The cost of forgetfulness

The greatest threat to Australian values may not be Islam itself but Australian forgetfulness. If Australians cease to prize freedom, equality, mateship, democracy, and the rule of law, they will surrender them easily. If younger generations believe these values are merely secular conveniences, they will not defend them with conviction.

The Bible warns of this danger. In Judges 2:10, after the death of Joshua, *"another generation grew up who knew neither the Lord nor what he had done for Israel."* They abandoned the faith and fell into idolatry. Likewise, if Australians forget the Christian roots of their values, they will lose the framework that sustains them. The challenge of Islam exposes this significant vulnerability. It forces Australians to ask: do we still believe in our own values? Are we willing to defend them, or will we compromise in the name of tolerance?

The future if values are defended

If Australians reaffirm their values, the future can be secure. Islam will remain a minority religion, and Muslims who embrace freedom will thrive. The cultural fabric will be tested but also strengthened. Diversity will enrich rather than fracture. Freedom of speech will allow robust debate, even when uncomfortable. Women will enjoy equality protected by law. The rule of law will remain unified.

Such a future requires intentional action. It requires teaching younger generations the true value of freedom. It also requires policymakers with courage to set limits. It requires citizens who refuse to be intimidated. It requires churches that proclaim the gospel clearly and live it out faithfully.

The future if values are compromised

If, however, Australians compromise, the future will look very different. Incremental accommodation of Sharia will create parallel societies. Free speech will shrink under pressure to avoid offence. Gender inequality will grow in enclaves where Sharia norms dominate. The rule of law will fracture, with informal arbitration replacing national courts.

Eventually, national identity will erode. Australia will no longer be defined by Western and Christian values but by cultural relativism. In such a vacuum, Islam will grow more assertive, pressing for further recognition. What began as tolerance will end in transformation.

This is not alarmism but observation of trajectories already visible in parts of Europe. The future will be determined not by intentions but by the cumulative effect of decisions.

A call to courage

The challenge of Islam is, at its very core, a test of courage. Do Australians believe in their own values strongly enough to defend them? Will they risk being called intolerant for the sake of truth? Will they draw firm lines while extending compassion to individuals?

Courage is not hostility. It does not mean demonising Muslims or abandoning compassion. It just means telling the truth about incompatibility while still treating people with dignity. It means saying no to practices that undermine freedom while saying yes to the personhood of Muslims made in God's image.

Joshua's words remain relevant: *"But if serving the Lord seems undesirable to you, then choose for yourselves this day whom you will serve… But as for me and my household, we will serve the Lord"* (Joshua 24:15). Australia must likewise choose whether it will serve the values that have preserved its freedom or compromise them away.

Conclusion

The future of Australian values is not predetermined. It will be shaped by choices—personal, communal, and national. Islam poses real cultural pressure, but the decisive factor will be whether Australians defend their foundations or forget them.

Freedom, equality, mateship, democracy, and the rule of law are worth defending. They are gifts of history, fruits of the gospel, and treasures for the future. If preserved, they will ensure Australia remains free, fair, and united. If surrendered, they will vanish more quickly than many imagine.

10. ISLAM AND MULTICULTURALISM

I have already addressed the issue of multiculturalism in a number of chapters. However, I feel it needs a more detailed examination in a chapter on its own because this could well be the one issue which will determine our future as a nation.

The history and philosophy of multiculturalism in Australia

Multiculturalism has become one of the defining features of modern-day Australia. For decades, politicians, academics, and media voices have celebrated it as the essence of the nation's identity. Cultural festivals, ethnic food, and stories of successful migrant families are held up as proof that multiculturalism works really well.

Yet this national philosophy is relatively recent and born out of particular historical circumstances. To understand its current challenges, especially in relation to Islam, we must first explore its origins, development, benefits, and assumptions.

The end of the White Australia Policy

At Federation in 1901, Australia's identity was framed largely in terms of race and heritage. The Immigration Restriction Act — the so-called White Australia Policy — ensured that migrants would overwhelmingly be of European origin, primarily British. For decades, this shaped the nation's character. Australians saw themselves as part of a global Anglo world, tied by loyalty to Britain and united by language, law, and culture.

World War II began to challenge this whole framework. Facing Japanese aggression and fearing invasion, Australian leaders realised that the nation's survival required population growth. The slogan "populate or perish" captured the urgency.

Massive post-war immigration programs then followed, initially focusing on British migrants but very soon expanding to include southern and eastern Europeans. Italians, Greeks, Poles, and others arrived in large numbers, transforming urban landscapes.

By the 1960s, it became clear that the White Australia Policy was unsustainable. International criticism mounted, especially from newly independent Asian nations.

Domestically, our economic growth required a broader labour supply. Social attitudes also shifted, with increasing recognition that racial discrimination was incompatible with democratic ideals.

The dismantling of the White Australia Policy was gradual but decisive. By the early 1970s, formal restrictions based on race were gone. Australia was entering a new era, one in which its identity would be reshaped by global migration.

The birth of multiculturalism

In place of racial exclusion, Australia adopted multiculturalism as its guiding philosophy. The term gained prominence in the 1970s, particularly under Prime Minister Gough Whitlam and his successor Malcolm Fraser. Both recognised that post-war migrants, especially from southern Europe, were struggling with integration. Their cultures were very distinct from the Anglo mainstream, and many were facing discrimination.

Multiculturalism promised a new approach. Instead of expecting migrants to assimilate fully into an Anglo identity, it encouraged them to maintain their cultural traditions while participating in national life.

Ethnic media, community organisations, and cultural festivals were then supported by government funding. Policies promoted equal opportunity, cultural recognition, and social cohesion.

This philosophy drew on broader global trends. In Canada, Prime Minister Pierre Trudeau championed multiculturalism as official policy in 1971.

In Britain, multicultural ideas gained traction in response to immigration from former colonies. So, Australia followed suit, framing itself as a modern, tolerant, and diverse nation.

The assumptions of multiculturalism

Multiculturalism rests on several key assumptions:

1. *Cultural diversity enriches society* – Different traditions, cuisines, and perspectives add to national life.
2. *All cultures are equally valid* – No one culture should dominate or be privileged over others.
3. *Integration is possible without assimilation* – Migrants can maintain their heritage while adopting civic participation.
4. *Shared democratic values are sufficient for unity* – Freedom, equality, and law provide a framework in which diverse cultures can coexist.
5. *Tolerance prevents conflict* – By respecting difference, societies avoid division and build cohesion.

These assumptions reflect optimism about human nature and society. They suggest that such cultural diversity is inherently positive, conflict is avoidable, and unity requires little more than tolerance and shared institutions.

The benefits of multiculturalism

Multiculturalism has brought real benefits to Australia.

➤ *Economic contributions* – Migrants have fuelled economic growth. Italian and Greek migrants built businesses; Vietnamese migrants revitalised declining industries; Indian and Chinese migrants have contributed to technology, medicine, and education.
➤ *Cultural enrichment* – Australian cuisine has been transformed by migrant food. Festivals, art, and music reflect global influences. Cities such as Sydney and Melbourne boast vibrant multicultural precincts that attract tourism and investment.
➤ *International connections* – Migrant communities link Australia to global markets, fostering trade and diplomacy. Indian IT professionals, Chinese entrepreneurs, and Middle Eastern traders expand Australia's global reach.

> *Social resilience* – Diversity has, in many cases, strengthened adaptability. Communities facing economic or social challenges have found renewal through new energy and ideas brought by migrants.

These benefits are undeniable. They explain to us clearly why multiculturalism has been embraced right across the political spectrum and celebrated in public discourse.

The challenges and blind spots

Yet from its inception, multiculturalism carried blind spots. By treating all cultures as equally valid, it downplayed questions of compatibility. It assumed that migrants would naturally adopt our democratic values while maintaining cultural practices. It overlooked the possibility that some cultural traditions might clash with freedom, equality, or the rule of law. For most migrant groups, these blind spots were manageable. Italians, Greeks, Vietnamese, and Indians, despite differences, adapted well to Australian society. Their traditions enriched the culture without severely undermining the foundations. Christianity, Buddhism, Hinduism, and secular traditions could coexist with democracy.

Islam, however, presents a very different case. Its comprehensive legal system, Sharia, challenges so many of the assumptions of multiculturalism. Islam does not easily separate culture from law, religion from politics, or community from ideology. Where multiculturalism assumes pluralism, Islam very often assumes exclusivity. Where multiculturalism prizes individual freedom, Islam often prioritises community conformity. The blind spot becomes apparent: multiculturalism assumes that all cultures fit within a clear democratic framework. Islam tests whether that assumption is true.

Political embrace of multiculturalism

Successive Australian governments have deeply entrenched multiculturalism as policy. The Office of Multicultural Affairs was established in the 1980s. Reports such as the *National Agenda for a Multicultural Australia* (1989) affirmed cultural diversity as central to national identity.

Public funding supported ethnic organisations, media, and cultural events. By the 2000s, both major parties endorsed multiculturalism, though debates about national security and social cohesion created tensions.

The Howard Coalition government emphasised integration and Australian values, while still affirming our rich diversity. Later governments reasserted multiculturalism as a positive good, framing critics as intolerant or xenophobic.

This bipartisan embrace reflects the now deep entrenchment of multiculturalism in national identity. To question it is often seen as questioning Australia itself. Yet this makes it difficult to have honest discussions about its limits.

The role of the media and academia

Media and academia have been loud and proud promoters of multiculturalism. Universities teach it as a model of progressive society. Media outlets celebrate migrant success stories and highlight cultural festivals. Critics are most often marginalised and portrayed as reactionary or racist.

This dominance of narrative shapes public perception. Many Australians equate multiculturalism with tolerance and fairness, assuming that rejecting it means embracing bigotry. The result is a climate where any genuine concerns about incompatibility — particularly with Islam — are silenced or dismissed.

The religious dimension

Multiculturalism has also reshaped religious life in Australia. Churches, once central to national identity, have been relativised within a much broader pluralism. Christianity is seen as one faith among many, not as the foundation of national values. Mosques, temples, and synagogues stand alongside churches in public recognition.

This relativism aligns with secular multicultural assumptions but neglects history. Australia's freedoms — speech, religion and equality — emerged from Christianity.

To treat all religions as equally foundational is to ignore the very roots of our nation's values. Islam, in particular, challenges these freedoms by advocating Sharia. By relativising Christianity, multiculturalism weakens the very source of the freedoms it claims to protect.

Multiculturalism as civic religion

In many ways, multiculturalism functions as a civic religion. It provides a narrative of identity, a moral framework, and a vision of the future. Australians are told that diversity is their greatest strength, that tolerance is the highest virtue, and that cultural equality is non-negotiable. This civic religion, however, is fragile. It relies on shared values of freedom and equality in order to function, yet it refuses to acknowledge their Christian roots. It assumes that all cultures will play by democratic rules, yet it struggles when cultures demand exceptions. Islam exposes these weaknesses, testing whether multiculturalism can survive its own assumptions.

Lessons from other nations

Australia is not alone in embracing multiculturalism. Britain, Canada, and much of Europe adopted similar philosophies. Their experiences offer some lessons. In Britain, multiculturalism allowed Muslim communities to establish parallel institutions, including Sharia councils. In France, policies of accommodation led to cultural clashes and segregation. In Sweden, high levels of immigration have strained welfare systems and sparked tension.

These examples reveal a pattern: multiculturalism works when cultures are broadly compatible with democracy, but falters when they are not. Islam is the decisive test case. Nations that fail to set firm boundaries find themselves confronting enclaves, radicalisation, and cultural conflict.

Why this history matters

Understanding the history and philosophy of multiculturalism is essential for assessing Australia's future. Multiculturalism was born as a response to the end of White Australia and the arrival of diverse migrants.

It has brought real benefits, enriching society and expanding opportunities. But it was built on assumptions that may not hold when faced with Islam.

The assumption that all cultures are equally valid ignores the reality that some practices undermine freedom and equality. The assumption that tolerance prevents conflict overlooks the need for clear boundaries. The assumption that shared democratic values are sufficient neglects the reality that some ideologies, like Sharia, reject democracy itself.

Islam within the multicultural framework

When multiculturalism became Australia's guiding philosophy, it was celebrated as a model for harmony in diversity. Politicians promised that cultural pluralism would strengthen the nation, enrich its identity, and prove that tolerance could triumph over division. For many migrant groups, this experiment succeeded.

The Italians, Greeks, Vietnamese, Indians, and others integrated well while preserving traditions. Their contributions reinforced national life without threatening its foundations.

But Islam has tested the framework more severely than any other culture. Its claims are not merely cultural but totalising. Sharia does not confine itself to cuisine or festivals; it extends to law, politics, gender, and society. Multiculturalism assumes equality of cultures, but Islam assumes supremacy. This fundamental clash creates persistent tension wherever Islamic communities grow under a multicultural policy.

The promise of multiculturalism and the reality of Islam

The promise of multiculturalism was simple: migrants could retain their heritage while embracing Australia's democratic values. Islam, however, challenges this by insisting that its heritage includes a comprehensive system of divine law. Where multiculturalism celebrates pluralism, Islam always proclaims exclusivity. Where multiculturalism assumes our voluntary coexistence, Islam often demands recognition and submission.

This does not mean all Muslims consciously seek to impose Sharia. Many of them are content to practise privately and live peacefully. Yet the ideology embedded in Islam inevitably shapes community expectations. Leaders, imams, and activists often press for recognition of Islamic practices, presenting them as rights within the multicultural framework. Thus, the very policy designed to foster harmony becomes a platform for cultural demands that undermine cohesion.

Demands for accommodation

Within multicultural policy, Muslim communities have made a series of demands for accommodation. Each may appear small, but together they illustrate how Islam always tests the limits of tolerance.

1. *Dress Codes* – The wearing of hijabs, niqabs, and burqas has sparked debate in schools, workplaces, and public spaces. While religious expression is protected, the covering of faces raises issues of security, communication, and social integration. Requests for exemptions from uniform policies highlight the tension between equality and accommodation.

2. *Education* – Schools face demands for halal meals, prayer rooms, gender-segregated activities, and curriculum adjustments. Islamic schools, funded by taxpayers, sometimes prioritise Sharia values over civic education. The question arises: should multiculturalism permit schools that reinforce separation rather than integration?

3. *Law and arbitration* – Informal Sharia councils already operate in some communities, especially for family disputes. While presented as voluntary, women often feel compelled to use them, forfeiting rights under Australian law. Advocacy for formal recognition of such councils occasionally surfaces, testing the principle of one law for all.

4. *Religious Sensitivities* – Campaigns against so-called Islamophobia often demand restrictions on speech. Cartoons, books, or lectures critical of Islam spark protests and calls for censorship. In the multicultural framework, respect for diversity is easily reinterpreted as protection from criticism.

5. *Public Life* – Recognition of Islamic holidays, provision of prayer facilities in workplaces, and accommodation of fasting during Ramadan are increasingly demanded. While flexibility is not inherently problematic, the cumulative effect is to normalise Sharia expectations in public life.

Each demand is framed as a matter of fairness or tolerance. Yet when taken together, they shift the cultural balance, embedding Islamic norms within the multicultural framework.

Case studies of tension

Some concrete examples illustrate how Islam interacts with multiculturalism in practice.

Halal Certification – The growth of halal certification has sparked controversy. For Muslims, halal food is a religious requirement. For businesses, certification opens markets. But for critics, it represents the embedding of Sharia into public commerce, often without any consumer knowledge. Campaigns against halal certification have been dismissed as intolerance, yet the debate reveals how Islamic demands are reshaping industries under multicultural accommodation.

Burqa Debates – In 2014, proposals to restrict full-face coverings in Parliament House raised some fierce debate. Supporters cited security and transparency; opponents cried discrimination. The issue revealed the clash between multicultural tolerance of religious expression and the broader societal concerns about cohesion and equality.

School Conflicts – In several public schools, Muslim students have demanded prayer rooms and exemptions from mixed-gender activities. In some cases, schools have yielded; in others, conflict erupted. The pattern illustrates how multicultural appeasing can undermine the principle of shared schooling.

Local Councils – The construction of Mosques has often sparked controversy in suburban areas. Residents raise concerns about noise, traffic, or overdevelopment, but underlying fears about cultural change are evident. Councils find themselves caught between planning regulations and multicultural commitments.

Media and Free Speech – Journalists and academics critical of Islam have faced backlash, sometimes including threats. Universities, under pressure, have cancelled speakers or censored content. The chilling effect shows how multicultural ideals of respect can become tools of suppression. These examples highlight a pattern: multiculturalism, designed to foster harmony, actually becomes a trigger for serious conflict when we are confronted with Islam's comprehensive claims.

The role of advocacy groups

Muslim advocacy groups play a central role in pressing for accommodation. Organisations like the Australian Federation of Islamic Councils (AFIC) and state-based Islamic associations often lobby governments, media, and institutions. They present demands in the language of multiculturalism: rights, equality, and respect.

By framing Islamic practices as cultural rights, they make it very difficult for governments to refuse. Politicians fear accusations of discrimination or racism. Media outlets, so wary of offending, then amplify the narrative of victimhood. Advocacy becomes effective not because demands are inherently reasonable but because multiculturalism makes them difficult to resist.

This dynamic creates imbalance. Other cultural groups, such as Italians or Vietnamese, rarely demand systemic accommodation beyond cultural festivals or perhaps language programs. Islam's demands extend much deeper, touching law, speech, and public institutions. Yet multiculturalism treats them all alike, blinding policymakers to the difference.

The paradox of multiculturalism

This reveals a central paradox: multiculturalism depends on the same shared freedoms — speech, religion, equality — that Sharia undermines. By protecting Islamic practices in the name of diversity, multiculturalism erodes its own foundations. The more it accommodates incompatible demands, the weaker its framework becomes. The very policy intended to strengthen cohesion risks producing fragmentation. Instead of harmony, it fosters enclaves, resentment, and cultural conflict.

Lessons from abroad

Other nations' experiences confirm this pattern.

➤ *United Kingdom* – Sharia councils operate with government tolerance. Multicultural policies allowed parallel legal systems to emerge, leaving women disadvantaged.

➤ *France* – Strong secularism clashes with Islamic demands, leading to repeated conflict over veils, schools, and public identity. Multiculturalism failed to integrate; instead, it produced segregation.

➤ *Sweden* – High immigration from Muslim-majority countries under multicultural ideals has strained welfare, created ghettos, and increased crime rates.

These examples show us that multiculturalism, when applied uncritically to Islam, produces tension, not harmony. Australia risks following the same path soon if it does not learn from these lessons.

Christian reflections

For Christians, this tension underscores the importance of truth. The gospel calls believers to love strangers and welcome migrants (Lev. 19:34), but also to guard against false teaching (Galatians 1:8). Compassion must not mean compromise.

The early church thrived in pluralistic societies by holding firmly to Christ while engaging neighbours with love. Likewise, Christians in Australia must distinguish between Muslims as people—worthy of dignity and compassion—and Islam as an ideology, which is incompatible with freedom.

Multiculturalism blurs this distinction, treating Islam as just another culture. The church must speak clearly: while Muslims are welcome, Sharia is not.

Toward honest debate

The interaction of Islam and multiculturalism exposes the need for honest debate. For too long, discussion has been stifled by fear of accusations.

Genuine concerns are dismissed as racism, while real conflicts are downplayed. But avoiding the issue only deepens division. Australians must ask: Can multiculturalism survive Islam's comprehensive claims? What boundaries are necessary to preserve our freedom and equality? Is cultural relativism even sustainable, or must Australia reaffirm its foundational values? These questions cannot be silenced forever. They will shape the nation's future.

The future of multiculturalism

Multiculturalism is often described as Australia's great success story. Politicians and academics alike often insist that it has transformed a once insular society into a vibrant, cosmopolitan nation. Yet beneath the celebration lies a growing unease. The rise of Islam within a multicultural framework has exposed very deep and divisive tensions. The question is no longer whether multiculturalism has worked in the past, but whether it can endure now into the future — especially when confronted with an ideology that resists the underlying premise of multiculturalism.

Multiculturalism at a crossroads

Australia stands at a crossroads. For decades, multiculturalism has functioned on assumptions that migrants, whatever their background, would broadly adapt to democratic values while enriching national life with cultural variety. For Italians, Greeks, Vietnamese, and Indians, this assumption held true. But Islam now complicates the picture.

Unlike other cultural traditions, Islam makes totalising claims. It offers not just food, festivals, or language but a complete system of law, governance, and morality. Sharia does not sit alongside other traditions; it seeks to replace them. This exposes the limits of multiculturalism's core assumption — that all cultures are equally valid within a pluralistic framework. If multiculturalism continues unchanged, it risks accommodating practices that undermine freedom, equality, and cohesion. If it is redefined, it may preserve its strengths while protecting national values. The future depends on which path Australia chooses.

Three possible futures

Looking ahead, three broad trajectories are possible:

1. *Uncritical continuation* – Multiculturalism continues as it has, treating all cultures as equally valid. Islamic demands for accommodation grow, and incremental concessions embed Sharia norms in public life. This risks fragmentation and the emergence of parallel societies.

2. *Backlash and retrenchment* – Growing tensions lead to a backlash. Politicians restrict immigration, limit cultural recognition, and emphasise assimilation. While this may protect national values, it risks alienating minorities and fuelling resentment.

3. *Redefinition with boundaries* – Multiculturalism is redefined to affirm diversity within limits. Cultural expression is welcomed, but practices incompatible with freedom, equality, and democracy are rejected. This path preserves the benefits of multiculturalism while protecting foundations.

The third path is the most sustainable, but it will require great courage and a renewed clarity.

The cost of uncritical continuation

If Australia persists with uncritical multiculturalism, several outcomes are likely:

➤ *Parallel societies* – Islamic enclaves will grow, with distinct norms and limited integration. Mosques, schools, and businesses will reinforce separation, creating societies within society.

➤ *Erosion of free speech* – Campaigns against Islamophobia will silence criticism of Islam. Media, academia, and politics will self-censor, undermining open debate.

➤ *Gender inequality* – Polygamy, forced marriage, and honour-based violence may persist within enclaves, tolerated in the name of cultural respect.

> *Fragmented law* – Informal Sharia councils will adjudicate family disputes, effectively creating parallel legal systems. Women in particular will suffer.

> *Weakened national identity* – Loyalty to the *ummah* will rival loyalty to Australia. National identity will be diluted into mere geographic residence rather than shared values.

These outcomes are already visible in parts of Europe. Britain's Sharia councils, France's urban ghettos, and Sweden's rising crime rates illustrate this trajectory. Australia risks the same future if it refuses to confront multiculturalism's blind spots.

The dangers of backlash

The opposite danger is backlash. Growing frustration with this Islamic infiltration could fuel harsh restrictions on immigration, cultural expression, or religious freedom.

Populist movements may try to scapegoat Muslims, treating all religions as threats to our nation rather than distinguishing between individuals and ideology.

Such backlash carries risks:

> Alienating moderate Muslims who value freedom and democracy.

> Fuelling radicalisation among disaffected youth.

> Undermining Australia's global reputation as a fair and welcoming society.

Backlash is a predictable reaction when legitimate concerns are ignored. If multiculturalism silences debate, resentment builds until it explodes. The challenge is to address incompatibility honestly before backlash becomes inevitable.

The path of redefinition

The most constructive future lies in redefining multiculturalism with some clear boundaries. Diversity can be celebrated in food, language, art, and traditions, while firmly rejecting practices that undermine national values. This requires that we can distinguish between cultural expression and ideological imposition.

Wearing a sari or celebrating Lunar New Year can be enriching for Australia. Practising polygamy or demanding blasphemy restrictions will only undermines it. The key is clarity about non-negotiable principles.

Redefined multiculturalism would affirm:

➢ *One law for all* – No recognition of Sharia arbitration. All disputes resolved under Australian law.

➢ *Freedom of speech* – Protection of criticism and debate, even when offensive.

➢ *Gender equality* – No tolerance for polygamy, forced marriage, or unequal rights.

➢ *National identity* – Affirmation of Australia's Christian and Western heritage as the foundation of freedom.

➢ *Integration as an expectation* – Migrants welcome, but assimilation into civic values required.

This model preserves the richness of diversity while defending the values that sustain it.

Policy implications

Redefining multiculturalism requires concrete policy shifts:

1. *Education reform* – Schools, especially Islamic schools, must be held accountable for teaching civic values. Public schools must not compromise shared experiences through excessive accommodation.

2. *Legal vigilance* – Governments must resist recognition of parallel systems. Informal Sharia councils should be monitored and discouraged.

3. *Immigration settings* – Selection criteria should consider cultural compatibility, not just skills. Humanitarian intakes must be balanced with capacity for integration.

4. *Public discourse* – Laws against hate speech must not become blasphemy laws. Debate about Islam must remain free. We used to have these debates years ago, but not so much now.

5. *Community Engagement* – Moderate Muslims who are willing to embrace Australian values should be supported, while radicals who reject them should be confronted.

These policies are not anti-Muslim; they are pro-freedom. They ensure that diversity strengthens rather than weakens Australia.

The role of churches and civil society

Redefining multiculturalism is not only a task for governments. Churches, schools, and civil society also play a vital role.

➤ *Churches* must seek to recover confidence in the gospel's contribution to freedom. They should remind the nation that its values are rooted in Christianity. They must also engage Muslims with love, offering friendship and witness while resisting Sharia.

➤ *Civil society* must foster open debate. Universities, media, and community organisations must resist intimidation and protect freedom of thought.

➤ *Citizens* must live out values daily. Mateship, fairness, and courage are not policies but practices.

A redefined multiculturalism requires a cultural renewal, not just policy reform.

The Biblical perspective

The Bible provides wisdom for navigating diversity. Israel was commanded to treat foreigners with justice (Leviticus 19:34), yet also to guard against idolatry (Deuteronomy 13). The early church welcomed Greeks and Romans into fellowship but rejected false teaching (Galatians 1:8). This balance—compassion without compromise—is essential. Christians are called to love Muslims as neighbours while refusing to accept Sharia as compatible with freedom. The gospel offers a better foundation for diversity: unity in Christ across cultures, grounded in truth.

A national choice

Australia must choose its future. Will it persist with uncritical multiculturalism, drifting toward fragmentation?

Will it embrace backlash, risking division and injustice? Or will it redefine multiculturalism, affirming diversity within firm boundaries?

The choice will not be made in a single moment but in countless decisions about school policies, immigration laws, community debates, and personal interactions. Yet the cumulative effect will shape the nation for generations.

The stakes are so high. If multiculturalism is redefined, Australia may be able to remain a free, fair, and united society. If not, it risks following Europe into division and conflict.

Conclusion

Multiculturalism has brought much good to Australia. But its future depends on honesty. Islam exposes its limits, forcing the nation to confront hard questions. Can all cultures truly coexist under one framework? Are all practices equally valid? Or must boundaries be drawn to protect freedom?

The answer will determine the future of multiculturalism but also the future of Australia itself as a nation. Diversity is only sustainable when anchored in shared values. Those values— freedom, equality, democracy, and the rule of law—are not negotiable. They must be preserved, even if it means redefining multiculturalism.

11. ISLAM AND RADICALISATION

The global context of Islamic radicalisation

The phenomenon of Islamic radicalisation cannot be understood in isolation. While radicalisation manifests locally — in suburbs, mosques, prisons, and in online spaces — it draws deeply from some global currents. The ideology of jihad is not just a fringe interpretation but an enduring strand of Islamic history, revived and reasserted in modern times. For Australia to grasp the risks posed by radicalisation, it must first understand the wider world that shapes it.

Historical roots of radicalisation

Radicalisation is certainly not some modern invention. From its earliest centuries, Islam contained an impulse toward militant expansion. Muhammad himself led many military campaigns. His successors, the caliphs, oversaw conquests stretching from Arabia to North Africa, Spain, and into Central Asia. The rapid spread of Islam was not solely spiritual but military.

This legacy established the concept of *jihad* — striving in the path of Allah — as both personal piety and armed struggle. While interpretations varied, the idea that Muslims could and should fight to defend or expand Islam became embedded in theology. Their Jurists distinguished between defensive jihad (protecting Muslim lands) and offensive jihad (expanding them). Both remained legitimate.

Throughout history, movements arose that emphasised militant jihad. The Almohads in North Africa, the Mahdist revolt in Sudan, and various caliphal expansions testify to this recurring theme. Radicalisation, in this sense, is not a departure from tradition but a reassertion of one of its long-standing strands.

The rise of modern Islamism

The nineteenth and twentieth centuries brought new challenges to the Islamic world. Colonialism, Western dominance, and secular nationalism eroded traditional authority.

In response, thinkers sought to revive Islam's political and legal supremacy. Out of this ferment emerged modern Islamism — the ideology that Islam is not just a religion but a total system that must govern politics, law, and society. Key figures shaped this movement:

> *Hassan al-Banna* (founder of the Muslim Brotherhood, 1928) argued that Islam must govern every aspect of life. His movement combined social welfare with political activism, laying the groundwork for global Islamist networks.

> *Sayyid Qutb* (executed in 1966) provided the theological justification for jihad against corrupt regimes and Western influence. His writings inspired generations of radicals.

> *Abul A'la Maududi* (South Asia) developed a comprehensive vision of an Islamic state governed by Sharia.

These thinkers rejected secularism and democracy, insisting that sovereignty belongs to Allah alone. Their writings still remain influential among radicals today.

Radicalisation in the late twentieth century

The twentieth century saw Islamist thought translated into many militant movements. The Iranian Revolution (1979) established a theocratic state under Ayatollah Khomeini, demonstrating that Islamism could seize power. In Afghanistan, the Soviet invasion (1979–1989) mobilised tens of thousands of Muslims worldwide. Fighters trained, networks formed, and jihad became globalised.

From this crucible emerged *al-Qaeda*, founded by Osama bin Laden. Its ideology declared war on the West, framing America and its allies as enemies of Islam. The September 11, 2001 attacks revealed the potency of this movement.

Al-Qaeda was not an aberration but the culmination of many decades of Islamist thought. It merged theological justification, organisational capacity, and global ambition. Radicalisation in Muslim communities worldwide then drew inspiration from its narrative: Islam under siege, Muslims obliged to fight, and martyrdom glorified.

The Islamic State and global jihad

If al-Qaeda globalised jihad, the Islamic State (ISIS) localised it with shocking intensity. Rising from the chaos of Iraq and Syria, ISIS declared a caliphate in 2014. It sought not only to fight the West but to govern territory under strict Sharia. Its brutality — beheadings, slavery, crucifixions — was broadcast online as both warning and recruitment.

ISIS attracted tens of thousands of foreign fighters, including from Australia. Its slick propaganda, often in English, targeted disaffected youth in Western societies. Videos glorified jihad, offered belonging, and promised eternal reward. Online forums became radicalisation incubators.

Though the caliphate was territorially defeated, its ideology endures. Lone-wolf attacks in Europe and elsewhere testify to its lasting appeal today. Radicalisation no longer requires travel to battlefields; it can occur in bedrooms via the internet.

Ideological currents

Several ideological currents feed radicalisation:

1. *Salafism* – A puritanical movement that seeks to return to the practices of the earliest Muslims. Not all Salafis advocate violence, but their strict worldview creates fertile ground for jihadist interpretations.

2. *Wahhabism* – Originating in Saudi Arabia, Wahhabism emphasises rigid monotheism and rejection of innovation. Its global spread through Saudi-funded mosques and literature has promoted intolerance of other all faiths and sects.

3. *Islamism* – The political ideology that Islam must govern the state. While some Islamists pursue this through elections, the overlap with jihadist goals is significant.

4. *Takfirism* – The practice of declaring other Muslims apostates, justifying violence against them. This ideology fuels intra-Muslim violence, as seen in Iraq and Syria.

Together, these four currents now form the intellectual soil of radicalisation. They are disseminated through mosques, schools, literature, and increasingly, digital media.

Radicalisation in the West

In Western nations, radicalisation takes some distinctive forms. Muslims in minority contexts face real identity struggles: caught between cultures, some now feel alienated from both. Radical ideologies exploit this tension, offering belonging and purpose. Common pathways to radicalisation include:

1. *Alienation* – Feeling excluded from society, whether due to racism, unemployment, or cultural dislocation.
2. *Identity crisis* – Young Muslims torn between Western freedoms and Islamic expectations may turn to radical groups for clarity.
3. *Community influence* – Radical preachers or networks can groom vulnerable youth.
4. *Online propaganda* – Social media platforms amplify jihadist messaging, bypassing traditional authority.
5. *Global solidarity* – Conflicts in Palestine, Syria, or Afghanistan resonate deeply, fostering anger and a sense of duty to act.

Case studies from Britain, France, and Germany illustrate how radicals often emerge from second-generation communities. They may appear well-integrated externally but harbour resentment, exploited by extremist recruiters.

The appeal of radicalisation

Why does radicalisation appeal? Several factors converge:

1. *Belonging* – Radical groups offer a sense of family and brotherhood, appealing to those who feel isolated.
2. *Purpose* – Jihad provides meaning, transforming frustration into heroic struggle.

3. *Certainty* – In a confusing world, strict ideology offers clarity.

4. *Revenge* – Perceived injustices against Muslims worldwide fuel anger.

5. *Reward* – Promises of paradise, martyrdom, and honour allure young recruits.

These appeals resonate particularly with the youth, who crave identity and purpose. Radicalisation thus thrives not only on ideology but on emotional and psychological needs.

The role of mosques and institutions

Not all mosques promote radicalisation, but some have served as incubators. Radical preachers, very often educated overseas, import intolerant ideologies. Sermons may emphasise Muslim victimhood, hostility toward the West, or glorification of jihad. Literature distributed in a number of mosques promotes Sharia supremacy.

Islamic schools and community organisations, when dominated by Islamist leaders, reinforce separation from broader society. While many operate responsibly, the risk of radical influence remains. Governments struggle to monitor these institutions without infringing religious freedom, creating a delicate balance.

Radicalisation in prisons

Prisons worldwide have become hotspots for radicalisation. Disaffected inmates, often already alienated, prove receptive to extremist ideologies. Charismatic recruiters exploit grievances, offering Islam as a path to dignity and purpose. Radicalised inmates then emerge as threats upon release.

France, Britain, and the United States report significant prison radicalisation. Australia faces many similar risks, with several convicted terrorists radicalising other prisoners behind bars. This dynamic complicates counter-terrorism efforts, requiring ongoing surveillance and rehabilitation attempts.

Online radicalisation

The internet has revolutionised radicalisation. Recent groups like al-Qaeda and ISIS mastered digital propaganda, producing glossy magazines, videos, and memes. Social media platforms then amplify this content globally. Encrypted apps allow private recruitment and coordination.

Online radicalisation can now bypass geography. A teenager in suburban Sydney can consume jihadist material as easily as someone in the Middle East. Algorithms amplify echo chambers, reinforcing these extremist views. Counter-narratives struggle to compete with the emotional power of jihadist propaganda. This digital dimension is now ensuring that radicalisation remains a persistent threat, even if physical networks are disrupted.

Impact on Muslim minorities in the West

Global jihadist movements profoundly affect Muslim minorities in the West. Even those who reject violence cannot ignore the pull of global identity. Events in Gaza, Iraq, or Kashmir resonate strongly. Radical groups exploit these grievances, framing Western Muslims as part of a worldwide struggle.

This creates a climate of tension. Non-Muslims grow suspicious, fearing hidden sympathies for jihad. Muslims feel stigmatised, resenting constant association with terrorism. The result is polarisation, which itself fuels radicalisation.

For Australia, this dynamic is especially concerning. Muslim communities, though a minority, are highly visible in certain suburbs. Global conflicts reverberate locally, shaping identity and sometimes fuelling extremism.

Christian reflections on radicalisation

From a Christian perspective, radicalisation clearly illustrates the bondage of legalism and the hunger for meaning apart from Christ. Paul wrote of his fellow Jews in Romans 10:2, *"They are zealous for God, but their zeal is not based on knowledge."* Radical Muslims are zealous, but their zeal leads to destruction, not life.

The gospel offers an alternative. In Christ, belonging, purpose, and reward are found not in violence but in grace. The church must therefore respond with truth, but also with compassion. Muslims must hear that salvation is a free gift, not earned through jihad.

The global context of Islamic radicalisation is sobering. Rooted in history, fuelled by ideology, and amplified now by modern technology, it shapes Muslim minorities worldwide.

For Australia, radicalisation cannot be treated as a purely local problem. It is part of a global movement, drawing inspiration and legitimacy from centuries of theology and many decades of activism. To confront it, Australia must understand its roots, recognise its appeals, and resist its encroachments. Only then can the nation prepare for the challenges of radicalisation at home.

Radicalisation in Australia

The story of radicalisation is not only global but local. While Australia is geographically distant from the Middle East and Africa — the epicentres of Islamist insurgency and terrorism — it has not been immune to their influence.

Radicalisation has taken root within many Australian Muslim communities, producing individuals who have travelled to fight overseas, plotted domestic attacks, and spread their extremist ideologies. The challenge for Australia is to understand how and why radicalisation occurs at home, and how it can be resisted without compromising freedom.

The early signs

Islamic radicalisation in Australia began to emerge visibly in the 1990s. Immigration from Lebanon, Turkey, and Afghanistan had created rapidly growing Muslim communities in Sydney and Melbourne. While most migrants pursued education, work, and family life, a small number gravitated toward radical ideologies imported from abroad. Reports began to surface of radical preachers influencing young men in suburban mosques.

Bookstores distributed Islamist literature by figures such as Sayyid Qutb and Abul A'la Maududi. International conflicts—in Bosnia, Chechnya, and later Iraq—resonated deeply, with some Australians travelling to fight. Though numbers were small, the pattern was significant: global jihadist narratives were finding local listeners.

The shock of September 11 and Bali

The attacks of September 11, 2001, really changed everything. Australians, like much of the world, awoke to the reality of global jihad. Yet for Australia, the wake-up call was even more personal the following year.

In October 2002, bombs exploded in Bali, killing 202 people, including 88 Australians. In this case, the perpetrators were members of Jemaah Islamiyah, a Southeast Asian jihadist network linked to al-Qaeda.

The Bali bombings exposed Australia's vulnerability. Citizens were targeted abroad, but the networks extended into Australia. Some perpetrators had studied in Australian universities or visited local mosques. The notion that terrorism was a distant threat collapsed.

Domestically, counter-terrorism became a priority. Intelligence agencies expanded, new laws were introduced, and community engagement programs were developed. Yet the seeds of radicalisation continued to grow, fertilised by global conflicts and local discontent.

Case studies of radicalisation in Australia

Several high-profile cases illustrate the reality of radicalisation:

➤ *The Pendennis Plot (2005)* – Police uncovered a network of young men in Melbourne and Sydney preparing for attacks. They had been radicalised by extremist sermons, videos, and peer reinforcement. The arrests prevented mass casualties, but the case revealed how radicalisation could flourish unnoticed in suburbs.

➤ *Man Haron Monis (Sydney Siege, 2014)* – An Iranian-born self-styled cleric, Monis took hostages in the Lindt Café in Sydney, resulting in two deaths. Though mentally unstable, he was motivated by jihadist ideology and pledged allegiance to ISIS during the siege. The event traumatised the nation, highlighting the unpredictable nature of lone-wolf radicalisation.

➤ *Foreign fighters in Syria and Iraq (2012–2016)* – Over 100 Australians travelled to join jihadist groups, primarily ISIS. Some became prominent propagandists or fighters. Many died; a few attempted to return. Their departure raised questions about how radicalisation had taken root in Australian suburbs.

➤ *Prison radicalisation* – Several convicted terrorists, including leaders of the Pendennis Plot, continued to spread ideology behind bars. Authorities reported radicalisation of other inmates, confirming prisons as incubators of extremism.

➤ *Plots foiled* – Numerous plots have been disrupted, including planned attacks on military bases, public events, and landmarks. While few succeeded, the persistence of attempts illustrates ongoing radicalisation.

These cases confirm that radicalisation is not hypothetical. It has produced violence, death, and lasting fear within Australia.

Recruitment patterns

How do individuals in Australia become radicalised? Research and investigations reveal common patterns:

1. *Identity struggles* – Many radicals are second-generation migrants, caught between cultures. They feel alienated from both their parents' traditions and broader Australian society. Radical Islam offers clarity and belonging.

2. *Peer groups* – Radicalisation often occurs in groups of friends. Shared grievances and reinforcement intensify commitment. The Pendennis Plot demonstrated this dynamic vividly.

3. *Charismatic preachers* – Radical imams, sometimes educated overseas, wield disproportionate influence. Their sermons, whether in mosques or online, inspire disaffected youth.

4. *Prisons* – As noted, prisons are hotspots of recruitment, where isolated individuals are drawn to radicalism as a source of meaning and protection.

5. *Online networks* – Perhaps most powerful today, online propaganda bypasses traditional authority. Social media spreads jihadist ideology, connecting Australians to global movements.

Each pathway reflects broader global trends but has specific Australian expressions.

The role of Mosques and religious leaders

The vast majority of mosques in Australia do not preach jihad. Many imams explicitly reject violence and emphasise civic participation. However, a minority of mosques and leaders have promoted radical interpretations.

Investigations have revealed many sermons glorifying jihad, condemning democracy, and fostering hostility toward all non-Muslims. Some mosques have distributed extremist literature or hosted controversial speakers. Even where violence is not openly advocated, a culture of separation, which strongly emphasises Muslim victimhood and Sharia supremacy, can easily pave the way for radicalisation.

Community leaders often face real dilemmas. Publicly, they condemn terrorism. Privately, some avoid confronting radicals for fear of division. Others, sympathetic to Islamist ideology, downplay the whole problem. This ambivalence undermines prevention efforts.

Radicalisation in prisons

As already mentioned, prisons can amplify the problem. Several convicted terrorists in Australia have continued to influence others while they are incarcerated. Young offenders, isolated and searching for identity, prove vulnerable to radical recruiters.

Islamic study groups, while not inherently problematic, can become platforms for extremist teaching when led by radicals. Authorities have responded with segregation units, surveillance, and some deradicalisation programs. Yet success is mixed. Some inmates feign rehabilitation to secure release, only to resume extremist activities. Others, hardened by prison, emerge more radical than before.

Online radicalisation in Australia

The digital realm has transformed radicalisation. Australian security agencies report that online propaganda is a primary driver of recruitment.

ISIS in particular targeted Australians with many English-language videos and magazines. Social media platforms amplified these messages, while encrypted apps facilitated direct contact with recruiters.

Teenagers in suburban homes consumed jihadist material, often without parental knowledge. Algorithms reinforced their exposure, drawing them deeper into echo chambers. Online forums provided belonging and validation. Some progressed to plotting attacks; others attempted to travel overseas.

Despite efforts by tech companies and governments to remove extremist content, the problem persists. Online radicalisation is diffuse, fast, and difficult to detect.

The response of law enforcement and intelligence agencies

Australia's response to radicalisation has been multi-faceted. Agencies like the Australian Security Intelligence Organisation (ASIO), the Australian Federal Police (AFP), and state police forces have expanded their counter-terrorism divisions. Key measures include:

> *Surveillance* – Monitoring of suspects, mosques, and online spaces.
> *Disruption* – Foiling plots through early intervention and arrests.

> *Legislation* – Laws enabling control orders, preventative detention, and citizenship revocation for dual nationals engaged in terrorism.

> *Community engagement* – Programs designed to build trust with Muslim communities and encourage cooperation.

> *International cooperation* – Sharing intelligence with allies, particularly the United States and United Kingdom.

These efforts have prevented major attacks but carry challenges. Balancing security with civil liberties is contentious. Critics will usually argue that Muslim communities are unfairly targeted; authorities insist the focus reflects real threats.

Challenges of deradicalisation

Deradicalisation programs seek to rehabilitate extremists, but success is limited. Ideology runs deep, and many radicals remain committed even when confronted with evidence of violence's futility. Programs involving counselling, mentorship, and even vocational training show some promise, but require long-term commitment.

A much deeper issue is theology. Unless radical interpretations of Islam are confronted and firmly discredited, deradicalisation will continue. Many programs avoid theological debate, fearing accusations of Islamophobia. Yet ideology cannot be countered by economics or psychology alone.

The cost of complacency

Radicalisation in Australia remains a minority phenomenon, but its cost is disproportionate. Billions of dollars are being spent on security, surveillance, and counter-terrorism. Communities live in fear of attacks. Social trust erodes as suspicion grows. Even failed plots create anxiety.

The cost of complacency is high. Ignoring radicalisation risks tragedies like Bali or the Sydney siege. Yet overreaction risks alienating many Muslims who reject extremism. Navigating this balance requires honesty about ideology, courage to confront it, and wisdom to distinguish individuals from systems.

Christian reflection

For Christians, radicalisation underscores the spiritual battle at the heart of culture. Paul described unbelievers as *"without hope and without God in the world."* (Ephesians 2:12). Radical Islam fills this void with counterfeit hope, offering martyrdom instead of grace.

The church must respond with both vigilance and mission. Vigilance, to defend freedom and protect society. Mission, to reach Muslims with the gospel of peace. Many former radicals testify that only the love of Christ broke their bondage. Australia's security, therefore, is not only political but spiritual.

Radicalisation in Australia is real, persistent, and dangerous. It manifests in plots, propaganda, and pressures on communities. It thrives in prisons, mosques, and online spaces. It challenges law enforcement, tests civil liberties, and exposes the limits of multiculturalism.

Australia's response has prevented many tragedies, but the struggle is ongoing. Unless the ideological roots of radicalisation are addressed, the threat will remain. The question is whether Australia has the clarity and courage to confront it honestly, without fear or compromise.

Security and freedom

Security and freedom are often seen as opposites in tension. A nation that prioritises security above all risks sliding into authoritarianism, with citizens under constant surveillance and liberty is lost.

A nation that prioritises freedom without vigilance risks naivety, leaving itself vulnerable to those who would exploit liberty to destroy it. Australia, like every democracy, must live in this tension.

The challenge of Islamic radicalisation intensifies the dilemma: how to protect citizens from terrorism while preserving the freedoms that define the nation.

The security–freedom balance

Australia's history shows a strong instinct for freedom. From its convict beginnings, Australians have distrusted heavy-handed authority. Our national character prizes independence, free speech, and *"a fair go."* Yet Australians also expect government to protect them from any harm. After events such as the Bali bombings and the Sydney siege, public pressure demanded strong security responses.

The balance is delicate. Too little security, and terrorism thrives. Too much, and freedom is eroded. The future of Australia's democracy depends on finding a sustainable equilibrium.

Legislative responses to terrorism

Since 2001, Australia has enacted extensive counter-terrorism legislation. These laws expand the powers of intelligence and law enforcement agencies, enabling them to act pre-emptively against suspected terrorists. Key measures include:

➤ *Control Orders* – Allow restrictions on movement, communication, and activities of individuals suspected of terrorism.

➤ *Preventive detention* – Authorises detention of individuals without charge for limited periods to prevent imminent attacks.

➤ *Extended surveillance* – Expands interception of communications, monitoring of internet activity, and use of metadata.

➤ *Citizenship revocation* – Permits stripping citizenship from dual nationals engaged in terrorism overseas.

➤ *Foreign fighters legislation* – Criminalises travel to conflict zones without authorisation.

These laws have disrupted plots and reduced risks. Yet they also raise concerns about civil liberties. Critics argue that they allow detention without trial, excessive surveillance, and seem to be disproportionately targeting Muslim communities.

Proponents insist they are necessary in an age of asymmetric threats. The tension remains unresolved: how much freedom should be curtailed to preserve security?

The role of Intelligence Agencies

Our intelligence community plays a central role in counter-terrorism. The Australian Security Intelligence Organisation (ASIO), the Australian Federal Police (AFP), and state agencies collaborate to monitor suspects, infiltrate networks, and disrupt plots.

Their work is often unseen but vital. Dozens of planned attacks have been foiled in recent decades. Surveillance of online activity has identified radicalisation early. International cooperation, particularly with the United States and United Kingdom, has provided crucial intelligence. Yet reliance on intelligence raises challenges:

➢ *Privacy Concerns* – Citizens fear constant monitoring of communications.

➢ *Discrimination fears* – Muslim communities often feel disproportionately targeted, eroding trust.

➢ *Resource strain* – Monitoring hundreds of suspects requires vast manpower and funding.

Balancing effectiveness with accountability is critical. Without oversight, intelligence risks overreach. Without vigilance, it risks failure.

Risks of complacency

Complacency is as dangerous as overreach. Radicalisation in Australia may appear small-scale compared to Europe or the Middle East, but its potential impact is severe. A single successful attack can cause mass casualties, economic disruption, and long-term fear. Complacency manifests in several ways:

➢ *Political fatigue* – As major attacks recede from memory, governments may reduce funding or soften vigilance.

- ➤ *Public naivety* – Many Australians assume terrorism is "someone else's problem," underestimating local radicalisation.
- ➤ *Cultural relativism* – Multicultural ideology may downplay the incompatibility of Sharia with freedom, hindering prevention.

History warns us against such complacency. The United States, after years of downplaying al-Qaeda, suffered 9/11.

Britain totally underestimated radicalisation until the London bombings of 2005. France ignored warnings until Paris was attacked in 2015. Australia must not repeat these mistakes.

Strategies for safeguarding security and freedom

How, then, can Australia balance security and freedom in the face of radicalisation?

Several strategies stand out:

1. Clear legal boundaries

Counter-terrorism laws must be firm yet accountable. Judicial oversight, sunset clauses, and regular reviews prevent abuse. Freedom must be limited only as necessary, never as convenience.

2. Community engagement

Muslim communities must be partners, not adversaries. Building trust encourages cooperation with law enforcement. Yet engagement must be honest: leaders who excuse or minimise radicalisation cannot be indulged. Moderate voices should be supported, radicals confronted.

3. Education and prevention

Schools are frontline defences. Teaching civic values, critical thinking, and media literacy can help inoculate youth against extremist propaganda. Islamic schools must be held accountable to national standards, ensuring they promote integration rather than separation.

4. Prison management

Segregating radical inmates, monitoring Islamic study groups, and providing credible deradicalisation programs are essential. Prisons should rehabilitate, not radicalise.

5. Digital vigilance

Tech companies must work with governments to remove extremist content more quickly. Counter-narratives have to be developed a lot faster to challenge jihadist propaganda. Online radicalisation requires digital solutions as well as community resilience.

6. Immigration policy

Future security depends on who enters. Immigration programs must assess cultural compatibility, not just skills. Humanitarian intakes should consider risks of radicalisation, ensuring capacity for integration.

7. Defence of free speech

Perhaps most importantly, free speech must be defended. Suppressing criticism of Islam in the name of harmony only strengthens radicals, who interpret it as weakness. Open debate allows truth to prevail and exposes extremist ideologies to scrutiny.

Learning from other nations

Australia can learn from others' successes and failures:

➤ *United States* – Aggressive counter-terrorism has prevented many attacks but sometimes overreached, undermining liberties. Australia must avoid mass surveillance without oversight.

➤ *United Kingdom* – Community engagement programs have been mixed; too often they empowered Islamist groups rather than moderates. Australia must choose partners carefully.

- ➤ *France* – Strong secularism confronts Islamic demands directly but has produced alienation and unrest. Australia must balance firmness with fairness.

- ➤ *Denmark* – Innovative deradicalisation programs, combining mentorship with accountability, show promise. Australia can adapt such models.

Comparative lessons highlight the need for nuance: firmness without brutality, engagement without naivety, freedom without complacency.

The role of the church

Christians have a distinctive role in this balance. The state bears the sword to restrain evil (Romans 13:4), but the church must proclaim the gospel that transforms hearts. No counter-terrorism strategy can succeed without addressing the spiritual void that fuels radicalisation.

Churches must therefore:

- ➤ Pray for leaders and security agencies.
- ➤ Model communities of love and inclusion that expose the emptiness of jihad.
- ➤ Reach out to Muslims with the hope of Christ.
- ➤ Speak truth about Sharia's incompatibility while showing compassion to individuals.

The gospel provides what jihad cannot: peace with God, forgiveness of sins, and true freedom. In Christ, zeal is redirected from violence to service, from hatred to love.

What does the future look like?

Australia's future depends on whether it can maintain freedom while resisting radicalisation. If it sacrifices freedom for security, it will lose its identity. If it sacrifices security for freedom, it will lose its safety. Only by holding both together can it remain the nation it is meant to be.

The stakes are certainly high:

➤ National security.
➤ Public trust.
➤ Civil liberties.
➤ The future of multiculturalism.
➤ The preservation of Western and Christian values.

Radicalisation is not only a security threat but a cultural and spiritual one. The balance of security and freedom will shape not only policies but the soul of the nation.

Conclusion

The challenge of radicalisation forces Australia to confront its deepest dilemmas. It is not just a matter of policing or legislation but of identity. What kind of nation does Australia want to be? Will it defend freedom courageously, even when threatened? Will it protect security without losing its soul?

The answer will determine whether Australia navigates the age of radicalisation with wisdom or succumbs to fear or folly. The task ahead requires clarity, courage, and conviction.

Above all, it requires remembering that true freedom is found not in the absence of threat but in the presence of truth. *"If the Son sets you free, you will be free indeed."* (John 8:36).

12. ISLAM AND THE MEDIA NARRATIVE

The rise of the media narrative on Islam

The way most Australians perceive Islam is shaped not only by personal encounters or academic debates but also, and perhaps most powerfully, by the media. Newspapers, television, radio, films, and digital platforms filter reality every day and shape public imagination.

Very few Australians visit the Middle East, study Islamic law, or read the Qur'an. Even less will read this book! Most learn about Islam from what they see and hear in the news or entertainment industry. This makes the media narrative decisive. It informs whether Australians perceive Islam as a peaceful religion, a looming threat, or something in between.

The power of media framing

The media does not simply report the facts. It frames those facts. Decisions about what to report, how to report it, and what language to use will create narratives. A bombing in Baghdad may be presented as *"sectarian violence"* or *"Islamist terrorism."* A new mosque in Sydney may be described as *"a sign of diversity"* or *"a challenge to cohesion."* The same event, framed differently, will produce radically different perceptions.

Framing also involves omission. What is left unsaid can shape perception as much as what is said (sometimes even more). A report on multicultural harmony that ignores honour killings or radicalisation presents a distorted picture.

A story about terrorism that avoids naming ideology can create confusion. So, Australians consume narratives that are partial, filtered, and shaped by editorial agendas.

This is not unique to Islam; all issues are framed. But the stakes with Islam are especially high, because the narrative influences immigration policy, security laws, community relations, and national identity.

The global backdrop

To understand the Australian media narrative, one must first look globally. In the wake of the September 11 attacks, global media outlets faced the challenge of reporting on Islam. The scale of the event demanded explanation. Why would Muslims fly planes into buildings? Was Islam inherently violent? Or was this the work of a fringe group?

Western leaders quickly promoted the narrative of Islam as *"a religion of peace."* President George W. Bush, within days of 9/11, declared that America was not at war with Islam. This framing set the tone. Mainstream media followed suit, emphasising that terrorism was the act of extremists, not reflective of Islam itself.

The repetition of this message created a dominant narrative: Islam is peaceful but hijacked by radicals. Criticism of Islam as a religion was therefore equated with bigotry. The category of *"Islamophobia"* emerged, discouraging any real scrutiny.

This global framing shaped the Australian media. Coverage of terrorism, immigration, and cultural conflicts adopted similar caution. The narrative was set: Islam must be separated from terrorism, and critics must be scrutinised for intolerance.

The Australian media landscape

Australia's media is diverse but dominated by a few major players. On one side, outlets such as the *ABC, SBS,* and *The Sydney Morning Herald* lean to the progressive side, emphasising multiculturalism and tolerance. On the other side we have outlets like *The Australian, Sky News,* and some regional papers which lean to the conservative side, raising sharper questions about Islam and security.

This division produces competing narratives. Progressive outlets highlight Muslim success stories, condemn Islamophobia, and frame critics as intolerant. Conservative outlets report more extensively on radicalisation, terrorism, and incompatibility. Yet even within conservative outlets, caution prevails. Few openly challenge Islam as a system; most confine critique to *"extremism."*

Entertainment media adds another layer. Films, dramas, and comedies often portray Muslims as either victims of prejudice or as villains linked to terrorism. Rarely do they depict ordinary Muslims grappling with Sharia or integration. The result is polarisation: Islam is seen either as a persecuted minority or as a looming threat, with little nuance.

Terrorism and the media

Nothing has shaped perceptions of Islam more than terrorism. Every major attack—Bali in 2002, London in 2005, Paris in 2015, Christchurch in 2019—has generated intense coverage. Images of the carnage, grieving families, and the emergency response sear themselves into our memory.

Yet the framing of terrorism is contested. Progressive outlets often downplay ideology, describing attackers as *"lone wolves,"* *"mentally unstable,"* or *"radicalised online."* Conservative outlets are more likely to identify Islamist ideology explicitly. This divergence confuses the wider public. Are terrorists motivated by Islam, or are they aberrations?

Moreover, saturation coverage of attacks paradoxically serves terrorists' aims. Radical groups seek publicity. Media attention magnifies fear, creating the perception of an omnipresent threat. The challenge for the media is unavoidable: to report without amplifying, to inform without sensationalising.

Immigration and multiculturalism in the media

Media narratives on Islam extend beyond terrorism to include immigration and multiculturalism. Reporting on refugee intakes, for example, often emphasises humanitarian suffering—images of Syrian children, Afghan families, or boats of asylum seekers.

This framing will appeal to people's compassion, portraying Islamic immigration as a moral duty. Seldom reported with equal emphasis, are those long-term integration challenges—enclaves, welfare dependence, or cultural conflict.

When such issues are covered, they are often framed as failures of Australian society to welcome migrants, rather than failures of migrants to assimilate.

Multicultural festivals, halal food expos, and mosque open days receive glowing coverage as symbols of harmony. Incidents of honour violence, forced marriage, or Sharia advocacy receive less attention, or are presented cautiously to avoid accusations of racism. The narrative thus tilts toward celebration rather than scrutiny.

Victimhood narratives

Another powerful strand in the media narrative is victimhood. Muslims are frequently portrayed as the victims of prejudice, discrimination, and hate crimes. After major terrorist attacks, the media often focus almost as much on potential backlash against Muslims as on the victims of the attack itself.

For example, after the Christchurch Mosque shootings in 2019, Australian media devoted extensive coverage to Islamophobia, right-wing extremism, and the need for tolerance. While this response was appropriate to the tragedy, the pattern is telling: coverage shifts quickly from Muslims as perpetrators to Muslims as victims. This framing reinforces the multicultural ideology: Muslims must be protected, not scrutinised. Criticism of Islam is conflated with hatred of Muslims. The effect is to shield Islamic practices from robust debate.

Political influence on media narratives

Governments influence media narratives through statements, funding, and access. Since 9/11, Australian leaders have consistently affirmed that Islam is peaceful and that terrorism represents only a perversion. This political framing discourages open critique. Public broadcasters such as the ABC and SBS, funded by government, reflect this narrative strongly. Programs highlight many Muslim achievements, challenge *"Islamophobic"* rhetoric, and emphasise harmony. Investigative journalism into radical mosques or Sharia advocacy is comparatively rare.

Conservative politicians occasionally challenge this narrative, emphasising security and assimilation. Yet even they avoid critiquing Islam as a system, focusing instead on "radical Islam" or "Islamist extremism." The political consensus thus narrows media debate.

The role of academia and experts

Media narratives often rely on academic experts. In the field of Islamic studies, many scholars emphasise Islam's diversity and peaceful traditions, downplaying connections to violence. Their commentary has significantly shaped our public understanding, providing intellectual support for multicultural narratives.

Critics of Islam, by contrast, are often marginalised. Academics who highlight incompatibilities will face accusations of bias or Islamophobia. Media outlets, wary of controversy, prefer "safe" experts who reinforce dominant frames.

This reliance on selective expertise reinforces a narrow narrative: Islam is complex, mostly peaceful, and always misunderstood. Radicalisation is attributed to poverty, alienation, or Western foreign policy, not to Islamic doctrine itself.

Entertainment media and pop culture

Beyond the news, entertainment shapes perceptions subtly but powerfully. Hollywood films often portray Muslims as either terrorists or victims. Television dramas include token Muslim characters to demonstrate diversity. Documentaries emphasise tolerance and resilience.

In Australia, SBS dramas and ABC feature stories often showcase Muslim families navigating prejudice, promoting empathy. Rarely are tensions over Sharia, gender roles, or radicalisation explored in depth. Entertainment thus contributes to a narrative of Islam as misunderstood minority. At the same time, online spaces can complicate the picture. Independent filmmakers, YouTube channels, and alternative media present harsher critiques of Islam, often sensationalised.

This counter-narrative has attracted audiences who are very suspicious of the mainstream outlets. The result is polarisation: competing realities shaped by competing media.

The global to local connection

Australian media narratives are shaped by global currents. Coverage of wars in Iraq, Afghanistan, Syria, and Gaza filters into the local debates. When images of suffering Palestinians dominate headlines, sympathy for Muslims in Australia grows. When ISIS atrocities are shown, suspicion intensifies. Global media frames reverberate locally, shaping public opinion on immigration, security, and multiculturalism.

This interconnectedness means that the narrative is never purely Australian. It is part of a global struggle over how Islam is perceived: as a peaceful religion, dangerous ideology, or both.

The Christian perspective on media narratives

From a Christian perspective, all media narratives must be evaluated through the lens of truth. The Bible warns against false witness (Exodus 20:16) and commends honesty. Christians must ask whether media portrayals of Islam reflect reality or obscure it. When the media shields Islam from critique, it fails in truth-telling. When it sensationalises terrorism, it feeds fear rather than wisdom. The task is discernment: separating narrative from fact, spin from substance.

Christians are called to speak truth in love (Ephesians 4:15). This means refusing both extremes: neither demonising Muslims indiscriminately nor denying the incompatibility of Islam with freedom. A biblical perspective insists on honesty, compassion, and courage.

Bias, censorship, and the silencing of criticism

If the rise of the media narrative on Islam revealed the power of framing, the second challenge is even deeper: the active shaping of discourse through bias, censorship, and the silencing of criticism. In modern Australia, to raise questions about Islam is to risk being labelled intolerant or *"Islamophobic."*

In public conversation, certain critiques are not merely debated but delegitimised, excluded as unacceptable. This shaping of discourse does not occur by accident. It is sustained by political correctness, reinforced by media practices, and entrenched in academic and cultural institutions.

The climate of 'Political Correctness'

Political correctness has become one of the defining features of Western discourse. Originating as an effort to promote respect for minorities, it has grown into a pervasive culture of speech regulation. In Australia, political correctness influences how journalists, politicians, and citizens talk about Islam. At its best, political correctness aims to prevent discrimination. It challenges racism, discourages inflammatory language, and protects the vulnerable groups. But at its worst, it just suppresses legitimate debate. When criticism of ideas is treated as hatred of people, public discourse suffers terribly.

This dynamic is particularly visible with Islam. Terms like "Islamophobia" only blur categories. They conflate criticism of Islamic ideology with bigotry against Muslims as individuals. The result is a paralysis: important questions about Sharia, radicalisation, or cultural incompatibility are silenced under fear of social stigma.

Consider the pattern:

➤ A journalist questions the role of Sharia councils → labelled Islamophobic.

➤ A politician raises security concerns about immigration from conflict zones → labelled Islamophobic.

➤ A citizen expresses discomfort with burqas in public spaces → labelled Islamophobic.

By deploying the label, critics are delegitimised without any engagement. The discussion ends before it begins. The term is asymmetrical. Criticism of Christianity, often harsh or mocking, is celebrated as free speech. Criticism of Islam is denounced as bigotry. This double standard reinforces the narrative that Islam is uniquely protected from scrutiny.

Media self-censorship

Fear of being labelled Islamophobic fosters self-censorship in the media. Some Journalists hesitate to investigate radical mosques, fearing the backlash. Editors avoid publishing critical pieces.

Self-censorship is often subtle. Stories are framed to emphasise harmony rather than conflict. Phrases like *"men of Middle Eastern appearance"* replace *"Muslim"* in crime reporting. Radical attacks are attributed to *"mental illness"* rather than radical ideology. This pattern distorts reality. It denies the public the full picture, undermines trust in media, and creates suspicion. Citizens begin to believe that truths are being hidden. Alternative media fills the gap, sometimes irresponsibly, further polarising society.

Academic reinforcement

Academia reinforces the silencing effect. Many scholars of Islam will emphasise diversity, peace, and victimhood. Their research highlights Islamophobia, racism, and colonial guilt, whilst downplaying any incompatibilities with democracy. University courses often present Islam as being misunderstood, oppressed, or perhaps progressive. Critical perspectives are marginalised. Students who question Sharia or gender roles may be shamed. Speakers critical of Islam are protested and shouted down.

This academic climate influences media. Journalists rely on the academic experts, who almost always represent the progressive consensus. Their commentary filters into news stories, framing Islam as peaceful and critics as prejudiced. The cycle of bias is then complete.

Case studies of silencing

Several Australian examples illustrate bias and censorship:

➤ *The Bendigo Mosque protests (2014–2015)* – Residents opposed a proposed mosque, citing concerns about cultural change and radicalisation. Media coverage overwhelmingly framed them as racists and bigots. While some protesters were indeed extreme, legitimate questions were drowned out by accusations of intolerance.

- ➤ *The Halal Certification debate* – Citizens raising concerns about halal certification, particularly its links to Sharia and possible funding of Islamic groups, were portrayed as paranoid or xenophobic. Investigative reporting on financial flows was minimal.

- ➤ *Academic conferences* – Scholars critical of Islam's incompatibility with democracy have faced disinvitation from conferences or campaigns against them. Their voices, rather than being debated, are excluded.

- ➤ *Christchurch Massacre response (2019)* – In the aftermath of the horrific mosque shootings, national media emphasised Islamophobia and right-wing extremism. While appropriate in context, the effect was long-term chilling: critiques of Islam became even harder to voice without association with violence.

These examples clearly illustrate a consistent pattern: critics are not engaged but delegitimised. The discourse always narrows, as dissenting voices are silenced, and the narrative remains unchallenged.

The role of advocacy groups

Muslim advocacy organisations play an active role in shaping the narrative. Groups such as the Australian Federation of Islamic Councils (AFIC) lobby government, engage media, and mobilise communities. Their strategy often involves highlighting Islamophobia and demanding protection.

By positioning Muslims as perpetual victims, advocacy groups gain influence. Governments provide funding for *"community cohesion"* programs. Media outlets then amplify their concerns. Universities host conferences on Islamophobia.

This advocacy is effective because it aligns with the multicultural ethos. It frames Muslims as vulnerable minorities needing protection. Critics, by contrast, are framed as aggressors. The effect is powerful: debate tilts heavily toward accommodation rather than scrutiny.

Bias in language and terminology

Language itself reveals bias. Terms like *"extremist"* or *"radical"* are used selectively. A jihadist inspired by the Qur'an is called an extremist, implying deviation from Islam, rather than an Islamist, which recognises serious ideological roots. Attacks are described as *"senseless violence,"* obscuring their real theological rationale.

The phrase *"men of Middle Eastern appearance,"* used frequently in crime reports, illustrates evasion. It conveys ethnicity without naming religion, avoiding controversy but leaving ambiguity. Citizens suspect concealment, undermining trust. This linguistic bias sanitises reality. It reassures progressive audiences while frustrating those who prefer honesty. Over time, it corrodes credibility, driving people toward alternative media.

The international dimension of censorship

Bias and censorship are not unique to Australia. Globally, Western nations struggle with similar dynamics.

➤ *In the United Kingdom*, police and media initially downplayed the scale of grooming gangs involving Muslim men, fearing accusations of racism. When revelations emerged, public trust collapsed.

➤ *In France*, coverage of Islamist violence is often framed as socio-economic struggle rather than ideology.

➤ *In the United States*, debates over terms like "Islamic terrorism" versus "violent extremism" illustrate political pressure on language.

These international patterns then shape Australia. Global media frames filter into local reporting. The reluctance to criticise Islam is reinforced by a shared Western narrative.

Consequences of silencing

The silencing of criticism has several obvious consequences:

1. *Erosion of free speech:* When critiques of Islam are delegitimised, free speech suffers. Citizens hesitate to speak openly, fearing labels of bigotry.

2. *Polarisation:* Mainstream media's bias drives citizens to alternative outlets, often less responsible, deepening division.

3. *Radicalisation of debate:* Suppression of moderate criticism leaves space for extremes. When ordinary concerns are ignored, frustration fuels radical opposition.

4. *Victim mentality:* Muslims, constantly framed as victims, are discouraged from confronting internal problems such as radicalisation or gender inequality.

5. *Weak policy:* Governments, influenced by skewed narratives, fail to address real challenges. Immigration, security, and multicultural policy are shaped by ideology rather than reality.

These consequences weaken society's capacity to respond to Islam honestly and effectively.

A Christian response

Christians must navigate this climate with wisdom. The call to speak truth in love requires courage when truth is censored. The apostles declared, *"We cannot help speaking about what we have seen and heard."* (Acts 4:20). Silencing is not new; the early church faced it constantly. The church must model respectful but honest and firm critique. The church really needs to distinguish between loving Muslims and critiquing Islam. It must refuse to accept the false charge that all criticism is hate. And it must defend free speech as essential for the gospel itself. If critique of Islam is silenced, critique of secular ideologies or even proclamation of Christ may be silenced tomorrow.

The consequences of the narrative

These media narratives do not merely describe reality; they shape it. The way Islam is reported in Australia and the West has consequences for how ordinary citizens think, how policymakers legislate, and how then Christians respond.

When narratives are biased, censored or incomplete, societies are forced to act on distorted information. Public confusion deepens, policymaking falters, and truth is obscured.

Public confusion

Perhaps the most immediate consequence of the media narrative on Islam is confusion. Ordinary Australians are left unsure of what Islam is, how it relates to terrorism, and whether cultural incompatibilities are real.

On the one hand, they see news of terrorist attacks, radicalised youth, and international conflicts. On the other hand, they hear repeated assurances that *"Islam is a religion of peace."* This contradiction produces dissonance. People know what they see, yet they are told to interpret it differently. This confusion has social costs:

> *Distrust of Media* – Citizens suspect that truths are being hidden.

> *Suspicion of Muslims* – Lacking clarity, people generalise, assuming all Muslims may be threats.

> *Polarisation* – Some adopt hostility, others embrace denial, with little middle ground.

In short, public understanding of Islam then becomes fractured, driven less by facts than by competing narratives.

The impact on policymaking

Media narratives profoundly influence policymakers. Politicians operate in a world of headlines, soundbites, and public pressure. When the dominant narrative portrays Islam as peaceful and critics as bigoted, politicians hesitate to enact firm policies.

Immigration is one area deeply shaped by media. Humanitarian programs are often presented through images of suffering children, generating pressure for generosity. Little space is given to discussions of integration, security, or cultural compatibility. Policymakers who raise such concerns are branded intolerant.

Counter-terrorism policy is another critical area. Governments frequently emphasise *"violent extremism"* rather than *"Islamic terrorism,"* reflecting the media framing. By avoiding explicit identification of ideology, policies will focus on socioeconomic causes rather than any theological ones. The result is partial strategies that address symptoms but not the roots.

Multiculturalism, too, is reinforced by media narratives. Stories of harmony, diversity festivals, and happy, successful migrants always dominate the media coverage.

Policymakers who challenge multiculturalism's assumptions risk media backlash. Thus, ideology entrenches itself not through evidence but through narrative pressure.

The chilling effect on debate

One of the most damaging consequences is the chilling effect on debate. Citizens, journalists, and politicians alike self-censor. Fear of being labelled Islamophobic stifles open conversation.

This chilling effect prevents societies from confronting real problems. Issues like Sharia advocacy, honour violence, or radicalisation in schools remain under-discussed. When they are raised, they are framed as isolated incidents or blamed on poverty rather than ideology.

The Bible warns against such silencing. *"Woe to those who call evil good and good evil, who put darkness for light and light for darkness"* (Isaiah 5:20). When societies suppress truth in the name of tolerance, they invite confusion and decay.

Consequences for Muslim communities

The media narrative also affects Muslims themselves. Constant portrayal as being victims will foster a mentality of grievance. Communities are encouraged to focus on Islamophobia rather than self-examination. Problems within — radicalisation, gender inequality, intolerance — are therefore deflected outward. At the same time, Muslims who reject radicalism or critique aspects of Islam find themselves being marginalised.

Reformers therefore are silenced by both conservative leaders and progressive allies. The narrative protects traditional Islam rather than encouraging change. This paradox leaves Muslims caught: blamed collectively by suspicious outsiders, portrayed as poor victims by sympathetic insiders, and then hindered from genuine reform by dominant narratives.

Cultural polarisation

The long-term consequence is cultural polarisation. When one side of society believes Islam is a religion of peace and the other sees it as an existential threat, common ground vanishes. Debates become hostile, trust erodes, and unity weakens.

Polarisation fuels extremism on both sides. Some citizens turn to far-right groups, convinced mainstream media hides the truth. Others embrace uncritical multiculturalism, unwilling to see incompatibility. In this climate, reasoned discussion is rare.

Polarisation is precisely what radicals desire. Islamist groups thrive on division, presenting themselves as defenders of Muslims against a hostile West. Biased narratives inadvertently strengthen their claims.

Finding our way in a confused culture

For Christians, navigating this landscape requires wisdom and courage. The church cannot rely on media narratives, whether progressive or conservative. It must turn to Scripture, truth, and discernment.

The gospel calls believers to love Muslims as neighbours, while rejecting Islam as false teaching. This dual stance is difficult in a polarised culture. To love Muslims risks being seen as naïve; to critique Islam risks being labelled intolerant. Yet Christians must do both. The apostle Paul provides an example. He engaged pagan cultures with respect, quoting their poets (Acts 17:28), while boldly declaring the truth of Christ. Likewise, the church must engage Muslims with compassion while clearly exposing the incompatibility of Sharia with freedom.

Christians must also defend free speech. The right to proclaim Christ rests on the same freedom that allows criticism of Islam. If critique is silenced, evangelism will follow. Defending free speech is not optional but essential for the gospel.

The need for truth

Ultimately, the media narrative highlights the central need of our time: truth. Without truth, freedom falters, policy fails, and culture collapses. Jesus declared, *"Then you will know the truth, and the truth will set you free."* (John 8:32). This applies not only spiritually but socially.

Truth requires honesty about Islam. It means acknowledging its doctrines, recognising its incompatibilities, and refusing to sanitise its challenges. Truth requires courage to say what is unpopular, trusting that clarity brings freedom.

At the same time, truth requires fairness. It means rejecting prejudice, protecting Muslims from unjust discrimination, and remembering they too are made in God's image. Truth is not cruelty, but clarity guided by love.

Toward a new media honesty

If Australia is to navigate Islam's challenge wisely, it needs a new media honesty. Journalists must recover the courage to report facts, even when uncomfortable. Academics must allow genuine debate, not just approved perspectives. Citizens must demand transparency rather than slogans.

A new honesty would acknowledge both realities: that many Muslims live peacefully, and that Islamic ideology contains inherent incompatibilities. It would refuse both extremes: neither demonising Muslims indiscriminately nor romanticising Islam as merely misunderstood.

This honesty would strengthen democracy. It would enable citizens to debate policies openly, shape immigration wisely, and confront radicalisation effectively. Above all, it would restore trust in institutions by showing that truth is valued above ideology.

Conclusion

The media narrative on Islam is not a side issue. It will shape perception, policy, and culture. Biased framing, censorship, and silencing distort truth, creating confusion and polarisation. The consequences are profound: weak policies, cultural division, and missed opportunities for reform. Christians, above all, must respond with truth. The church cannot be captive to narratives but must always proclaim Christ, defend freedom, and expose falsehood. In a world where lies abound, the gospel offers truth that liberates.

Australia's future depends on recovering honesty. Only by naming realities clearly, confronting ideologies courageously, and defending freedoms steadfastly can the nation preserve its values. The media must no longer dictate narratives divorced from truth. Citizens must demand clarity. And the church must shine as a beacon of truth in a culture of confusion. The task before Australia is precisely this: to expose falsehood, defend truth, and ensure that freedom is not lost to silence.

It is frightening to see the extent to which the media has shaped the collective thinking of Australians today. If you want to see how hard it is to promote intelligent, honest, measured debate in this nation on Islam and its impact, then I suggest you hand this book to any media outlet and ask them to publish their review. I am under no illusion about the end result.

The truth of the matter is this, my final motivation to write this book came one morning as I listened to a television news story about the rise of Islamophobia in our great nation. It was not the outright bias and distortion in the story that raised my blood pressure – it was the fact that the people reporting genuinely and passionately believed what they were saying!

The frightening thing about constantly peddling such a false narrative, is that it doesn't take long for you to accept it as truth and defend it against all critique. Tragically, millions of people will be exposed to that bias every day, but only a handful will ever read this book.

13. THE QUESTION OF LOYALTY: NATION OR UMMAH?

The Islamic concept of the ummah

At the heart of Islam lies an idea both spiritual and political, individual and collective: the *ummah*. It is not merely a religious congregation or some vague sense of belonging. The *ummah* is the worldwide community of Muslims, bound by faith, loyalty, and law. For Muslims, this concept is not optional but intrinsic. To be a Muslim is to be part of the *ummah*. Its reach transcends every border, language, and culture. Its claims are stronger than any national identity, any citizenship, or any political allegiance. Understanding the *ummah* is essential for grasping the challenge that Islam poses to national unity in Australia and beyond.

The theological roots of the ummah

The Qur'an itself lays the foundation for the *ummah*. Several verses emphasise the unity of believers as one community distinct from all others.

"Indeed this, your religion, is one religion, and I am your Lord, so worship Me." (Qur'an 21:92).

"You are the best nation produced for mankind. You enjoin what is right and forbid what is wrong and believe in Allah." (Qur'an 3:110).

These texts present the Muslim community as divinely chosen, tasked with moral superiority and global mission. Belonging to the *ummah* is not a matter of choice but divine decree.

Hadith traditions reinforce this. Muhammad is reported to have said, *"The believers are like one body; if one part feels pain, the whole body suffers."* The metaphor of the body emphasises solidarity. Injury to one Muslim anywhere in the world is injury to all.

From its beginning, then, Islam embedded the idea that Muslims form a single, indivisible community, united in worship, law, and destiny.

The ummah in early Islam

The first Muslim community under Muhammad in Medina became the prototype for the *ummah*. Known as the *ummah al-Madinah*, it was both religious and political. Muhammad acted as prophet, judge, and also political leader. Law and faith were inseparable.

The Constitution of Medina, a document attributed to Muhammad, formalised this arrangement. It bound all Muslims together, distinguished them from Jews and pagans, and set principles of loyalty. Even in its earliest form, the *ummah* was not merely spiritual but political: allegiance to Islam superseded tribal or ethnic ties.

Following Muhammad's death, the caliphs carried this vision forward. The caliph was not only a ruler but also the leader of the *ummah*. Expansion through conquest soon brought diverse peoples under Islamic rule, but their identity was reshaped. Arabs, Persians, Berbers, and Turks all became part of one community defined by Islam.

Ummah as universal community

Unlike Judaism, tied to ethnic lineage, or Christianity, which distinguished between church and state, Islam insisted on comprehensive unity. The *ummah* is universal, transcending race and geography, yet exclusive: only Muslims belong.

This exclusivity shapes Muslim identity. Loyalty is not first to family, tribe, or nation – it always to Islam. The *ummah* provides belonging stronger than nationality. For many Muslims today, being part of the *ummah* matters more than being Indonesian, Pakistani, or Australian.

This universality has enduring appeal. A Muslim in Sydney feels solidarity with a Muslim in Gaza or Kashmir. Shared rituals — prayer, fasting, pilgrimage — all reinforce unity. The Qur'an is recited in Arabic worldwide, binding millions in a common language. The sense of belonging is profound, transcending distance and difference.

The Ummah and Sharia

Central to the *ummah* is Sharia. Law unites this worldwide community, ensuring consistency across cultures. Whether in Saudi Arabia, Nigeria, or Australia, Sharia defines what it means to live as a Muslim.

Theological unity, therefore, is not abstract. It is legal and practical. Muslims obey the same rituals, dietary laws, and moral codes. Sharia courts, where permitted, adjudicate disputes not by national law but by Islamic principles.

This creates tension with modern nation-states. Citizenship requires loyalty to national law; Islam requires loyalty to Sharia. Where conflicts arise, devout Muslims are expected to prioritise the *ummah*. This principle is enshrined in Islamic jurisprudence, where allegiance to non-Muslim states is permitted only as a temporary necessity, never as ultimate loyalty.

Historical caliphates as Ummah in practice

Throughout history, the caliphate embodied the *ummah*. From the Rashidun Caliphs (7th century) to the Ottoman Empire (ending in 1924), the caliph was regarded as leader of all Muslims. Even when fragmented politically, the ideal of unity persisted.

The Ottoman caliphate, in particular, symbolised this. Stretching across three continents, it governed diverse peoples under the banner of Islam. Though local identities remained, ultimate loyalty was expected to the caliph and the Islamic order.

The abolition of the caliphate in 1924 by Mustafa Kemal Atatürk was a seismic shock. For many Muslims, it marked a betrayal of Islam's unity. Movements such as the Muslim Brotherhood emerged partly in response, seeking to revive the *ummah* and restore Islamic governance.

To this day, the longing for a restored caliphate remains very powerful. Groups like al-Qaeda and ISIS explicitly frame their mission as revival of the *ummah*. Even moderate Islamists invoke the memory of lost unity as a source of inspiration.

The modern resurgence of the Ummah

In the twentieth and twenty-first centuries, globalisation has now intensified Muslim consciousness of the *ummah*. Satellite television, the internet, and social media connect Muslims worldwide instantly. Events in one country resonate globally.

Whenever Muslims suffer in Palestine, Kashmir, or Myanmar, protests erupt in Sydney, London, and New York. Social media campaigns mobilise solidarity. Charities raise funds across borders. The idea that Muslims are one body is more visible than ever before.

This global solidarity can inspire compassion, but it also fuels radicalisation. Jihadist recruiters appeal to loyalty to the *ummah*, urging Muslims in the West to fight for their brothers and sisters abroad. The *ummah* becomes not only a spiritual ideal but also a political rallying cry.

Tensions with national identity

The strength of this *ummah* loyalty creates tension with national identity. In Western democracies, citizenship requires allegiance to the nation, respect for its laws, and participation in its political community. For devout Muslims, however, ultimate loyalty belongs elsewhere.

This tension is visible in several ways:

➤ *Dual Allegiance* – Muslims may profess loyalty to the nation while privately prioritising the *ummah*.

➤ *Selective Citizenship* – National laws are followed when convenient but resisted when conflicting with Sharia.

➤ *Political Advocacy* – Muslim organisations lobby for recognition of Islamic practices, framing demands as religious rights but grounded in *ummah* loyalty.

In some cases, this tension leads to outright conflict. Muslims who join jihad abroad explicitly reject any national allegiance, declaring loyalty only to the *ummah*. But even short of violence, the pull of *ummah* identity hinders integration.

Ummah in Muslim minority communities

For Muslim minorities, such as those we have in Australia today, the *ummah* provides real strength and solidarity as communities establish mosques, schools, and cultural centres to preserve identity. This ensures continuity but also fosters separation.

In multicultural societies, Muslims will often live in enclaves where *ummah* identity is dominant. Local politics, media, and education reinforce global solidarity. Children grow up with a strong awareness of being Muslim first, Australian second.

This identity is reinforced by transnational networks. Imams trained overseas import teaching which emphasises loyalty to the *ummah*. Islamic charities link local mosques to global causes. Diaspora Muslims remain deeply connected to their homeland politics, whether in Lebanon, Turkey, or Afghanistan.

For host nations, this creates challenges. Integration becomes partial at best. Muslims participate in civic life but maintain distinct identity and allegiance. The *ummah* becomes a parallel nation, invisible yet powerful.

The appeal of Ummah in a fragmented world

The persistence of the *ummah* reflects its very deep appeal. In a fragmented, individualistic modern world, belonging to a global community offers real meaning. While Western societies grapple with loneliness and identity crises, Muslims find solidarity in the *ummah*.

Friday prayers, Ramadan fasts, and Eid celebrations connect millions simultaneously. The great pilgrimage to Mecca gathers Muslims from every nation, reinforcing unity. In an age of nationalism and secularism, the *ummah* offers a very real sense of belonging.

For many young Muslims in the West, caught between cultures, the *ummah* provides clarity. It resolves identity crises by offering a higher allegiance. Jihadist recruiters exploit this, framing participation in the *ummah* as heroic and meaningful.

Christian reflection on the Ummah

From a Christian perspective, the *ummah* is both a counterfeit and a real challenge. It mimics aspects of the church—unity, solidarity, global identity—but without Jesus Christ. It offers belonging without salvation, purpose without grace.

The New Testament describes the church as being one united body (1 Corinthians 12:12-13), united across nations in Christ. Christians find ultimate loyalty not in ethnicity or nation but in the kingdom of God. The *ummah* echoes this, but its foundation is law, not the gospel; coercion, not grace.

This contrast highlights the high stakes. For Muslims, loyalty to the *ummah* will demand submission to Sharia. For Christians, loyalty to Christ produces freedom. Where the *ummah* divides Muslims from non-Muslims, the gospel unites Jew and Gentile, slave and free.

For Australia, the question is which vision will shape national life. Will the unity of the *ummah* infiltrate and divide, or will the freedom of Christ sustain and integrate? The answer requires honesty about the power of the *ummah* and its incompatibility with national loyalty.

The clash of loyalties in practice

The concept of the *ummah* is not merely theoretical. It shapes lived experience, guiding how Muslims navigate their identities in societies where national loyalty is expected. In Western democracies, including Australia, citizenship involves rights and duties: obedience to law, respect for institutions, and allegiance to the nation.

Yet for many Muslims, the pull of the *ummah* complicates these expectations. The clash of loyalties then manifests in daily life, politics, law, and even matters of war and peace. To understand the implications for Australia, one must examine how this conflict plays out in practice.

Dual identity in minority contexts

Muslim minorities in the West often describe themselves in dual terms: British Muslims, French Muslims, Australian Muslims. Yet the ordering of those identities is not always clear. For some, "Muslim" always comes first. Belonging to the *ummah* must outweigh national citizenship.

Sociological studies reveal this tension. Surveys in Britain, for instance, show that a significant proportion of Muslims feel more loyalty to fellow Muslims worldwide than to the British state. Similar findings appear across Europe. For many, national identity is functional — a passport, a set of civic duties — but ultimate allegiance belongs elsewhere. In Australia, anecdotal evidence suggests the same pattern. Muslims may embrace the benefits of citizenship — healthcare, education, welfare — yet feel solidarity with the global *ummah*.

Case study: The Iraq and Afghanistan wars

The wars in Iraq and Afghanistan highlight the clash of loyalties. When Australian troops joined the U.S.-led coalition, many Muslims in Australia opposed the campaigns. Protests in Sydney and Melbourne denounced the wars as an attack on Islam. For some Muslims, loyalty to the *ummah* demanded opposition to their own nation's policies.

Radical groups exploited this tension. Recruiters framed the wars as proof that the West was at war with Islam. Young Muslims, torn between citizenship and solidarity, sometimes chose the latter. A minority travelled overseas to fight alongside insurgents. Others provided ideological or financial support. While many Muslims rejected violence, the underlying loyalty conflict remained. The *ummah* was not an abstract idea but a living allegiance that shaped responses to war.

Case study: Palestine and Israel

The conflict in Palestine resonates deeply across the Muslim world. For Muslims in Australia, loyalty to the *ummah* often translates into passionate identification with Palestinians.

Rallies in support of Gaza have attracted tens of thousands, drawing participants from diverse Muslim backgrounds. For Australian Jews and supporters of Israel, this creates tension. The conflict is imported into Australian institutions and campuses, straining national unity. Universities see clashes between pro-Palestinian and pro-Israeli groups. Political parties face lobbying to adopt positions aligned with Muslim solidarity.

This raises a question: when foreign conflicts dominate domestic politics, where does our loyalty lie? For many Muslims, their identification with the *ummah* in Palestine always far outweighs identification with Australia's interests or neutrality. The conflict demonstrates how global solidarity competes with national cohesion.

Case study: foreign fighters in Syria

The Syrian civil war provided perhaps the starkest test of loyalty. Between 2012 and 2016, over 100 Australians travelled to Syria and Iraq to fight, most joining ISIS. These individuals explicitly rejected national allegiance, declaring loyalty only to the *ummah*.

Their actions shocked the nation. How could citizens, raised in Australian schools and communities, abandon their country to fight for a terrorist caliphate? The answer lies in the power of *ummah* identity.

For these radicals, being Muslim transcended being Australian. The suffering of Syrians was their own suffering; the cause of jihad was their own cause.

Not all who sympathised went overseas. Some raised funds, spread propaganda, or plotted some domestic attacks. Each case revealed the same dynamic: loyalty to the *ummah* always trumps loyalty to the nation.

Everyday expressions of divided loyalty

The clash of loyalties is not limited to dramatic cases of war and terrorism. It surfaces in everyday life.

- ➤ *Law and arbitration* – When disputes arise, some Muslims prefer Sharia councils or imams rather than Australian courts. This reflects loyalty to the *ummah*'s legal framework over national law.
- ➤ *Education* – Islamic schools often emphasise global Muslim identity. Students grow up more conscious of their belonging to the *ummah* than to Australia.
- ➤ *Politics* – Muslim candidates sometimes campaign explicitly on issues affecting the global *ummah* — Palestine, Kashmir, or Islamophobia — rather than domestic concerns.
- ➤ *Charity* – Zakat (almsgiving) is often directed overseas, supporting causes linked to the global *ummah* rather than local needs.

Each practice reinforces a divided loyalty. While not all are subversive, collectively they weaken national cohesion.

Muslim political mobilisation

In several Western nations, Muslim political mobilisation reflects the power of *ummah* identity. Voting patterns often cluster around issues affecting global Islam. In Britain, the Muslim vote is courted by parties who are promising support for Palestine or protection against Islamophobia. In Canada, similar patterns appear.

In Australia, Muslim communities have begun to exercise some political influence, particularly in western Sydney and Melbourne's northern suburbs. Politicians seek their support by adopting sympathetic stances on Middle Eastern conflicts or multicultural policies.

Muslim organisations leverage this influence to press for accommodations — halal certification, recognition of Islamic holidays, or protection from criticism.

This mobilisation is framed as civic participation, yet its orientation toward the *ummah* distinguishes it from any other minority advocacy. Italian or Vietnamese communities rarely lobby over foreign conflicts. Muslim mobilisation is unique in its global solidarity.

National symbols and identity

Another arena of significant tension is national symbols. For many Australians, the flag, the anthem, and Anzac Day embody national unity. However, participation by Muslims is sometimes ambivalent. Some schools with large Muslim populations report reluctance among students to sing the anthem or observe Anzac commemorations. This ambivalence reflects a deeper identity conflict. If loyalty lies with the *ummah*, national symbols carry less weight. They may even be seen as hostile, representing colonial or Western power. Such detachment undermines shared identity, eroding the glue that binds citizens together.

The pressure of global events

Global events repeatedly expose this divided loyalty. When cartoons of Muhammad were published in Denmark (2005), protests erupted worldwide, including in Australia. Muslims identified not with their host nation's free speech traditions but with the global *ummah*'s outrage.

When military interventions occur in Muslim lands, loyalty to the *ummah* is stirred up. Even humanitarian crises, such as the Rohingya in Myanmar, evoke intense solidarity. None of these events are Australian, yet they dominate Muslim identity within Australia. The global reach of media and the internet intensifies this. A sermon in Cairo or a speech in Islamabad can often shape attitudes in Sydney within a few hours. The *ummah* transcends borders, mediated by technology.

The dilemma of integration

For host nations, the clash of loyalties poses a very real dilemma. Integration requires that migrants adopt national identity while preserving cultural traditions. Yet for those devout Muslims, integration into secular, democratic nations is partial at best. The *ummah* demands ultimate allegiance. Some Muslims resolve this tension pragmatically, living peacefully while retaining inner solidarity with the *ummah*. Others embrace a hybrid identity, balancing loyalties uneasily. But for radicals, the choice is clear: the *ummah* comes first, the nation is irrelevant or hostile.

This dilemma is sharper than for other minorities. Italians, Greeks, or Vietnamese may retain their cultural pride, but their loyalties are not globalised like Islam. The *ummah* uniquely creates a supranational identity that competes directly with national unity.

Voices of dissent within Islam

It must be noted that not all Muslims prioritise the *ummah*. Some reformers advocate for contextualised Islam that affirms national loyalty. They argue that Muslims should also be good citizens, respecting secular law while practising faith privately. However, such voices are often marginal. Traditionalist leaders denounce them as compromised. Advocacy groups emphasise victimhood and solidarity, not reform. The weight of history and theology favours loyalty to the *ummah* over national integration. For reform to succeed, it would require a radical rethinking of Islamic theology — something that remains rare and contested.

Christian reflection on divided loyalty

The clash of loyalties illustrates the contrast between Islam and Christianity. Jesus taught, *"Give back to Caesar what is Caesar's, and to God what is God's."* (Mark 12:17). This principle established a distinction between earthly authority and divine allegiance. Christians can be loyal citizens while continuing to worship God supremely. Islam, by contrast, does not permit such distinction. Allegiance to Allah encompasses politics, law, and society. The *ummah* demands loyalty above nation. This totalising claim creates perpetual conflict in pluralistic societies.

For Christians, the lesson is very clear: true freedom requires separation of ultimate allegiance from political structures. The gospel liberates individuals to love their nation without absolutising it. Islam binds individuals to a political community that supersedes all others.

Implications for Australia

The clash of loyalties between nation and *ummah* is not a minor matter of personal preference. It cuts to the heart of citizenship, integration, and the cohesion of a free society.

For Australia, a country which prides itself on multiculturalism and civic harmony, the challenge is pressing. Can a nation built on Western democratic foundations remain cohesive when a growing minority pledges ultimate allegiance to a transnational religious community? What does divided loyalty mean for national security, for political unity, and for the preservation of shared values?

Integration under strain

Integration in Australia has historically meant that migrants bring their cultural traditions while embracing national identity. Italians, Greeks, Vietnamese, and Indians maintained language, food, and festivals while proudly identifying as Australians. Their loyalties were local, tied to family heritage, not global movements.

Muslim migration is uniquely different. The *ummah* introduces a supranational identity that competes with Australian identity. While many Muslims live peacefully, the pull of the *ummah* means integration is often partial. Muslim enclaves in Sydney and Melbourne clearly reflect this. Within them, Islamic schools, mosques, and businesses reinforce *ummah* identity more than national identity. This produces two consequences:

1. *Partial assimilation* – Muslims participate economically but maintain distinct cultural and legal practices.
2. *Cultural segregation* – Enclaves become parallel societies, where loyalty to the *ummah* outweighs loyalty to the nation.

The result is significant strain on integration, testing the limits of multiculturalism.

Security concerns

Divided loyalty has direct implications for security. If allegiance to the *ummah* outweighs national citizenship, then conflicts involving Muslim nations reverberate domestically. When Australian forces engage overseas, segments of the Muslim population will often side emotionally or materially with the other side.

This is not hypothetical. Australians have travelled to fight in Afghanistan, Iraq, and Syria, citing loyalty to the *ummah*. Others have raised funds or spread propaganda. Even those not engaging in violence may withhold support for national policies, weakening unity in times of crisis.

Security agencies recognise this. ASIO monitors communities where radicalisation is most likely, aware that divided loyalty creates vulnerabilities. Prisons, mosques, and online networks become battlegrounds of allegiance. The nation's safety depends on whether citizenship or *ummah* loyalty prevails.

Political fragmentation

The political sphere is also affected here. Muslim communities, mobilised around *ummah* identity, press for policies aligned with global solidarity rather than national interests. Demands for recognition of Palestine, opposition to foreign wars, and many campaigns against Islamophobia dominate political life.

This mobilisation differs from other migrant groups, whose advocacy is primarily local. It introduces foreign conflicts into domestic politics, fracturing national debate. Politicians, seeking votes, adjust policies not to serve Australia as a whole, but to appease *ummah*-driven constituencies. As Muslim populations grow, this influence will increase. Parties will face pressure to adopt stances favourable to Islamic causes. National unity will be compromised by global loyalties.

Erosion of shared identity

A nation depends on shared identity. Without common values, laws, and loyalties, it fragments. Australia's identity is rooted in democracy, freedom, equality, and rule of law — values drawn from our Christian heritage. Divided loyalty to the *ummah* undermines this identity.

When Muslims see themselves first as members of the global *ummah*, national belonging becomes secondary. National symbols lose meaning. Social trust erodes as citizens perceive neighbours whose ultimate allegiance lies elsewhere.

The erosion of shared identity threatens the very fabric of Australia. Diversity enriches only when anchored in unity. Without unity, it produces division.

Policy implications

The implications for policy are profound. If Australia ignores divided loyalty, it risks repeating Europe's mistakes. If it confronts it honestly, it may preserve unity. Several measures are necessary:

1. *Clear Expectation of citizenship* – Citizenship must involve more than rights; it must involve allegiance. Oaths of citizenship should emphasise loyalty to Australia above all other communities.
2. *Integration standards* – Immigration and settlement programs must prioritise integration, not just economic need. Enclaves that reinforce *ummah* identity should be discouraged through housing, education, and employment policies.
3. *Education reform* – Islamic schools must be required to teach civic values, loyalty to Australia, and respect for its laws. Curricula that emphasise *ummah* over nation must be reformed.
4. *Transparency in advocacy* – Muslim organisations must disclose overseas ties and funding. Advocacy rooted in foreign conflicts must be distinguished from genuine civic participation.
5. *Firm legal framework* – Sharia arbitration must never be recognised. One law for all must remain non-negotiable. Loyalty to national law is the bedrock of unity.

These policies are not anti-Muslim. They are pro-Australian, designed to protect the cohesion of the nation for all citizens.

Christian responsibility

For Christians, divided loyalty highlights the need to model true allegiance. Jesus Christ declared, *"No one can serve two masters."* (Matthew 6:24). While He spoke of God and money, the principle applies: ultimate loyalty cannot be divided.

For Christians, it belongs to Christ, yet this loyalty liberates them to honour earthly authorities. *"Let everyone be subject to the governing authorities."* (Romans 13:1).

The church must teach this distinction clearly. It must defend freedom by showing that ultimate allegiance to Christ produces good citizenship, not conflict. Christians must also engage Muslims with compassion, offering them a better loyalty — one that frees rather than enslaves.

Evangelism in Muslim communities should not shy away from addressing the *ummah*. The gospel offers a superior belonging: the church of Jesus Christ, a global body that transcends borders but affirms good citizenship. Christians must invite Muslims into this new community where allegiance is not divided but rightly ordered.

The future of national unity

Looking ahead, the question of loyalty will shape Australia's future. If the *ummah* continues to grow as a primary identity, national unity will weaken. Parallel societies will deepen, political fragmentation will intensify, and security risks will multiply.

If, however, Australia confronts the issue now — affirming one law, one identity, one loyalty — then unity can be preserved. Diversity will flourish within boundaries of shared allegiance.

Muslims will be welcome as citizens, but only if they accept the primacy of national loyalty. The choice is stark. National unity or global allegiance. Australia cannot have both.

Conclusion

The question of loyalty is not abstract. It is lived daily in schools, mosques, workplaces, and politics. For Muslims, the pull of the *ummah* is powerful, demanding allegiance that competes with national identity. For Australia, this creates strain on integration, security, politics, and unity.

The implications are clear: divided loyalty cannot sustain a nation. A house divided against itself cannot stand (Mark 3:25). Australia must choose clarity over confusion, unity over fragmentation.

Christians must lead the way in speaking the truth. They must defend freedom, model good citizenship, and invite Muslims to a greater loyalty: allegiance to Christ, which alone brings peace. For the nation, policymakers must set firm expectations: one law, one nation, one loyalty.

The *ummah* will remain very powerful, but Australia must be stronger. Its identity must be rooted in values that cannot be compromised. Its future depends on ensuring that loyalty to the nation, under God, is not supplanted by allegiance to a global religious community.

14. ISLAM AND AUSTRALIAN LAW IN PRACTICE

Legal fault lines emerging in Australia

Australia prides itself on being a nation ruled by one law, equally applied to all. The principle that every citizen, regardless of background, is subject to the same justice is foundational to our democracy. Yet as Islamic communities grow, questions emerge about how Australian law interacts with Islamic practices. While debates about Sharia in the Middle East are very well known, the more pressing concern for Australia is how these tensions might surface here, in family courts, food regulation, finance, and community governance.

This chapter does not repeat theological arguments or distant case studies but turns directly to the Australian context. How do Muslim practices challenge the integrity of one legal system? Where are the pressure points? And how might these tensions reshape our nation's future?

Polygamy and marriage law

One of the clearest areas of friction is marriage law. Under Australian law, marriage is strictly monogamous. Bigamy is criminal offence under the Marriage Act 1961. Yet within Islam, polygamy is permissible—men may marry up to four wives.

In practice, some Muslim men in Australia maintain multiple "wives" through Islamic ceremonies not recognised by the state. Only one marriage may be legally registered, but the others are conducted informally by imams. This creates a legal grey zone. The additional wives often have no legal rights—no claim to property, inheritance, or child custody in the event of separation.

Courts have struggled with cases where polygamous unions abroad are later recognised for practical purposes. For example, in some inheritance disputes, judges have had to determine whether "wives" from overseas marriages should share estates. In family law, custody battles become complex when children come from unregistered polygamous households.

Though technically illegal, polygamy persists in communities, tolerated under the veil of multicultural sensitivity. Of course this undermines the principle of one law for all. If a community can practise what law forbids, equality under law is weakened.

Divorce and custody disputes

Related tensions appear in divorce and custody issues. Under Australian law, divorce is granted by civil courts, with property and custody decided on the basis of fairness and best interests of children. Islamic practice, however, provides for *talaq,* which is unilateral divorce pronounced by a husband.

While not legally binding in Australia, *talaq* continues within communities. Some Muslim women are abandoned without civil divorce, leaving them in limbo: unable to access property rights, welfare support, or legal remarriage. In some cases, imams issue religious divorces that contradict court rulings, creating dual systems of authority.

Custody disputes reveal much sharper clashes. Australian law emphasises shared parental responsibility, but some Islamic interpretations prioritise paternal authority. Courts have faced cases where fathers demand custody based on Sharia principles, rather than Australian law. Even when judges uphold national law, communities sometimes ignore rulings, following imams instead. These situations erode confidence in legal system. They also place women and children in vulnerable positions, caught between two competing authorities.

Sharia arbitration proposals

In recent years, some Muslim leaders in Australia have proposed formal recognition of Sharia arbitration in family and financial matters. The argument is framed around multicultural respect: if Jewish Beth Din courts can arbitrate disputes within a Jewish community, why not allow Sharia councils to arbitrate for the Muslims? Advocates insist these would be voluntary, applying only to willing participants. They claim such councils could ease pressure on courts by handling divorces, inheritance disputes, or financial disagreements internally.

Yet critics point to some dangers. Overseas experience shows "voluntary" quickly becomes coercive. Women pressured by families or communities often submit unwillingly. Outcomes frequently favour men, undermining equality. In Britain, Sharia councils have been accused of denying women fair divorce settlements, forcing them into reconciliation with abusive husbands, or disadvantaging them in custody cases.

Introducing such structures in Australia would create two legal systems: one under secular law, another under Islamic law. Even if framed as arbitration, the practical effect would be recognition of Sharia within national system. That would directly contradict the principle of indivisible law for all.

Halal certification controversies

Another area where Islam intersects with Australian law is halal certification. To access Muslim markets at home and abroad, food producers seek certification that products comply with Islamic requirements.

On surface, this seems a commercial matter. Yet controversies arise over transparency, funding, and fairness. Certification fees often go to Islamic organisations; some accused of links to extremist groups overseas. Investigations have not always proven these claims, but suspicion remains.

Critics also argue that halal certification forces non-Muslim consumers to subsidise Islamic practices, since costs are passed into pricing. In effect, Australian law compels everyone to participate in religious system through commerce.

Defenders say certification is no different from kosher for Jews, simply meeting market demand. Yet scale differs. While kosher remains niche, halal has become widespread across many supermarkets, all airlines, and a lot of restaurants. This ubiquity normalises Islamic standards within public life. Parliamentary inquiries have examined halal certification, but no uniform regulation has emerged. This leaves space for abuse and deepens perception of dual standards.

For many Australians, halal debates symbolise broader concern: that Islamic norms are creeping into mainstream through law and commerce without proper debate.

Islamic finance in Australia

Islamic finance presents another emerging tension. Traditional banking involves interest *(riba)*, which Islam strictly prohibits. To accommodate Muslims, financial institutions have developed *"Sharia-compliant"* products — profit-sharing mortgages, interest-free loans, sukuk bonds.

These remain niche in Australia, but as the Muslim population grows, pressure increases for wider accommodation. Some universities now teach Islamic finance; some banks experiment with products.

The concern is not financial creativity but legal implications. Sharia-compliant contracts require oversight by Islamic scholars who certify compliance. This effectively introduces religious authority into commercial law. If Islamic finance expands significantly, parallel regulatory structures may then develop, creating subtle dual system. Again, the issue is principle: should Australian law adapt to religious codes, or should migrants adapt to national law?

Religious arbitration in local councils

Beyond courts and commerce, Islamic influence sometimes appears in local governance. In certain councils with large Muslim populations, debates arise about prayer rooms, gender segregation at public events, or recognition of Islamic holidays. While often framed as multicultural accommodation, the cumulative effect is the informal recognition of Sharia norms.

Some local councils have been pressured to provide separate swimming sessions for women, halal-only catering, or facilities for ritual washing. Individually, these may seem minor. Collectively, they normalise separate standards, eroding the principle that public institutions serve all equally.

Case studies from Australian courts

Australian case law already reflects these tensions.

➤ *In inheritance disputes,* judges have had to navigate claims by multiple wives from overseas marriages.

➤ *In custody disputes,* parents have invoked Islamic principles, forcing courts to clarify supremacy of national law.

➤ *In fraud cases,* misuse of halal certification has been prosecuted, raising questions about regulation.

These cases reveal that Islamic practices are not abstract but already shaping Australian jurisprudence. Each ruling sets precedent, gradually adjusting legal landscape.

The multicultural dilemma

Underlying all this is the multicultural dilemma which we have covered extensively already. Australia celebrates diversity, but when diversity collides with equality, which prevails? Allowing Sharia practices undermines equality. Enforcing one law may alienate whole communities. Politicians, fearing accusations of intolerance, often avoid clear decisions.

This paralysis benefits Islamists, who exploit ambiguity. What often begin as accommodation becomes a foothold for further demands. Once concessions are granted, they are difficult to reverse.

Christian reflection

Christians, the lesson is sobering. God's law is one and universal. Israel was warned not to adopt practices of surrounding nations but to remain distinct (Deuteronomy 12:29–32). Likewise, the church is called to live under Christ's lordship, not compromise with competing authorities. Australia's legal system, though secular, was built on biblical principles of justice and equality. To dilute these by importing Sharia norms is to erode the very soil in which freedom grew. Christians must therefore defend one law for all, while also proclaiming the gospel that alone brings true justice and peace.

Deepening legal tensions in the Australian context

The intersection of Islam and Australian law is not theoretical — it plays out daily in courts, welfare systems, workplaces, and prisons. These are the places where principles are tested, and where multicultural ideals are confronted by hard realities. In these practical arenas, it becomes clear that a single legal system is difficult to maintain when cultural and religious groups seek to live by their own codes.

Welfare and immigration loopholes

One recurring controversy involves welfare and immigration benefits connected to Islamic family structures. Since Australian law recognises only one legal spouse, polygamous unions pose challenges. Yet in practice, multiple wives may claim support through welfare system if classified as *"single mothers."* This loophole has been documented in communities where men with several wives, married under Islamic law, register only one legally but support others through welfare payments. The state thus subsidises polygamy indirectly, even though it is illegal.

Immigration law also faces a lot of strain. Family reunion visas sometimes involve multiple spouses or various children from polygamous households overseas. While only one spouse can be officially recognised, pressure mounts to allow others to enter as dependants. Bureaucrats, reluctant to appear discriminatory, often process applications with leniency.

These examples show how any legal system, which is designed for monogamous society, bends under the weight of such Islamic practices. Loopholes erode consistency and fuel resentment among other citizens who see law applied unequally.

Workplace rights and religious accommodation

Another fault line lies in workplace rights. Australian law prohibits discrimination on the basis of religion. This is rightly intended to protect individuals from unfair treatment.

Yet it is increasingly used to push Islamic accommodations beyond reasonable boundaries. Examples include:

- Demands for prayer breaks during shifts, even when disruptive to productivity.
- Requests for gender segregation in staff facilities.
- Refusals to handle alcohol, pork, or gambling-related products, creating difficulties in supermarkets, abattoirs, or logistics.
- Pressure for halal-only catering at corporate events.

Employers face a real dilemma: accommodate demands and risk fragmenting their workplace standards, or resist demands and risk discrimination claims. Some tribunals have ruled in favour of accommodation, setting precedents that tilt balance. In effect, Islamic practices reshape workplace law, not through legislation but through incremental rulings. Other employees may resent unequal treatment, undermining cohesion.

Uniforms and identification

Islamic dress also intersects with law in schools, workplaces, and public safety. The most famous case was the 2014 incident in Parliament House when a woman in full burqa entered the gallery, sparking debate about security and identification. The Prime Minister at the time, Tony Abbott, questioned whether full-face coverings should be allowed in secure environments.

Courts and commissions have grappled with cases involving hijabs in schools, niqabs in driver's licence photos, and burqas in courtrooms. While modest dress can be accommodated, full-face coverings raise undeniable security risks. Judges have struggled to balance religious freedom with open justice. Some rulings have permitted women to testify while veiled, provided a female officer confirmed identity privately. Others insist on removal for fair trial. Inconsistency leaves uncertainty.

Prisons and criminal law

Islam also intersects with criminal justice, particularly in prisons. Muslim inmates often request halal meals, prayer times, and imams. While many accommodations are reasonable, some authorities report problems:

➤ Radicalisation in prisons, where Islamic study groups become recruitment hubs.

➤ Segregation demands, creating tension among inmates.

➤ Refusals to participate in rehabilitation programs conflicting with Islamic norms.

In some cases, Muslim prisoners have challenged requirements of rehabilitation courses involving alcohol awareness or mixed-gender participation, claiming religious grounds. Courts and corrections must decide then whether to grant exemptions, potentially weakening rehabilitation.

Terrorism cases further highlight tension. Convicted extremists often cite Sharia in defiance of Australian law, refusing to recognise our court's authority. While judges rightly insist on supremacy of our national law, spectacle of such defiance undermines public confidence.

Child protection cases

Another sensitive area is child protection. Reports have surfaced of forced marriages among Muslim communities in Australia. Though rare, these cases expose clash between Islamic cultural practices and Australian child protection law.

Courts have intervened in instances where underage girls were taken overseas for marriage or pressured into Islamic ceremonies locally. In 2014, police in New South Wales charged a sheikh with conducting a marriage between a 12-year-old girl and a 26-year-old man.

The case shocked the nation and forced authorities to confront uncomfortable reality: forced marriage is not just a distant issue but a domestic one.

The Commonwealth has since strengthened laws against forced marriage, making it specific offence. Yet enforcement remains difficult, as victims are often pressured into silence by families and communities. These cases show how Islamic practices can threaten rights of children, demanding robust legal response.

Zoning and local governance

Local councils face challenges when Islamic organisations seek approvals for mosques, schools, or cemeteries. Opposition often arises, not from religious prejudice, but from concerns about traffic, noise, or the cultural impact. Councils that resist may face discrimination claims.

Some proposals include gender-segregated facilities, raising questions about compliance with Australian equality laws. Others involve foreign funding for mosques, prompting security concerns. Councils, ill-equipped to navigate such complexities, often capitulate to avoid controversy.

This reveals a broader issue: Islamic groups are skilled at using Australia's anti-discrimination laws to push boundaries. Local governance, intended for planning matters, becomes arena for cultural conflict.

Criminal defences and Islamic arguments

Occasionally, defendants in Australian courts have invoked Islam in mitigation of crimes. In domestic violence cases, some have claimed cultural norms allowed harsher discipline of wives or children. In fraud or assault cases, others argue ignorance of Australian law due to religious background.

Judges rightly reject such defences, but even their appearance illustrates risk of dual standards. If culture is allowed to mitigate crime, equality before law is lost. High-profile cases have drawn attention to *"cultural defences,"* sparking public concern that legal system may bend. Courts must remain firm that Australian law applies equally, regardless of cultural or religious norms.

Asylum claims and Islamic persecution

Immigration courts also face Islamic complexity. Many asylum seekers are Muslims fleeing persecution by other Muslims—Shia from Sunni-majority countries, women escaping forced marriage, or apostates who are fearing death. While compassion demands refuge, these cases create legal puzzles.

Some claimants practise Islam only nominally, raising questions about credibility. Others arrive with views hostile to Australian law yet still gain entry as refugees.

This highlights a paradox: Australia offers safety to victims of Islam while also importing adherents who may promote the very same practices. Law struggles to distinguish between genuine victims and those likely to perpetuate conflict.

Anti-discrimination law and blasphemy pressures

Although more directly related to free speech (addressed in later chapters), anti-discrimination law already shapes many Islamic interactions with courts. Muslim groups have lodged complaints against critics, alleging offence or vilification. While courts often dismiss extreme claims, the process itself is very punishing, and defendants endure costly hearings. This creates a chilling effect, discouraging open discussion. Though technically under human rights commissions, these cases will demonstrate how Islamic sensitivities pressure Australian law to act like blasphemy codes.

Incrementalism and legal drift

What ties these examples together is incrementalism. Rarely does Islam confront Australian law head-on. Instead, it pushes gradually — through welfare loopholes, workplace claims, local council proposals, or discrimination complaints.

Each concession seems minor, yet together they form trajectory toward parallel systems. This is legal drift. Without decisive action, Australia may find itself with fragmented legal order, where some citizens live by one standard, others by another. The principle of *"one law for all"* is eroded not by revolution but by attrition.

Christian reflection

From a Christian perspective, justice must be consistent. God warned Israel in Leviticus 19:15: *"Do not pervert justice; do not show partiality to the poor or favouritism to the great but judge your neighbour fairly."* Justice requires equal treatment under law.

When Islamic practices exploit certain loopholes or demand accommodation, justice is distorted. Christians must advocate for fairness, not allowing religious privilege to undermine law. At the same time, they must show compassion to individuals caught in tension, pointing them to Christ as the true source of justice and mercy.

One law for all – safeguarding the foundations

Australia's legal system is one of its greatest achievements. Rooted in the English common law tradition, it embodies principles of fairness, equality, and accountability. It is the framework through which citizens live together in peace, resolve disputes, and protect rights. But this very system is now being tested. As Islamic practices intersect with Australian law, the nation faces a choice: will it hold firmly to the principle of one law for all, or will it drift toward fragmented legal order?

The risk of legal pluralism

The gravest danger is legal pluralism—the existence of multiple legal systems within one nation. Already, in Britain, Sharia councils operate alongside civil courts. In practice, women and children are often pressured into these forums, denied rights they would have under national law. Critics argue this creates second-class citizens.

If Australia tolerates similar structures, the principle of equality collapses. Citizens will not live under one standard but under competing codes. Muslims will be judged by Sharia norms, others by civil law. This is not multicultural harmony – this is fragmentation. Legal pluralism undermines national unity. Law ceases to be unifying authority, becoming instead a patchwork of competing jurisdictions. Once a precedent is set, other groups may demand their own legal recognition. The nation then drifts toward Balkanisation.

The creep of informal Sharia

Even without official recognition, informal Sharia authority already exists in Australia. Imams are conducting divorces, issuing rulings, and mediating disputes.

While it's not legally binding, communities often treat them as decisive. Women, in particular, are pressured to accept the outcomes. This shadow system thrives in legal ambiguity. Authorities often turn blind eye, preferring not to intervene in *"cultural matters."* Yet this abdication only empowers Islamic authorities at expense of vulnerable individuals. Over time, informal authority gains practical force, undermining the law.

The weakening of women's rights

The greatest victims of Islamic encroachment are often women. Where Sharia is applied, women's rights in marriage, divorce, custody, and inheritance are curtailed. Even in Australia, women abandoned under talaq divorces, forced into marriages, or pressured into Sharia councils experience injustice. If national law fails to intervene decisively, women in Muslim communities will live under de facto second-class status. This contradicts Australia's commitment to equality and betrays those who most need protection.

The normalisation of Islamic standards

Another long-term risk is normalisation of Islamic standards in public life. Halal certification, prayer accommodations, dress exemptions, and workplace adjustments gradually become default expectations. Though individually minor, together they reshape our cultural and legal norms. Once normalised, these standards create new baselines. Future generations accept them as ordinary, forgetting that they once conflicted with Australian law and custom. The nation drifts incrementally toward Islamic influence, not by dramatic imposition but by cultural seepage.

The paralysis of political leaders

Legal drift is exacerbated by political cowardice. Leaders, fearing accusations of racism or Islamophobia, hesitate to enforce one law for all. Instead, they appease, compromise, and postpone. Yet in doing so, they empower Islamic demands. History shows appeasement never satisfies. Each concession invites the next. Leaders who refuse to draw firm lines discover too late that lines have already shifted.

Safeguarding one law for all

What then must be done? How can Australia safeguard its legal heritage against fragmentation?

1. *Reaffirm legal equality:* Parliament must declare unequivocally that Australian law applies equally to all, without exception. Polygamy, forced marriage, and talaq divorces must be prosecuted consistently.

2. *Resist parallel systems:* No recognition of Sharia arbitration or councils. Religious bodies may provide spiritual guidance, but legal authority must remain solely with state.

3. *Strengthen oversight:* Loopholes in welfare and immigration law must be closed. No subsidising polygamy or tolerating fraud. Consistency is essential.

4. *Support vulnerable individuals:* Women and children in Muslim communities must be protected. Hotlines, shelters, and legal aid must be accessible, ensuring national law prevails over community pressure.

5. *Regulate certification and finance:* Halal certification and Islamic finance must be transparent, accountable, and subject to same oversight as other industries. No private religious authority should wield unchecked power.

6. *Educate citizens:* Public awareness campaigns should explain principle of one law for all. Citizens must understand that freedom depends on equal law.

7. *Empower courts:* Judges must consistently reject cultural defences. Criminal acts cannot be excused by religious or cultural background.

Safeguarding requires vigilance. Legal equality is never self-sustaining; it must be defended.

The role of the church

Christians have unique responsibility in this struggle. While state enforces law, church proclaims truth. Believers must remind society that justice flows from God. They must speak against compromise, support the vulnerable, and always model integrity.

The prophet Micah declared: *"He has shown you, O mortal, what is good. And what does the Lord require of you? To act justly and to love mercy and to walk humbly with your God"* (Micah 6:8). Justice and mercy are inseparable. The church must defend justice while showing mercy to Muslims as people loved by God. This means not only opposing Sharia encroachment but also reaching out to Muslims with gospel. For while law can restrain, only Christ can transform. Legal reforms are necessary, but spiritual renewal is ultimate solution.

A warning from history

History offers warnings. Nations that tolerated parallel systems suffered division. In Lebanon, separate religious codes fractured society. In Nigeria, recognition of Sharia led to violent conflict. In Britain, appeasement bred enclaves where national law is weak. Australia must learn from these examples. It cannot allow sentimentality or fear to blind it to consequences. To preserve unity, it must insist: one nation, one law.

A vision for the future

Yet the vision is not only defensive. By upholding one law for all, Australia can remain beacon of freedom and justice. It can provide refuge for Muslims fleeing oppression overseas. It can demonstrate that equality and fairness are possible under law grounded in Christian principles.

This vision requires courage. It requires leaders who will act, citizens who will speak, and churches that will pray. It requires nation to remember that its legal foundations were laid in soil enriched by gospel.

Conclusion

The challenge of Islam to Australian law is real and growing. From polygamy to welfare, from arbitration to halal, from prisons to councils, Islamic practices are pressing against boundaries of legal system. If unchecked, these pressures will fracture unity, undermine equality, and normalise dual authority. The choice is clear.

Australia must decide whether it will tolerate parallel systems or reaffirm one law for all. This is not only legal necessity but moral imperative. For without equal law, freedom dies. Christians, citizens, and leaders alike must resolve to defend principle that has sustained democracy for centuries: one people, one nation, one law.

As Proverbs 29:4 reminds us: *"By justice a king gives a country stability, but those who are greedy for bribes tear it down."* Justice, consistently applied, stabilises nation. Injustice, tolerated in name of multiculturalism, tears it down.

May Australia choose justice. May it resist fragmentation. May it remain a nation where law is equal, freedom secure, and truth honoured.

15. A CLASH OF CULTURES: DAILY LIFE IN AUSTRALIA

Everyday frictions emerging

Culture is lived not only in laws or institutions but in the daily rhythms of life: school routines, workplace expectations, family life and neighbourhood interactions. It is here, in the ordinary spaces of society, that the deepest clashes between Islam and Australia are often felt. For while politicians debate policy and scholars analyse ideology, it is the everyday Australian who experiences cultural difference most directly.

This chapter examines how Islam intersects with Australian life in these ordinary arenas. From classrooms to shopping centres, from community events to suburban streets, the collision of values surfaces not in abstract theory but in practical frictions.

Schools and education

One of the first places this cultural clash emerges is in schools. Children carry values from home into classrooms, and teachers must navigate competing expectations. With Muslim students increasing in number, Australian schools face real tensions that reflect broader societal divides.

Religious observances: Muslim students often request time for daily prayers, fasting accommodations during Ramadan, or exemption from certain activities. While schools rightly seek inclusivity, these accommodations sometimes disrupt schedules or place strain on teachers. For instance, sports carnivals during Ramadan spark conflict when Muslim students are pressured not to participate.

Curriculum disputes: In subjects such as history or religious studies, Islamic parents often object to portrayals of Christianity, evolution, or Western civilisation. In some cases, they request teaching be altered to avoid offending Islamic beliefs. Teachers, caught between parental demands and curriculum standards, face difficult choices.

Gender segregation: Reports have emerged of Muslim parents demanding that daughters be excused from swimming lessons, dance classes, or school camps due to modesty concerns. While some schools accommodate this, critics argue this undermines equality and inclusion. The result is always division, with Muslim students set apart from peers.

Bullying and peer pressure: Conversely, non-Muslim students will sometimes face accusations of disrespect or Islamophobia for normal behaviour. A child with a ham sandwich or joking about Christmas may be told they are offending Muslim classmates. This breeds resentment, eroding cohesion.

These frictions reveal a deeper clash: Australian education has been built on shared curriculum and equal participation, while Islamic expectations often demand separation.

Workplaces and employment

The workplace is another key arena where cultural differences emerge. While religious diversity is protected by law, Islamic practices often require accommodations that challenge norms of equality and efficiency.

Prayer breaks: Some Muslim employees request multiple daily breaks for prayer, in addition to their standard rest periods. Employers must balance their religious rights with operational demands. In warehouses or factories, frequent absences disrupt workflow, creating tension with colleagues.

Dress code: Uniform requirements will sometimes conflict with Islamic dress. Hijabs in hospitals or factories raise serious safety concerns; niqabs or burqas create issues of identification or communication. Employers who enforce reasonable rules will now risk discrimination claims, while those who relax them risk inconsistency.

Refusal of duties: Cases have arisen where Muslim workers refuse to handle alcohol, pork, or gambling products. In retail or food industries, this limits flexibility. Some employers accommodate; others face accusations of insensitivity. Once again, equality is strained.

Ramadan adjustments: During Ramadan, fasting employees may struggle with fatigue. Employers who reduce their hours or alter rosters to accommodate, risk resentment from other staff who see unequal treatment.

Gender relations: Some Muslim men will resist taking instructions from female managers, citing cultural norms. In rare but real cases, this undermines workplace hierarchy, creating division.

These examples show that Islamic practices, while personal in origin, often require real structural adjustments. The result is workplace tension and a perception of double standards.

Neighbourhoods and community life

Cultural clash is perhaps most visible at a neighbourhood level, where communities live side by side.

Mosques and noise issues: Proposals for new mosques often spark debate, not only about traffic and parking but about cultural impact. Calls to prayer, though rarely broadcast in Australia, are sometimes requested, raising noise and religious neutrality concerns.

Housing patterns: Muslim communities often cluster in specific suburbs, creating enclaves. While natural to some degree, this can foster segregation. Non-Muslim neighbours report feeling excluded as local shops, signage, and events become dominated by Islamic culture.

Festivals and holidays: Public recognition of Islamic festivals such as Eid raises questions of balance in society. Schools and councils sometimes give prominence to Eid, downplaying Christmas to avoid any offence. Many Australians perceive this as a reversal of heritage.

Community tensions: Street-level interactions also reveal friction. Reports include Muslim men objecting to women jogging in sports attire, disputes over dogs in parks (considered unclean in Islam), or pressure on local shops to provide halal products. While isolated, these incidents symbolise a much deeper cultural divergence.

Gender roles and public spaces

Gender roles present particularly sharp clash between Islam and Australian norms.

Public segregation: Some Islamic groups organise specific gender-segregated events in community halls or local swimming pools. Councils accommodating such requests will face backlash from citizens who see segregation as contrary to equality.

Modesty norms: Muslim women in niqabs or burqas can provoke strong reactions in public areas. For some Australians, full-face coverings represent rejection of openness. For some Muslim women, this is an act of faith. The resulting tension very often escalates into confrontation.

Male dominance: In certain communities, women are discouraged from public leadership, sport, or socialising. This jars with Australia's strong emphasis on gender equality and also female empowerment. Neighbours and colleagues observing these dynamics often feel cultural the divide deepen.

These gendered expectations create two worlds within one nation: one where equality is assumed, one where it is resisted.

The role of media and public perception

As detailed in chapter 12 of this book, daily life clashes are amplified by media. Reports of disputes in schools, workplaces, or neighbourhoods attract headlines, fuelling perceptions of Islam as incompatible with Australian culture. Muslim leaders will often respond defensively, accusing critics of Islamophobia. Non-Muslims feel silenced, unable to express concerns without being labelled intolerant. This dynamic increases resentment, widening the gulf between communities.

The impact on social cohesion

The cumulative effect of all these daily frictions is erosion of cohesion. Trust between neighbours weakens, workplaces will become divided, schools fragment along cultural lines. Instead of integration, the separation just grows.

Multiculturalism was intended to enrich, but when cultures resist assimilation, it fractures. Daily life becomes battleground of competing values.

Christian reflection

For Christians, these cultural clashes raise urgent questions. How should believers respond to Muslim neighbours? With hostility? With silence? With gospel witness?

Scripture calls for both truth and love. Paul urged believers: *"If it is possible, as far as it depends on you, live at peace with everyone."* (Romans 12:18). Yet peace does not mean compromise with falsehood. Christians must resist cultural accommodations that undermine truth, while also showing kindness toward individuals.

Daily life thus becomes the main arena for mission. Neighbours, colleagues, classmates—these are not enemies, but people for whom Christ died. This clash of cultures presents an opportunity for the gospel, if the church is ready.

Culture in the public square

Culture is not only lived out in private homes, schools, and workplaces; it is also displayed in the public square—stadiums, concert halls, town festivals, and civic rituals. These shared arenas provide the glue of society, places where people from diverse backgrounds come together around common practices and identities. But it is precisely in these spaces that Islam's incompatibility with Australian norms often emerges.

When expectations of modesty, gender relations, religious symbolism, or dietary laws enter public culture, tension arises. What most Australians consider to be neutral or inclusive is sometimes interpreted by Muslims as offensive or unacceptable.

Conversely, demands for accommodation often appear to others as preferential treatment. The result is a steady erosion of shared culture.

Sport and Islamic accommodation

Sport is central to Australian identity. From backyard cricket to AFL grand finals, sport unites communities across class and ethnicity. Yet Islamic practices increasingly create friction in this arena.

Team uniforms: Some Muslim athletes request modifications to uniforms to maintain modesty. In soccer and netball, female players have sought permission to wear long sleeves, leggings, or hijabs. While some leagues accommodate, others face criticism for inconsistency. The broader issue arises when entire teams demand changes, altering image of sport for everyone.

Mixed-gender Teams: Community sports often encourage boys and girls to play together at the younger levels. Some Muslim parents object, withdrawing daughters from participation. This reduces inclusivity and creates segregated spaces.

Ramadan scheduling: Those matches which are scheduled during Ramadan present challenges. Muslim players fasting during daylight struggle with performance, leading to calls for altered schedules. Professional clubs occasionally adjust training times to accommodate, but grassroots leagues cannot. This fosters resentment among other players.

Celebrations and alcohol: Post-match celebrations often involve alcohol. Muslim athletes sometimes refuse to participate, and teams are pressured to remove alcohol sponsors or alter their traditions. The clash between Australia's drinking culture and Islam's prohibition creates ongoing friction.

While individual accommodations may seem minor, together they change the sporting culture. What was once unifying soon becomes contested.

Entertainment and the arts

Entertainment — music, film, theatre, literature — reflects national values and creativity. Yet Islam frequently challenges these spaces.

Music and dance: Some Islamic interpretations discourage music and dance as immoral. Muslim parents object to school concerts, discos, or theatre excursions. This isolates Muslim children from peers and pressures schools to alter programs.

Film and censorship: Films depicting Islam critically often spark protests. Cinemas will avoid screenings to prevent controversy. Writers and comedians will self-censor, fearing backlash. The freedom of artistic expression is curtailed.

Literature and curriculum: Novels studied in schools, such as those exploring sexuality or religion, have been challenged by Islamic groups. While objections from conservative Christians will also occur, the intensity of many Islamic demands often intimidates institutions into compliance.

Public performances: Gender norms also intrude. At multicultural festivals, Muslim performers may insist on segregated audiences or restrictions on female participation. Councils, desperate for inclusivity, will often concede, undermining equal participation.

The arts thrive on freedom and provocation, but under Islamic pressure they bend toward caution, reducing creativity.

Public events and civic festivals

Local festivals, ANZAC commemorations, Christmas parades, and Australia Day celebrations are cornerstones of civic life. Yet these also face tension with Islamic communities.

Christmas and Easter: While broadly cultural as well as religious, these holidays often meet with resistance. Councils sometimes downplay Christmas symbols just to avoid offending Muslims, replacing nativity scenes with generic "holiday" displays. This frustrates the majority who see their traditions diluted.

ANZAC Day: National remembrance ceremonies will emphasise unity and sacrifice. However, some Islamic groups will object to participation, citing conflicts with their Muslim history. Schools occasionally exempt Muslim students from services, weakening shared national memory.

Australia Day: Already contested by many indigenous groups, Australia Day faces additional critique from Islamic activists who portray it as colonial and un-Islamic. Some Islamic groups boycott celebrations, fracturing unity even further.

Multicultural festivals: Intended to celebrate diversity, these often become platforms for Islamic assertion. Halal food dominates stalls, stages feature Islamic cultural shows, and some councils showcase mosques as symbols of inclusivity. Other communities feel overshadowed, turning what was meant to unite into a stage for competition. Public events are supposed to build national cohesion. Instead, under pressure, they expose division.

Food and public life

Food is central to our culture, and in Australia's multicultural landscape, diverse cuisines flourish. But halal requirements complicate public catering.

School canteens: Some schools serve halal-only meat, effectively imposing Islamic standards on all students. Parents object that their children are being forced to comply with religious requirements.

Festivals and functions: Councils, universities, and some corporate events often provide halal-only catering to avoid exclusion. Yet this excludes those who would prefer to not subsidise religious requirements.

Restaurants and retail outlets: Large chains increasingly seek halal certification, normalising Islamic standards in mainstream commerce. While commercially rational, the social impact is one of Islamic influence extending into daily consumption.

Food, once a source of celebration, becomes another flashpoint of cultural clash.

Interfaith dynamics

In response to tensions, many institutions promote interfaith dialogue between Christians, Muslims, and others. While well-intentioned, these forums will often blur rather than clarify the differences.

Superficial harmony: Interfaith events most often will emphasise commonalities—charity, family, prayer—while ignoring those irreconcilable doctrines. This creates the illusion of unity but conceals real incompatibility.

Suppression of evangelism: Christians at interfaith events are often discouraged from proclaiming Jesus Christ as the only way. To maintain harmony, the gospel is silenced or corrupted.

Public messaging: The media coverage of interfaith gatherings reinforces the false narrative that Islam and Christianity are essentially the same. This confuses public and weakens Christian witness. While dialogue has place in fostering civility, when it obscures truth, it becomes dangerous.

Civic rituals and oaths

Another area of friction is civic rituals such as citizenship ceremonies or parliamentary openings.

Oaths of allegiance: New citizens pledge loyalty to Australia. Some Islamic activists have called for exemptions from swearing oaths under the flag, seeing it as un-Islamic. Proposals to allow alternative pledges undermine national unity.

Parliamentary prayers: Australia's parliaments traditionally open with Christian prayer. Islamic groups have lobbied for inclusion of Quranic readings, challenging heritage. Some parliaments have considered neutral "moments of reflection" instead, diluting Christian influence.

*Military service***:** Questions have arisen about whether Muslims can serve loyally in conflicts against Islamic states. While many do serve honourably, doubts persist, and debates about dual loyalty continue.

These civic rituals, designed to bind citizens, are contested by Islamic influence, further eroding unity. Each example—sport, entertainment, festivals, interfaith forums, civic rituals—may seem isolated. But together, they illustrate a serious cumulative clash.

In daily life, Islam resists assimilation, always pressing for accommodation. Institutions, fearing offence, concede ground. The result is cultural shift. Australians who are accustomed to shared spaces and a common identity, will find themselves negotiating differences at every turn. Instead of unifying, public culture fragments.

Christian reflection

For Christians, this cultural clash is opportunity as well as challenge. While Islamic demands strain institutions, they also expose hunger for meaning. Muslims pressing for recognition are revealing their search for identity.

Christians must respond with both firmness and compassion. Firmness in defending the truth — Jesus Christ alone is Lord, not multicultural relativism. Compassion in reaching out — Muslims are neighbours to be loved, not enemies to be despised.

Paul reminded the Corinthians: *"Though I am free and belong to no one, I have made myself a slave to everyone, to win as many as possible"* (1 Corinthians 9:19). Christians must engage culture not by compromise but by witness.

Long-term cultural implications and the way forward

The daily frictions described in previous parts — whether in schools, workplaces, neighbourhoods, or public events — may appear at first to be isolated incidents, temporary adjustments in the name of diversity. Yet when viewed collectively, they reveal trajectory. Cultural clash between Islam and Australian society is not passing inconvenience but long-term challenge.

The key question is whether Australia can sustain unity under such pressure. If cultural practices remain irreconcilable, the nation risks fragmentation.

To see the stakes clearly, we must look at cultural implications over time, examining failures of assimilation elsewhere, and consider how Christians should respond with both clarity and compassion.

The failure of assimilation

One of the defining features of Australian multiculturalism has been the expectation of integration. Migrants from Europe, Asia, and Africa brought their traditions but embraced common civic identity. Italians, Greeks, Vietnamese, Chinese — all enriched our culture while then adopting national norms. This integration produced true unity in diversity.

Islam, however, has proven resistant to assimilation. In many cases, Islamic identity is preserved not only privately but also publicly, with demands for recognition of Sharia norms, gender roles, dietary laws, and festivals. Instead of blending into our national identity, Islamic communities often form parallel societies.

Overseas evidence confirms this. In Britain, Muslim enclaves maintain Sharia councils, segregated schools, and distinct cultural practices. In France, *"no-go zones"* have emerged where national law is weak and Islamic norms dominate. In Sweden, mass migration has produced ghettos marked by crime and deep cultural separation. These serious failures of assimilation warn Australia. Without clear expectations, multiculturalism will just degenerate into tribalism. The myth of seamless harmony simply collapses.

Cultural fragmentation

The result of failed assimilation is fragmentation. When daily life is divided — separate schools, separate sports, and separate neighbourhoods — the shared identity of our nation will dissolve. Citizens no longer see themselves primarily as Australians but as members of ethnic or religious blocs.

Fragmentation breeds mistrust. Neighbours become strangers, institutions lose authority, and unity weakens. Social cohesion, essential for democracy, erodes. Once fractured, it is difficult to restore. Australia is not yet at this point, but trends suggest direction. Suburbs dominated by Islamic culture, schools adjusting curricula, councils bending to demands — all signal gradual shift. Unless addressed, fragmentation will deepen.

The impact on women and children

Long-term cultural implications are particularly severe for our women and our children. When Islamic norms can dominate communities, women often face restrictions on dress, movement, and education. Children are raised with values contrary to Australian equality, producing a generational divide.

Girls denied participation in sport or certain excursions grow up excluded from mainstream culture. Boys taught male dominance struggle to respect gender equality. Over time, these values entrench inequality, undermining national progress toward fairness.

The tragedy is that women and children, who could benefit most from Australian freedoms, are often those most trapped by cultural isolation.

The strain on our national identity

National identity depends on shared stories, symbols, and values. ANZAC Day, Australia Day, sporting heroes, the flag — these unify citizens. When Islamic groups resist participation in these rituals, identity strains.

If significant portions of the national population abstain from these traditions, unity weakens. Identity becomes contested, not celebrated. The question of *"what it means to be Australian?"* is severely fractured. This opens the door to ideological battles where Islam competes for allegiance.

The erosion of freedom

Ironically, cultural accommodation in name of tolerance often erodes freedom. When schools alter lessons, workplaces adjust rosters, councils segregate events, and festivals censor art to appease Islamic sensitivities, freedom diminishes for everyone else. Non-Muslims lose freedom to eat what they choose in public canteens, to express artistic ideas without fear, to celebrate heritage without apology. Freedom of majority shrinks as minority demands expand. This inversion of tolerance will undermine democracy itself.

The risk of hostility

As frustrations grow, backlash becomes likely. Non-Muslims who feel their culture eroding may react with hostility. Far-right movements in Europe thrive on resentment against Islamic influence. Violence and riots erupt when citizens feel silenced. Australia must avoid this cycle. But the risk is very real. Cultural clash, if not addressed with fairness and firmness, will breed division not only between Muslims and others but within broader society.

Lessons from overseas

Australia can learn from Europe's recent mistakes. Nations that indulged unchecked Islamic demands now face chronic tension. Key lessons include:

1. *Do not tolerate parallel systems* – Britain's Sharia councils undermined women's rights and fragmented law.
2. *Defend national symbols* – France's attempts to suppress Christian heritage while appeasing Islam deepened division.
3. *Control migration* – Sweden's mass intake without integration strategy produced ghettos and crime.
4. *Insist on integration* – Canada's policy of multicultural relativism produced communities resistant to assimilation.

Australia must heed these warnings, setting clear expectations for integration and resisting appeasement.

Safeguarding cultural cohesion

What, then, should Australia do? Several measures are essential:

➢ *Reassert shared values* – Schools, councils, and media must teach and celebrate national heritage unapologetically.

➢ *Set firm boundaries* – Institutions must resist demands for segregation or censorship. Equality and freedom must remain non-negotiable.

➢ *Promote integration* – Migrants must be encouraged to adopt national norms, not isolate in enclaves.

- ➤ *Support women and children* – Specific policies must empower those vulnerable to cultural restrictions.
- ➤ *Encourage open debate* – Citizens must be free to discuss Islamic influence without fear of censure.

These steps can strengthen cohesion, preventing fragmentation before it takes root.

The Christian response

For Christians, cultural clash is not only political issue but gospel opportunity. The presence of Muslims in Australia, though very challenging, is also a great mission field. While resisting cultural accommodation, believers must engage with love.

This involves three commitments:

1. *Bold witness* – Refusing to be silenced by accusations of intolerance, proclaiming Christ as Lord.
2. *Practical hospitality* – Befriending Muslim neighbours, inviting them into homes, showing kindness that reflects Christ.
3. *Compassionate advocacy* – Speaking for women and children trapped by oppressive norms, defending their dignity in Christ's name.

The cultural clash, therefore, is not merely danger but divine appointment. God has brought Muslims to Australia where they can freely hear gospel. The church must seize the moment.

A prophetic warning

Christians must speak prophetically to nation. Accommodation of Islam is not merely harmless multiculturalism but a path to fragmentation. Isaiah warned ancient Israel not to mix truth with lies: *"Woe to those who call evil good and good evil, who put darkness for light and light for darkness."* (Isaiah 5:20).

Australia must hear same warning. If nation continues to forget foundations, Islam will grow bold. But if it remembers truth, freedom can endure.

Conclusion

Daily life in Australia is changing right in front of our faces. In schools, workplaces, neighbourhoods, festivals, and civic rituals, Islam presses for recognition. These demands, though often presented as cultural or religious rights, erode unity, equality, and freedom.

The long-term implications are extremely serious. If unchecked, assimilation will fail, fragmentation will grow, women and children will suffer, national identity will fracture, and freedoms will erode. Australia risks repeating Europe's mistakes.

But it is not too late ... yet. By reasserting our shared values, setting boundaries, promoting integration, and defending the vulnerable, Australia can preserve cohesion. More importantly, by proclaiming Christ, the church can turn a cultural clash into a gospel opportunity.

For ultimately, hope is not found in politics or culture but in Christ. Only He can reconcile divided communities, transform hearts, and establish true peace. The challenge of Islam is very real but so is power of gospel.

May the church rise to meet this challenge with courage and compassion, and may Australia remember its foundations before they are forgotten forever.

16. DEMOGRAPHICS AND THE CHALLENGES AHEAD

Immigration has always been central to Australia's story. From the first European settlers to waves of post-war migrants, this nation has been shaped by those who arrived from elsewhere. Diversity is part of our heritage. Yet immigration is not merely about culture or cuisine—it is about numbers, demographics, and the long-term character of the nation.

In the twenty-first century, few issues carry as much weight for Australia's future as immigration. For while newcomers enrich society, the scale, origin, and integration of migrants determine the trajectory of our national identity. As addressed already in various chapters in this book, Islam, in particular, raises some unique challenges. Not because Muslims are migrants—many are now second or third generation migrants—but because Islamic identity will often resist assimilation, creating enduring demographic enclaves.

It is important that we understand how immigration patterns and demographic trends are reshaping Australia, and what they mean for the nation's future. It is not alarmist speculation but sober analysis of numbers, policies, and projections.

Australia's immigration landscape

Australia is undoubtedly one of the most multicultural nations on earth. Nearly 30% of residents were born overseas, and over half have at least one parent born abroad. Migration from Europe once dominated, but in recent decades migration from Asia and the Middle East have surged.

Muslim migration, in particular, has grown significantly. While Muslims remain a minority (around 3–4% of the population), their growth rate outpaces the national average. Higher fertility rates, continued migration, and growing family reunions drive this increase. In certain suburbs of Sydney and Melbourne, Muslims already form significant local majorities. The question is not whether Islam will shape future, but how profoundly. Numbers matter, for demographics is destiny.

Fertility and family patterns

One key factor is fertility. Muslim families in Australia generally have more children than national average. While our overall fertility rate currently hovers around 1.6 — below replacement level — Muslim communities often maintain rates closer to 2.5 or higher.

This gap, compounded over the generations, produces striking demographic shift. Even without new migration, higher fertility ensures continued growth of the Muslim population. In suburbs where communities cluster, the effect is exponential. Schools, shops, and local politics reflect majority presence long before national average rises significantly.

This is not just theoretical. In parts of western Sydney, Islamic families already shape the cultural rhythm through mosque attendance, halal commerce, and Islamic schooling. Fertility ensures their influence endures.

Migration streams

Australia's migration system includes skilled migration, family reunion, and humanitarian intake. Muslims enter through all three, but the humanitarian category is particularly significant. Refugees from Afghanistan, Iraq, Syria, and Sudan include large Muslim populations.

Humanitarian intake is always noble, reflecting compassion for the persecuted. Yet it also introduces concentrated groups with strong Islamic identity, often traumatised and resistant to any assimilation. When settled in enclaves, these groups struggle to integrate, reinforcing cultural separation.

Political implications

Demographics will inevitably shape our politics. As the Muslim communities grow, they form voting enclaves which are capable of influencing elections. Already, in several federal electorates, Muslim populations now exceed 15–20%. Candidates court the voter's support, softening rhetoric on Islamic issues, avoiding criticism, and promising accommodation.

Local councils in those Muslim-majority suburbs often approve Islamic schools, mosques, and cultural festivals with very little debate, reflecting electoral realities. State and federal leaders tread cautiously, wary of alienating significant constituencies.

This political influence magnifies beyond numbers. Minority, concentrated demographics deliver Muslims disproportionate leverage. Parties reliant on marginal seats adjust policies to secure support. Thus, immigration shapes not only culture but governance.

Education and identity transmission

Another demographic factor is education. Muslim families are increasingly enrolling their children in Islamic schools, where teaching combines Australian standards with Quranic teaching. These schools, while legally compliant, often reinforce distinct identity. Students grow up fluent in Islamic doctrine, sometimes with limited exposure to broader Australian culture.

University presence also grows, with separate Muslim student associations becoming active across campuses. These groups, while providing community, sometimes propagate Islamist ideology. The combination of fertility, education, and activism ensures Islamic identity is transmitted robustly to next generation.

By contrast, secular Australian families will often transmit little religious or cultural depth. This asymmetry means that Islamic identity remains strong while national identity weakens.

Long-term projections

What does future hold? Projections suggest the Muslim share of our population may double by mid-century. While still only a minority, their concentration in many urban centres will ensure a disproportionate influence. In those suburbs where Muslims form 40–50% of population, cultural dominance is already a reality. Shops, signage, schools, and politics reflect Islamic norms. If trend continues, multiple suburbs may function as de facto Islamic zones within broader Australia.

This does not imply some kind of national takeover, but it does mean cultural fragmentation. Australia will increasingly consist of parallel societies with limited shared identity.

International comparisons

Australia's trajectory resembles that of Europe two decades ago. France, Britain, and Sweden once welcomed Muslim migrants in small numbers. Over time, higher fertility rates and continued migration transformed the demographics. Today, those nations grapple with enclaves, cultural clashes, and political unrest. France's banlieues, Britain's Birmingham, Sweden's Malmö—these are warnings. Demographics, left unchecked, reshape nations irreversibly. Australia still has opportunity to act, but time is limited.

The challenge of loyalty

Demographic growth also raises questions of loyalty. While many Muslims embrace Australia, others retain strong ties to global ummah. This dual identity complicates integration. In times of international conflict—Israel-Palestine, Afghanistan, Iraq—Muslim communities sometimes prioritise solidarity with overseas Muslims over national unity. As demographics grow, such tensions may escalate. National identity weakens when significant bloc feels stronger allegiance elsewhere.

Christian reflection

For Christians, these demographic realities are sobering but also missional. The presence of Muslims in Australia, however challenging, is also an opportunity. God has brought people from nations closed to gospel into a land where they can freely hear. Believers must respond with concern and with mission. Demographic growth is a reason for urgency not despair. The church must evangelise boldly, disciple faithfully, and pray fervently. Numbers matter, but God's power transforms hearts.

Psalm 22:27 promises: *"All the ends of the earth will remember and turn to the Lord, and all the families of the nations will bow down before him."* Demographics may shift, but ultimate destiny belongs to Christ.

Immigration policy, refugee intake, and national cohesion

Immigration is never a neutral act. Each new arrival changes the demographic balance, cultural texture, and political dynamics of a nation. For Australia, which relies heavily on migration for economic and population growth, the stakes are especially high.

Immigration policies today shape society for decades to come. When migrants come from strong Islamic backgrounds, the implications extend beyond economics into identity, security, and cohesion.

The policy landscape

Australia's immigration program is among the most carefully managed in the world. It combines economic priorities with humanitarian compassion, balancing skilled migration with family reunions and refugee resettlement.

Yet beneath the orderly framework lie contentious debates about scale, source, and settlement. Critics argue that Australia accepts too many migrants too quickly, straining infrastructure and housing.

Others argue our intake is too restrictive, denying refuge to those in need. Beneath these arguments lies deeper issue: cultural compatibility. While some groups integrate smoothly, others resist assimilation. Islam, in particular, tests assumptions of multicultural harmony.

Refugee intake controversies

The most contested element is humanitarian intake. Australia resettles thousands of refugees annually, many from Muslim-majority nations torn by conflict—Afghanistan, Iraq, Syria, Sudan.

➤ *Integration challenges:* Refugees often arrive traumatised, lacking English, education, or work experience. Settlement services strive to support them, but integration is slow. Concentrated resettlement in suburbs creates enclaves where Islamic culture dominates, hindering assimilation.

> *Cultural tensions:* When cases of forced marriage, gender inequality, and radicalisation occasionally emerge among refugee communities, this fuels public concern. While most refugees seek peace, minority engaged in Islamist activism undermines trust.

> *Public backlash:* High-profile crimes involving some Muslim refugees — such as assaults or terrorism links — spark media storms. Though statistically rare, they shape perception disproportionately, eroding public support for humanitarian intake.

> *Moral dilemma:* Compassion for the persecuted collides with concern for national cohesion. Christians, in particular, wrestle with tension between biblical call to welcome the stranger and duty to protect community.

Family reunion pressures

Refugee intake often triggers chain migration through family reunion. A single refugee arrival may sponsor multiple relatives, multiplying numbers beyond original allocation. In Islamic contexts, large extended families accelerate demographic concentration.

Family reunion can also complicate integration. Older relatives will often resist assimilation, retaining Islamic traditions more strongly. Women, in particular, may live isolated lives with limited English or civic engagement. This reinforces enclave culture.

Skilled migration and Islamic professionals

Not all Muslim migration is humanitarian. Many arrive through skilled streams, particularly from Pakistan, Malaysia, and the Middle East. These Muslim migrants often have education and professional skills, contributing economically. Yet even among skilled migrants, Islamic identity remains strong. Many seek out mosques, schools, and halal networks, reinforcing communal cohesion. Thus, skilled migration does not necessarily dilute cultural tension. In some cases, it strengthens Islamic presence in professional sectors, from medicine to finance, amplifying influence.

Impact on social services

Immigration places pressure on social services—housing, healthcare, education, welfare. When intake includes large numbers of low-skilled or refugees, the strain increases.

➤ *Housing:* Refugee families, often large, require affordable housing. Concentration in certain suburbs pushes demand, inflating rents and reducing availability for others. Overcrowding becomes common, straining community infrastructure.

➤ *Healthcare:* Many refugees arrive with untreated conditions or trauma. Healthcare systems, already stretched, struggle to meet demand. Language barriers complicate care.

➤ *Education:* Schools in resettlement areas face influx of non-English-speaking students. Teachers must adapt, slowing pace of learning for others. Islamic parents sometimes demand cultural accommodations, adding complexity.

➤ *Welfare:* Unemployment rates among refugees are high. Welfare dependency, while understandable initially, often persists. This fuels resentment among taxpayers who perceive unfair burden.

These pressures are not unique to Muslims, but concentrated intake from Islamic nations certainly intensifies them.

National cohesion and trust

Beyond services, immigration affects intangible but vital asset: trust. Social cohesion depends on citizens believing they share common identity and values. When communities resist assimilation, trust erodes.

➤ *Parallel societies:* Enclaves where Islamic culture dominates foster perception of "two Australias." Non-Muslims feel alienated in suburbs where English is scarce, shops are exclusively halal, and mosques dominate landscape.

➤ *Security concerns:* Radicalisation, though affecting minority, casts long shadow. Citizens worry that welcoming refugees may import extremism. This fear undermines trust in immigration system.

> *Political Polarisation:* Immigration debates fuel division. Some advocate open borders in name of compassion; others demand strict limits to preserve culture. The middle ground erodes, weakening national unity.

Demographic momentum

Even modest annual intakes, when sustained, produce long-term shifts. Combined with higher fertility rates, Islamic share of population rises steadily. Demographic momentum ensures growth even if immigration slows. This momentum challenges the policymakers. Decisions today, though appearing minor, shape demographics for future generations. Once established, communities are self-sustaining, with schools, mosques, and businesses reinforcing identity. Reversing trajectory becomes nearly impossible.

The economics vs culture debate

Pro-immigration advocates will emphasise economic benefits: migrants fill skill gaps, boost consumption, and offset ageing population. Critics respond that culture, not economics, is decisive. A prosperous but divided nation cannot endure.

Islam highlights this tension. While Muslim professionals will contribute economically, cultural resistance will all too often undermine cohesion. Economics may justify a high intake, but culture will determine sustainability.

Lessons from Europe and North America

Other nations offer sobering lessons:

> *Germany:* The decision to admit over a million mostly Muslim refugees in 2015 reshaped demographics overnight. Integration struggles, crime spikes, and political polarisation followed. Chancellor Merkel later admitted: "Multiculturalism has utterly failed."

> *France:* Decades of Muslim immigration produced banlieues where Islamic identity dominates. Terrorism, riots, and cultural clashes plague society. Attempts at assimilation falter against demographic realities.

- ➤ *United States:* – Muslim communities are smaller relative to population, but concentrated areas face similar tensions. Post-9/11 security fears continue to shape debate.
- ➤ *Canada:* With generous intake, Canada embraces multiculturalism but faces same long-term question: will cohesion survive when values diverge?

Australia's trajectory mirrors these nations in so many ways. The time to learn, therefore, is now.

Policy options for Australia

Given these realities, what should Australia do? Options include:

1. *Reduced intake from high-risk regions:* Prioritise migrants more likely to integrate, while limiting intake from areas with strong Islamist influence.
2. *Stricter screening:* Assess not only skills but cultural compatibility, language ability, and commitment to integration.
3. *Decentralised settlement:* Avoid concentration in urban enclaves by distributing migrants across regions.
4. *Integration requirements:* Mandate English classes, civic education, and participation in national traditions.
5. *Conditional welfare:* Tie benefits to integration milestones, incentivising participation.
6. *Transparent debate:* Allow open discussion of immigration impacts without fear of censorship.

These measures, though quite controversial, may be necessary to preserve cohesion.

The Christian tension

For Christians, immigration policy poses a very significant moral tension. On the one hand, Scripture demands that we care for the foreigner: *"Do not mistreat or oppress a foreigner, for you were foreigners in Egypt"* (Exodus 22:21). On the other, government is called to protect its people and uphold justice (Romans 13:4).

The challenge therefore is to balance compassion with wisdom. Welcoming refugees is noble, but not if it endangers national unity or imports oppression. True compassion considers both newcomers and citizens. Christians must therefore advocate policies that protect the vulnerable while preserving freedom. The gospel offers eternal refuge, but government must steward earthly responsibility.

Christian hope

Despite challenges, Christians should not despair. Immigration brings Muslims into contact with the gospel. What nations resist overseas, they encounter freely here. Churches have opportunity to reach the unreached without crossing any oceans. Thus, while advocating wise policy, believers must embrace the mission opportunities. The presence of Muslims in Australia is not only a threat, but an opportunity ordained by God.

The cost of inaction

Failure to address immigration challenges invites long-term crisis. If intake continues without integration, we may face:

➤ Expanding enclaves which are hostile to national identity.

➤ Increased welfare burdens straining economy.

➤ Rising cultural clashes eroding cohesion.

➤ Political instability as citizens lose trust.

These outcomes are not inevitable but probable if trends remain unchecked. Immigration is not merely humanitarian gesture but nation-shaping decision.

Projections, Politics, and a Christian Vision

Immigration and demographics are not passing concerns; they shape the long-term destiny of nations. Laws can be amended, policies reformed, and governments replaced, but demographic change endures for generations. When children are born into a culture and raised with its values, trajectory is set. This is why Islam's growth in Australia through immigration, fertility, and community consolidation represents not merely social change but a decisive shift in the nation's future.

As we now look ahead, what do projections suggest about Australia's demographic future? How will politics respond to shifting numbers? What lessons does history provide? And how should Christians face the coming decades with both clarity and hope?

Demographic projections

Current figures place Muslims at roughly 3–4% of Australia's population. This seems comparatively small, but the growth rate is disproportionate.

Demographers project Muslim share could double by mid-century, reaching 8–10%. In specific suburbs, it will be far higher. In western Sydney and northern Melbourne, Muslims may comprise between 40 and 50% within a generation. While still a minority nationally, concentration ensures influence far beyond their numbers. Suburbs with Islamic majorities shape schools, councils, commerce, and local politics decisively.

Political ramifications

Demographics drive politics. As Muslim communities grow, they consolidate into voting blocs. Politicians seeking election in key electorates must court their support.

This produces several ramifications:

➤ *Policy softening:* Parties avoid criticism of Islam to protect votes. Discussion of Sharia, radicalisation, or cultural tension is muted. Policies shift toward accommodation rather than resistance.

➤ *Representation:* Muslim candidates gain prominence, elected to councils, parliaments, and ministries. While diversity in itself is not negative, candidates aligned with Islamic organisations may prioritise community demands over national principles.

➤ *Foreign policy pressure:* Muslim blocs may influence Australia's stance on Middle East conflicts, Israel, or counterterrorism. Already, debates over Palestine polarise electorates with large Muslim populations.

➤ *Polarisation:* Non-Muslim citizens, feeling neglected, gravitate toward parties promising firmer stance. Politics becomes divided along cultural lines, weakening unity.

These dynamics are not simply speculative — they already shape key electorates in Sydney and Melbourne. With demographic momentum, influence will only grow.

Lessons from history

History confirms demographics determine destiny. The Roman Empire, though powerful militarily, was reshaped by waves of migration that diluted cohesion. Lebanon, once majority Christian, became fractured as Muslim population grew. In each case, demographic change altered culture irreversibly.

Europe provides our most recent lesson. Nations that welcomed Muslim migration decades ago now face entrenched enclaves, political polarisation, and cultural conflict. Leaders who once promised smooth integration now openly admit failure. France's repeated riots, Britain's grooming scandals, Sweden's crime surge — all stem from demographic shifts left unaddressed.

Australia, though geographically quite distant, follows a similar trajectory unless corrective action is taken.

Identity at the crossroads

Demographics not only shift numbers but redefine identity. If a significant portion of the nation identifies primarily with Islam, what is means to *"be Australian"* changes considerably. National holidays, traditions, and values become contested. Already, debates over Australia Day, ANZAC services, and Christmas reflect this contest. As Muslim share grows, pressure to reframe national identity intensifies. A secular elite, eager to appease, may dilute Christian heritage further.

The result is a hollow identity, vulnerable to ideological capture. The question becomes: will Australia remember its foundations or reinvent itself under pressure?

Long-term risks

If trends continue without response, several risks emerge:

1. *Enclave society:* Large suburbs operate as Islamic zones, with little integration.
2. *Eroded freedoms:* Free speech and expression curtailed to avoid offending Muslim communities.
3. *Weakened national identity:* Shared traditions diluted to accommodate Islamic sensitivities.
4. *Political instability:* Polarisation intensifies, with conflict between blocs.
5. *Security concerns:* Radicalisation risks persist, amplified by demographic growth.

These risks are not inevitable, but they are highly probable if policies remain unchanged.

Possible futures

Australia faces three broad futures:

1. *Assimilation success:* Muslims integrate fully, adopting national values while retaining private faith. This scenario is ideal but rare, given Islamic resistance to assimilation globally.
2. *Peaceful separation:* Enclaves function with minimal interaction, avoiding conflict but eroding unity. Australia becomes patchwork nation.
3. *Conflict and polarisation:* Tensions escalate into open hostility, with political unrest or even violence. This is Europe's path, and one Australia must avoid.

Which future unfolds depends on decisions made today.

A Christian vision

For Christians, demographic change is both a challenge and an opportunity. The challenge is obvious: Islam's growth threatens freedoms, identity, and unity.

But the opportunity is quite profound: never before have so many Muslims lived within reach of the gospel in Australia. Instead of withdrawing in fear, the church must see the mission. While governments debate numbers, Christians must proclaim Christ. While politicians court blocs, believers must reach individuals.

Every Muslim family in Australia is divine appointment for witness. The early church thrived in pluralistic Roman Empire, surrounded by paganism and hostility. Yet gospel advanced through faithful witness. Likewise, the Australian church must rise with courage.

Practical commitments for Christians

1. *Proclaim boldly:* Refuse silence. Share Christ with Muslim neighbours, trusting Spirit to work.
2. *Disciple deeply:* Equip believers to answer Islamic objections with Scripture.
3. *Support converts:* Provide community for Muslims who turn to Christ, often rejected by families.
4. *Pray earnestly:* Intercede for revival among Muslims, for courage among Christians, and for wisdom for leaders.
5. *Engage politically:* Advocate for policies that preserve freedom, integration, and justice.

In this way, the church responds not with fear but with faith.

The hope of the gospel

Demographics may seem daunting, but gospel transcends numbers. While Islam grows by birthrate, Christianity grows by rebirth. Every conversion is miracle of grace, altering eternal destiny. History shows revival can transform nations in single generation.

Psalm 2 reminds us: *"Ask me, and I will make the nations your inheritance, the ends of the earth your possession."* God rules history. Demographic trends are real, but not final. Christ is sovereign.

Conclusion

Immigration and demographics shape Australia's future more than any other factor. Muslim growth through migration, fertility, and enclaves ensures that Islam will remain a significant force. If left unaddressed, this trend will bring fragmentation, weakened identity, and political instability.

However, the future is not fixed. Wise policy, firm leadership, and courageous Christian witness can alter the current trajectory. Australia must insist on integration, resist appeasement, and preserve shared values. The church must rise in mission, seeing demographic challenge as gospel opportunity.

The crossroads is very clear: will Australia drift into fragmented future or choose unity grounded in truth? Will the church retreat in fear or advance in faith? The numbers may be a little daunting, but the gospel is greater. In Christ, there is hope—not only for Muslims, but for Australia itself.

17. ISLAM AND HUMAN RIGHTS

Global contrasts

Human rights are the bedrock of any democratic society. They safeguard the dignity of the individual, restrain tyranny, and ensure equality before the law.

In Australia, though imperfectly applied, human rights are enshrined in our institutions, laws, and culture. They reflect the Christian heritage that affirms every person is made in the image of God (Genesis 1:27). Yet when one looks to Islamic societies around the world, a starkly different picture emerges. Rights we take for granted are absent, restricted, or redefined.

So, let's explore the global contrasts between Islamic regimes and Australia. By surveying women's status, treatment of minorities, freedom of expression, and justice systems, we see how deeply Islam diverges from the universal human rights norms. These examples are not abstract but instructive, for they reveal what happens when Islam is given legal and cultural dominance.

Women's rights under Islam

One of the clearest contrasts lies in treatment of women.

➤ *Saudi Arabia* – Until recently, women could not drive. Guardianship laws still require male permission for travel, marriage, and sometimes medical treatment. Employment opportunities are restricted, with gender segregation enforced in workplaces and universities.

➤ *Afghanistan* – Under Taliban rule, women are excluded from secondary education, barred from public office, and confined to homes. Female judges, journalists, and activists have been silenced, often violently.

➤ *Iran* – Compulsory veiling is enforced by morality police. Women who protest face arrest, lashes, or imprisonment. Custody laws favour fathers, inheritance gives daughters half share of sons, and female testimony in court only counts half that of a man.

By contrast, Australian law affirms gender equality. Women can hold political office, lead companies, and pursue all education freely. Discrimination is prohibited, and domestic violence is criminal. While Australia still faces challenges, the baseline of equality is indisputable. The gulf between Islamic regimes and Australia reveals incompatibility of Sharia norms with universal human rights.

Treatment of religious minorities

Islamic regimes also restrict rights of non-Muslims.

➤ *Pakistan:* Blasphemy laws impose the death penalty or life imprisonment for insulting Islam. Christians and Hindus live under constant threat of false accusations. Churches are attacked and converts from Islam face violent persecution.

➤ *Egypt:* Coptic Christians, though an historic community, face discrimination in building churches, accessing jobs, and seeking justice. Mob violence against Christians often goes unpunished.

➤ *Saudi Arabia:* Non-Muslim worship is banned in public. Churches cannot be built, Bibles cannot be imported, and conversion from Islam is punishable by death.

By contrast, Australia protects freedom of belief. Citizens may worship, convert, or reject religion altogether without any legal penalty. Churches, mosques, synagogues, and temples coexist under Australian law. This freedom, though increasingly being pressured, remains foundational. The difference is not small but fundamental. Islam, when dominant, denies minorities the rights Australia enshrines.

Freedom of expression

Free expression is cornerstone of democracy. Without it, truth is suppressed and accountability lost. Yet in those Islamic regimes, expression is tightly controlled.

➤ *Iran:* Journalists critical of regime are imprisoned or executed. Social media is censored. Satire or art deemed offensive to Islam is criminalised.

- *Saudi Arabia:* Blogger Raif Badawi was sentenced to 1,000 lashes and 10 years in prison for advocating liberal reforms. Criticism of Islam or monarchy is outlawed.

- *Turkey:* Once more secular, Turkey now prosecutes journalists and academics for insulting Islam or government. Freedom of press has collapsed under Islamist influence.

By contrast, Australia protects free expression, even when it is offensive. Citizens may criticise government, religion, or leaders without fear of imprisonment. While defamation laws exist, they are civil, not criminal. The gulf is stark. Islam's demand for such blasphemy restrictions is irreconcilable with our freedom.

Justice and punishment

Justice systems under Sharia often conflict with universal human rights.

- *Hudud punishments:* In countries like Iran, Saudi Arabia, and Sudan, crimes such as theft, adultery, or apostasy incur brutal penalties: amputations, stoning, flogging, execution.

- *Due process:* Accused individuals often lack presumption of innocence or fair trial. Testimony of women or non-Muslims may carry less weight. Confessions under torture are common.

- *Political Use:* Rulers frequently employ Sharia selectively, punishing opponents while excusing allies. Justice becomes tool of tyranny.

By contrast, Australia affirms rule of law. Punishments are proportionate, trials are fair, and rights of accused are protected. While flaws exist, the framework is designed for equity. Islamic justice systems reveal what happens when law is not rooted in equality but in religious supremacy.

International human rights instruments

Most Islamic regimes will resist any international human rights standards. While Australia has affirmed the United Nations' Universal Declaration of Human Rights (UDHR), Islamic nations often qualify it or reject it outright.

In 1990, the Organisation of Islamic Cooperation adopted the Cairo Declaration on Human Rights in Islam. While appearing to endorse rights, it subjects them to Sharia. In effect, rights exist only insofar as they align with Islamic law. This means freedom of religion excludes conversion, equality excludes women, and expression excludes criticism of Islam. The Cairo Declaration demonstrates incompatibility. Where Australia sees rights as universal, Islam sees them as conditional.

The illusion of reform

Some argue Islamic regimes are reforming. Saudi Arabia allows women to drive, UAE hosts global events, and Turkey maintains elections. Yet beneath surface, fundamental restrictions remain. Reforms are only cosmetic, designed to appease international criticism while preserving Sharia supremacy.

Real reform requires abandoning Sharia's restrictions. Yet to do so is to abandon Islam's claim of divine law. Thus, true reform remains an illusion. It will never happen.

Implications for Australia

Why do these global contrasts matter? Because they reveal what Islam produces when allowed to be dominant. If given legal or cultural supremacy, Islam curtails women's rights, suppresses minorities, censors expression, and enforces brutal justice. These are not aberrations but consistent applications of Sharia.

Australia must recognise this reality. To assume that Islam will behave differently here is really naïve. Immigration from Islamic regimes imports values shaped by these systems. Unless firmly integrated, those values will influence Australian culture.

Christian reflection

For Christians, global contrasts highlight the absolute necessity of the gospel. Where Islam suppresses, Christ liberates. Where Sharia enslaves, grace redeems. Jesus declared: *"Then you will know the truth, and the truth will set you free"* (John 8:32). Freedom is not human invention but divine gift.

The church must therefore speak boldly. It must expose injustice abroad and defend people's rights at home. It must advocate for the persecuted, especially women and minorities under Islam. And it must proclaim Christ as the true source of human dignity.

Case studies of Islamic regimes

If human rights are the measure of a nation's moral health, then Islamic regimes offer some sobering lessons. While each country interprets Islam in its own political and cultural way, common patterns emerge wherever Sharia is given legal supremacy. Women are restricted, minorities are persecuted, free expression is silenced, and justice is harsh. These are not random abuses, they are systemic outcomes of Islamic law applied in society. By examining specific nations, we see clearly how Islam functions when dominant — and why Australia must be vigilant.

Saudi Arabia: The custodian of Sharia

Saudi Arabia presents the clearest case of Islam enshrined in law. As the birthplace of Islam and home to Mecca and Medina, it claims authority as custodian of the faith. Its legal system is explicitly based on the Wahhabi interpretation of Sharia.

➢ *Women's rights:* Until recently, women could not drive or travel without a male guardian. Though some reforms have eased restrictions, guardianship remains in many areas. Women's testimony in court carries less weight, inheritance is unequal, and marriage requires male consent.

➢ *Religious freedom:* Non-Muslim worship is banned in public. Churches cannot be built. Conversion from Islam is punishable by death. Foreign workers may worship privately but risk deportation if gatherings are discovered.

➢ *Justice System:* Punishments include beheadings, amputations, and floggings. Trials are often opaque, with limited rights for accused. Blasphemy or sorcery can result in execution.

➢ *Freedom of expression:* Critics of regime or religion are jailed. Blogger Raif Badawi's 1,000 lashes sentence illustrates brutality against dissent.

Saudi Arabia demonstrates what happens when Sharia is not moderated but applied in its purest form: human rights are systematically denied.

Iran: Islam and authoritarianism

Iran combines Shia Islam with authoritarian theocracy. Since the 1979 revolution, clerics have ruled with an iron grip, blending political power with religious authority.

➢ *Compulsory veiling:* Women must wear hijab in public. Morality police patrol streets, arresting violators. Protests in recent years have been met with violence, imprisonment, and death.

➢ *Political repression:* Opposition parties are banned. Activists, journalists, and minorities face execution or exile. Elections exist but are controlled by clerics who vet candidates.

➢ *Minorities:* Christians, Baha'is, and Sunnis face discrimination. Apostasy is punishable by death. Churches are raided, converts imprisoned.

➢ *Justice:* Public executions, amputations, and flogging persist. Courts operate under Islamic judges, with little due process.

Iran illustrates how Islam merges with authoritarian politics to crush rights comprehensively.

Afghanistan: Taliban rule and collapse of freedom

Afghanistan under the Taliban reveals the extremity of Sharia when applied by militants. After the US withdrawal back in 2021, the Taliban reinstated Islamic Emirate.

➢ *Women's exclusion:* Girls banned from secondary schools, women excluded from universities and workplaces. Travel requires male escort. Public spaces segregated.

➢ *Violence against dissent:* Journalists arrested, activists executed. Music, film, and art banned. Freedom of expression non-existent.

- ➤ *Religious minorities:* Christians forced underground. Converts face death. Hazara Shias targeted with violence.

- ➤ *Justice:* Public stoning, amputations, and floggings have resumed. Taliban claim to enforce divine justice, but the reality is tyranny.

Afghanistan demonstrates the regression possible when Islam dominates unchecked: society quickly collapses into medieval authoritarianism.

Pakistan: The blasphemy state

Pakistan, though officially democratic, enforces some of the harshest blasphemy laws in the world. These laws embody Islamic intolerance toward dissent.

- ➤ *Blasphemy laws:* Insulting Islam or Muhammad carries the death penalty. Accusations, often false, lead to mob violence. Asia Bibi, a Christian woman, spent years on death row before acquittal. Others were killed by mobs before trial.

- ➤ *Minorities:* Christians, Hindus, and Ahmadis face systemic discrimination. Forced conversions of Hindu and Christian girls are common. Police often fail to intervene.

- ➤ *Women:* Honour killings persist. Domestic violence laws are weakly enforced. Sharia-based family laws disadvantage women in divorce and custody.

- ➤ *Expression:* Journalists critical of Islam or military face assassination. Freedom of expression is precarious.

Pakistan reveals how even democratic institutions collapse under the weight of Islamic law. Rights vanish when Islam dominates.

Sudan: Sharia and civil strife

Sudan long enforced Sharia, particularly in the north. Apostasy carried the death penalty, floggings were common, and women faced harsh restrictions. While recent reforms repealed apostasy law, instability persists.

- ➤ *Civil conflict:* Sharia enforcement contributed to a decades-long civil war, as the Christian and animist south resisted Islamic dominance. Conflict killed millions and led to independence of South Sudan.
- ➤ *Women and minorities:* Under Sharia, women faced restrictions on dress and movement. Christians suffered persecution, particularly in Darfur and Nuba Mountains.

Sudan shows how Sharia destabilises nations, fuelling conflict and division.

Nigeria: Sharia and violence

Nigeria offers us a hybrid example. In the north, several states implemented Sharia law alongside national constitution.

- ➤ *Justice:* Amputations and stonings have been sentenced under Sharia courts, though sometimes overturned nationally.
- ➤ *Conflict:* The Boko Haram insurgency seeks a full Islamic state. Violence against Christians includes massacres, kidnappings, and church bombings.
- ➤ *Women:* Schoolgirls are kidnapped, forced into marriage or slavery. Gender-based violence is widespread.

Nigeria demonstrates how the implementation of partial Sharia fractures nations, producing conflict between Muslim north and Christian south.

Turkey: erosion of secularism

Turkey once symbolised secularism in Muslim world. Founded by Atatürk, it separated mosque and state. Yet under President Erdoğan, Islamism is resurging.

- ➤ *Freedom of press:* Journalists critical of the government or Islam face arrest. The media is tightly controlled.
- ➤ *Women's rights:* While freer than the Middle East, Turkey has rolled back protections. Domestic violence persists, and political Islam pressures women into traditional roles.

> ➤ *Expression:* Criticism of Islam or government is often prosecuted.

Turkey reveals how fragile secularism is in an Islamic context. Even modern democracies slide toward authoritarianism when Islam asserts itself.

Common patterns

Across these nations, despite their differences, common themes emerge:

➤ Women are restricted in rights and freedoms.

➤ Religious minorities are persecuted or excluded.

➤ Free expression is curtailed; blasphemy criminalised.

➤ Justice systems are harsh, unequal, and politicised.

➤ Human rights instruments are subordinated to Sharia.

These are not cultural quirks but systemic outcomes of Islam controlling society.

Why should Australians care about human rights overseas? Because these regimes represent values many Muslim migrants bring with them. While individuals vary, cultural norms persist. If Islam gains more influence in Australia, pressures will grow to normalise similar restrictions. Already, demands for censorship, gender segregation, and halal standards echo global patterns.

If unchecked, Australia risks importing not only people but values hostile to human rights. These case studies serve as a warning: what happens elsewhere under Islam can happen here.

Christian reflection

For Christians, these global abuses demand both lament and mission. Lament for millions suffering under Sharia. Mission to proclaim Jesus Christ as the only true liberator of humanity.

Isaiah 61:1 declares: *"The Spirit of the Sovereign Lord is on me, because the Lord has anointed me to proclaim good news to the poor. He has sent me to bind up the broken-hearted, to proclaim freedom for the captives and release from darkness for the prisoners."*

Only Jesus Christ offers the freedom Sharia denies. The church must therefore support the persecuted, advocate for justice, and preach the gospel boldly.

Lessons for the world and warnings for Australia

Human rights are not simply abstract ideals debated in the UN chambers or academic conferences. They are the daily bread of freedom, the moral oxygen of a healthy society. Where they are denied, people suffocate under tyranny; where they are upheld, people flourish in dignity. By now it is clear: wherever Islam is given legal and cultural dominance, human rights are eroded. This is not an occasional failure – it is a consistent pattern.

As we turn now from specific case studies to global implications, these questions arise, what does Islam's record on human rights mean for international order? What lessons must Australia learn from these examples? And how should Christians respond, both politically and spiritually?

Global implications of Islam's human rights record

The first implication is that Islam is incompatible with universal human rights. The very notion of universality — that all people, regardless of their creed, gender, or background, possess equal rights — contradicts Sharia's hierarchy. In Islam, Muslims hold a higher status than non-Muslims, men above women, believers above apostates. Rights are conditional, not inherent.

This incompatibility destabilises international consensus. While Western nations boldly affirm the UN's Universal Declaration of Human Rights, Islamic nations insist on the Cairo Declaration, which subjects all rights to Sharia. This creates parallel systems, undermining global unity on human rights.

The second implication is regional instability. Wherever Islam dominates, suppression of rights breeds unrest. Women are denied education, minorities are persecuted, and dissidents are silenced. These conditions fuel conflict and extremism. Refugees flee, terrorism grows, and instability spreads.

The third implication is global security. Islamic regimes that deny rights often export ideology. Saudi Arabia funds madrassas abroad; Iran sponsors militias; Pakistan's blasphemy laws embolden radicals worldwide. Denial of rights at home breeds aggression abroad. Thus, Islam's human rights record is not domestic matter but global challenge.

Why Australia must pay attention

Some argue these issues are distant asking why should Australia concern itself with abuses in Iran or Nigeria? The answer is twofold: moral responsibility and national interest.

➤ *Moral responsibility:* As a free nation, Australia has a duty to speak for the oppressed. Silence in the face of persecution is complicity. To ignore the plight of women in Afghanistan or Christians in Pakistan is to abandon the principle of universal dignity.

➤ *National interest:* More pragmatically, what happens abroad does not stay abroad. Refugees fleeing Islamic regimes arrive on Australia's shores. Migrants bring cultural norms shaped by human rights denial. Extremist ideologies, funded globally, influence local mosques. Ignoring global record is naïve; consequences reach Australia inevitably.

The myth of *"Moderate Islam"*

One common defence is an appeal to *"moderate Islam."* Advocates insist human rights abuses are only cultural distortions, not true Islam. They claim that Sharia can be interpreted flexibly, aligning with modern norms.

Yet the evidence says otherwise. Across nations, from Sunni Saudi Arabia to Shia Iran, from Arab Egypt to Asian Indonesia, patterns persist today. While severity varies, denial of rights is consistent.

So, the problem is not the culture – it is Islam itself. Moderate individuals exist, but moderate Islam as a system is just a myth. Wherever Islam governs, rights diminish. To believe otherwise is to ignore mountains of evidence.

Warnings for Australia

In light the global evidence, allow me to stress again what we need to do in Australia if we are to heed the warnings:

1. *Do not allow parallel systems:* Even limited recognition of Sharia risks entrenching inequality, as seen in Britain's councils.

2. *Protect freedom of expression:* Pressure to censor "Islamophobia" mirrors blasphemy laws abroad. Australia must resist drift toward speech restrictions.

3. *Defend women's rights:* Practices tolerated in name of diversity — forced marriage, gender segregation — mirror global abuses. Firm boundaries are essential.

4. *Safeguard minorities:* As Muslim communities grow, non-Muslim neighbours may feel pressure. Law must protect equality without fear of offence.

5. *Screen migration wisely:* Refugees from Islamic regimes may carry values hostile to rights. Screening must include cultural compatibility, not only security risk.

These warnings are not hypothetical — they are already emerging in schools, workplaces, councils, and courts. Without vigilance, Australia could replicate patterns of human rights erosion seen globally.

The Christian responsibility

Christians cannot observe these realities with detached analysis. We are called to act.

➤ *Advocate for the persecuted:* Hebrews 13:3 commands us : *"Continue to remember those in prison as if you were together with them in prison, and those who are mistreated as if you yourselves were suffering."* Believers must speak up for the oppressed, whether in Iran, Sudan, or Pakistan.

➤ *Support refugees wisely:* Compassion is essential, but wisdom too. Churches must welcome refugees while advocating policies that protect national cohesion. True love considers both guest and host.

➤ *Defend human rights at home:* Christians must resist erosion of freedoms in Australia. If criticism of Islam is silenced, if gender segregation is normalised, if cultural relativism prevails, rights will shrink. Believers must contend for liberty grounded in gospel.

➤ *Proclaim the Gospel:* Ultimately, human rights are secured not by documents but by Christ. Only when people see others as image-bearers of God will dignity endure. The gospel transforms oppressors into servants, persecutors into brothers. Saul became Paul; enemies became family in Jesus Christ.

A theology of rights

From a biblical perspective, rights are not a human invention but a divine gift. They flow from the truth that every person is made in God's image and accountable to Him. When societies reject this truth, rights begin to crumble. Islam's failure on human rights is theological. By denying the image of God in humanity, by subordinating dignity to Sharia hierarchy, it undermines foundation of rights. Australia must recognise that its freedoms rest on biblical soil. Remove the roots, and rights wither.

The role of the church in Australia

As Islam grows, Australian church faces critical task:

➤ *Educate congregations:* Many believers are naïve about Islam's global record. Churches must teach truth, equipping members to discern.

➤ *Engage politically:* Christians should advocate policies that defend rights, resisting pressure to appease. Silence is not neutrality but surrender.

➤ *Reach out missionally:* While resisting ideology, believers must love individuals. Muslims in Australia are not enemies but neighbours God has brought within reach of gospel.

➤ *Prepare for opposition:* As Islam gains influence, Christians who speak the truth may face legal pressure. Churches must prepare to suffer faithfully, remembering Acts 5:29: *"We must obey God rather than human beings!"*

Hope in Christ

Despite sobering realities, hope remains. Human rights may fail under Islam, but Christ reigns. His kingdom is not shaken by tyranny. Revelation 7:9 envisions great multitude from every nation, tribe, people, and language worshipping before throne. Among them will be countless Muslims who turned to Christ, liberated from Sharia's bondage.

Therefore, Christians labour not in despair but in hope. Even as we expose Islam's abuses, we proclaim Christ's grace. Even as we defend rights, we extend gospel. Even as we resist cultural encroachment, we love Muslim neighbours.

Conclusion

Islam's global record on human rights is one of consistent failure. Women oppressed, minorities persecuted, expression silenced, justice corrupted — these are the fruits of Sharia in power. This is not a cultural accident – it's a theological necessity.

For Australia, the lesson is urgent: do not assume Islam will behave differently here. What happens abroad can happen at home if our vigilance lapses. Rights, once eroded, are difficult to restore.

Yet for Christians, this is also a moment of clear calling. We are summoned to defend human rights, advocate for the oppressed, and proclaim Christ as the true source of dignity. The church is a voice of truth in a culture of compromise. The challenge is real, but so is the gospel. While Islam enslaves, Christ sets free. While Sharia divides, the Spirit unites. While human rights crumble under tyranny, they are restored under the cross.

May Australia heed the warnings of history, defend the dignity of all, and remember the foundation of our freedom. And may the church rise, not with fear but with faith, proclaiming that in Christ alone true liberty is found.

18. ISLAM AND RELIGIOUS FREEDOM IN AUSTRALIA

Freedom of belief under pressure

Australia has long been regarded as a nation where freedom of religion is woven into the very fabric of national life. Though the Constitution's Section 116 provides only limited protection, the broader culture has historically celebrated liberty of belief and worship. Churches have flourished, synagogues and temples stand openly, and people are free to embrace or reject religion without fear of punishment. This atmosphere, though imperfect, has been one of Australia's greatest strengths.

Yet this freedom is never guaranteed. Rather, it relies on cultural confidence and legal vigilance. When challenged by ideologies that seek dominance rather than coexistence, it quickly erodes. Islam, in particular, presents a unique challenge. For while it demands freedom to practise its rites in Australia, it often resists extending the same liberty to others, especially when Islamic norms are criticised or contradicted. The result is an asymmetry that strains the principle of equal freedom for all.

We need to understand how Islam intersects with freedom of belief in Australia, focusing on the rights to convert, to worship without intimidation, and to live out faith without coercion. The issue is not whether Muslims have freedom here—they clearly do—but whether the presence of Islam endangers the equal freedom of others.

Freedom to convert

At the heart of religious freedom lies the right to change belief. In theory, every Australian may leave one faith and embrace another. In practice, for Muslims, this path is perilous.

➤ *Family pressures:* Converts from Islam to Christianity often face severe rejection. Families may cut ties, disown children, or in some cases even threaten violence. While law protects individual rights, social reality can impose coercion. Many converts live in secrecy, fearing exposure.

- ➤ *Community hostility:* Churches that baptise believers with a Muslim background, sometimes report harassment. Pastors speak of intimidation, graffiti, or online abuse. Converts themselves may be followed or threatened, particularly in tightly knit communities where leaving Islam is seen as a betrayal.

- ➤ *Psychological toll*: For converts, pressure is not only external but internal. The fear of dishonouring family, losing identity, or facing isolation creates a real burden. Though legally free, they soon feel trapped by the invisible chains of community expectation.

These realities mean that while religious freedom still exists on paper, for Muslim-background Australians it is all too often compromised. True liberty is hollow if fear prevents its exercise.

Freedom of worship

Freedom of worship is constitutionally and culturally affirmed. Yet Islamic influence increasingly complicates this principle. These double standards erode freedom by privileging one faith. True liberty requires consistency, not selective accommodation.

- ➤ *Council decisions:* Local councils, so eager to appear inclusive, will sometimes fund Islamic festivals or permit the building of mosques while restricting Christian expressions at the same time. In some areas, Christmas carols are scaled back in schools or parks to avoid offence, yet Eid events receive official endorsement. Equality of treatment is undermined.

- ➤ *Schools:* In public education, Christian observances such as nativity plays are frequently curtailed, while Ramadan activities are promoted. Students may be discouraged from overtly Christian expression while encouraged to respect Islamic practice. The imbalance suggests freedom for one faith at expense of another.

- ➤ *Workplaces:* Employers often provide prayer rooms for Muslim staff yet may reprimand Christians for displaying Bibles or speaking about faith. While Islamic expression is accommodated, Christian practice is marginalised.

Religious liberty and public institutions

The interaction of Islam with public institutions raises further concerns.

➤ *Chaplaincy and hospitals:* Islamic chaplains are welcomed into hospitals, prisons, and universities. Christian chaplaincy, however, faces increasing restrictions, particularly in schools where secular activists object. The net effect is greater access for Islam, reduced space for Christianity.

➤ *Universities:* Muslim prayer rooms are common on campuses, often funded by institutions. Christian groups, by contrast, sometimes face obstacles in hiring venues or promoting events. Religious liberty is unevenly applied.

➤ *Government agencies* – Sensitivity training for staff often emphasises Islamic needs—halal catering, gender considerations—while Christian convictions are dismissed as outdated.

These patterns suggest a cultural bias. Institutions bend over backwards for Islam while constraining Christianity.

Silencing dissent

Religious freedom is also threatened when criticism of Islam is silenced. While this overlaps with free speech (to be covered in Chapter 18), here the concern is specifically with freedom of religion—the right to proclaim faith without fear of reprisal.

➤ *Church preaching:* Pastors warning against Islam sometimes face complaints to authorities. Sermons are scrutinised for *"hate speech,"* discouraging honest engagement.

➤ *Evangelism:* Christians sharing the gospel with Muslims may be accused of proselytising aggressively, even when conversations are voluntary. The fear of backlash can silence witness.

➤ *Public perception:* In media and politics, Islam is often framed as victim. Criticism is labelled intolerance, while genuine evangelism is portrayed as coercion. This distorts freedom, portraying Christian mission as threat and Islamic expansion as right.

Conversion the other way

It is worth noting a contrast. Muslims converting to Christianity face ostracism, but Christians converting to Islam are celebrated. Universities even host conversion ceremonies, councils highlight Muslim *"reverts"* as signs of diversity, and the media portray such stories positively. This imbalance reveals the underlying issue: freedom is not applied equally. One faith is free to gain adherents; the other is penalised for doing so.

The implications for Australia

The implications of these trends are serious. If religious freedom becomes uneven, national unity suffers. Citizens will no longer believe rights are equal but perceive favouritism. Once equality is lost, resentment grows, and liberty erodes for all.

Australia must ask: will it defend consistent freedom of belief, or will it allow Islamic sensitivities to dictate terms? True pluralism requires one standard, not two.

Christian reflection

For Christians, erosion of freedom is both warning and call. Warning that liberties long assumed may not endure. Call to defend not only our rights but principle of liberty for all.

Paul wrote to Galatians: *"It is for freedom that Christ has set us free. Stand firm, then, and do not let yourselves be burdened again by a yoke of slavery"* (Galatians 5:1). Though speaking of spiritual freedom, the principle applies: freedom must be guarded, lest it be lost.

The church must:

> Support converts from Islam, offering community when families reject them.
> Advocate for equal treatment of all faiths in schools, workplaces, and councils.
> Proclaim Christ boldly, refusing to be silenced by fear of offence.

Religious freedom is a gift to steward, not an assumption to take for granted.

Principles of freedom are only as strong as their practice. While Australia continues to affirm religious liberty in law, the lived reality often reveals subtle erosion.

Islam, when active in public life, frequently exerts pressure that limits Christian practice and reshapes institutions. These pressures may be legal, cultural, or social. They involve councils, schools, workplaces, and communities. Each case demonstrates how the principle of equal freedom is compromised when one faith claims privilege.

Case Study 1: Schools and education

Schools are among the most contested spaces in Australian society, for they shape future generations. Freedom of religion in schools has increasingly been tested by Islamic expectations.

➤ *Curriculum adjustments:* Reports exist of schools downplaying Christian teaching to avoid offending Muslim students. Christmas concerts are rebranded as "end-of-year celebrations," nativity plays omitted, or Easter references muted. Meanwhile, Ramadan events and Eid festivals are highlighted with enthusiasm.

➤ *Sport and swimming:* Muslim parents in some schools request exemptions for daughters from swimming lessons, dance classes, or sport carnivals due to modesty concerns. While framed as accommodation, these exclusions undermine the principle of equal participation. Girls grow up segregated, cut off from opportunities enjoyed by peers.

➤ *Prayer facilities:* Some schools provide prayer rooms specifically for Muslim students. Yet Christian students often have no equivalent support, or requests for Bible studies on campus are denied. Equality is compromised when one faith is given special provision.

➤ *Bullying and peer pressure:* Conversely, non-Muslim children sometimes feel pressured to respect Islamic practices without reciprocity. Eating ham sandwiches, celebrating Christmas, or even mentioning Jesus as Son of God can provoke accusations of *"disrespect."* Teachers, anxious to avoid offence, side with Muslim sensitivities.

These school-based pressures reveal slow but steady narrowing of Christian freedom. What was once shared celebration of national heritage becomes contested ground.

Case Study 2: Local Councils and community events

Councils, entrusted with managing local communities, often find themselves arbiters of religious freedom. Their decisions frequently privilege Islam at expense of Christianity.

➤ *Festivals:* Councils have funded Eid celebrations while reducing public emphasis on Christmas. Decorations once proudly displayed are now modest or absent, justified as "inclusive." Yet at same time, Islamic cultural festivals are promoted extensively.

➤ *Mosque approvals:* Planning applications for mosques often bypass normal scrutiny under pressure of anti-discrimination law. Residents raising concerns about traffic or noise are labelled bigoted. Meanwhile, churches applying for similar approvals face stricter requirements.

➤ *Prayers in meetings:* Some councils have removed Christian prayers from official meetings to appear neutral. Yet those same councils fund Islamic prayer facilities or permit Islamic call to prayer at community events. Neutrality is replaced by imbalance.

Such decisions reveal a trend: freedom of religion redefined as freedom for Islam but restriction for Christianity.

Case Study 3: Workplace challenges

Religious freedom must extend beyond private worship into workplaces. Here too, Islamic influence is producing a double standard.

➤ *Prayer breaks:* Employers will sometimes adjust rosters to accommodate Muslim prayer schedules. While flexibility is not wrong, the refusal to extend similar support for Christian practices — such as attending Bible study or sharing faith — creates inequality.

- ➤ *Dress codes:* Islamic headscarves are accommodated even in roles with safety concerns. Yet Christians wearing cross necklaces have been told to remove them in professional settings. Equality of expression is compromised.

- ➤ *Halal demands:* Staff catering in large organisations often defaults to halal. Employees uncomfortable with funding certification or restricted options feel pressured to comply.

- ➤ *Gender relations:* Some Muslim men resist taking instructions from female supervisors, citing religious norms. Employers, anxious to avoid discrimination claims, sometimes adjust structures rather than uphold equality.

Workplace examples demonstrate how Islam pushes institutions to bend, narrowing Christian liberty by contrast.

Case Study 4: Converts under pressure

Perhaps the most serious threat to religious freedom lies with Muslim-background Australians who embrace Christianity.

- ➤ *Social Ostracism:* Converts often lose family connections, inheritances, and community standing. In tightly knit suburbs, they are shunned entirely.

- ➤ *Threats and intimidation:* Some report harassment or even violence. Stories circulate of converts being followed, threatened online, or pressured by community leaders to return to Islam.

- ➤ *Church security:* Churches that baptise Muslim-background believers sometimes face graffiti, protests, or threats. Pastors have increased security for fear of reprisals.

- ➤ *Psychological cost:* Converts live in fear, often worshipping in secret. Though legally free, they feel trapped by cultural coercion.

In theory, Australia protects freedom to change faith. In practice, however, Islamic communities will enforce informal blasphemy codes, punishing apostasy socially and sometimes violently. This totally undermines the core principle of liberty.

Case Study 5: Public institutions

Freedom is also tested in public institutions — hospitals, prisons, universities.

➤ *Chaplaincy:* Muslim chaplains are welcomed, while Christian chaplains facing increased scrutiny. In hospitals, Islamic chaplaincy is funded to meet cultural needs, while Christian presence is reduced in secular push.

➤ *Universities:* Muslim prayer rooms are common, often built with institutional funds. Christian groups, however, must fight for access to rooms for Bible studies or worship. Universities justify provision for Muslims as inclusion but restrict Christians as proselytism.

➤ *Prisons:* Inmates often receive halal meals and Islamic chaplaincy. Christian services exist but with less institutional enthusiasm. Reports suggest radicalisation thrives under cover of religious freedom, while Christian evangelism is sometimes curtailed.

Public institutions thus reveal imbalance: Islam accommodated, Christianity restrained.

Case Study 6: Community intimidation

Freedom of religion is not only about law but about cultural climate. In some communities, Islamic dominance creates atmosphere where Christians feel silenced.

➤ *Neighbourhood pressure:* In suburbs with strong Muslim presence, Christians sometimes report harassment for visible symbols such as crosses. Street preachers face hostility, while Islamic events dominate public space.

➤ *Business pressure:* Shops unwilling to sell halal products or display Islamic symbols risk boycott. Meanwhile, Christian businesses expressing faith are targeted under anti-discrimination laws.

➤ *Public Perception:* Media portray Muslims as victims, Christians as aggressors. This narrative discourages open Christian witness, narrowing liberty indirectly.

Community intimidation reveals a chilling effect: Christians who are free in law, are constrained in practice.

The role of Anti-Discrimination laws

Many of these case studies intersect with anti-discrimination frameworks. While designed to protect minorities, these laws are often weaponised. Complaints brought against Christians for *"vilification"* are multiplying, while genuine Christian concerns are dismissed.

The result is a paradox we have mentioned many times already: laws meant to protect liberty end up restricting it, particularly when applied asymmetrically. Islam gains a shield against criticism, while Christianity loses the freedom to proclaim truth.

The erosion of equal liberty

What unites these case studies is erosion of equal liberty. Freedom no longer means one standard for all, but double standard privileging Islam.

➤ *In schools,* Christian traditions are curtailed, Islamic festivals are promoted.
➤ *In councils,* churches are restricted, mosques are encouraged.
➤ *In workplaces,* Christian expression is silenced, Islamic practice is accommodated.
➤ *In communities,* converts are threatened, critics are intimidated.

This erosion is subtle but dangerous. Liberty dies not in dramatic collapse but in quiet compromises, until freedom once assumed is gone.

Christian reflection

For Christians, these case studies highlight urgent mission. The church must support those most vulnerable—converts under threat, children excluded, believers silenced. It must advocate for equal freedom, insisting that one law and one liberty apply to all.

Jesus warned His disciples: *"If the world hates you, keep in mind that it hated me first"* (John 15:18). Persecution is not new, but it calls for faithfulness. The church must neither retreat into silence nor lash out in anger. Instead, it must proclaim truth with courage and love, defending freedom not only for itself but for all Australians.

Long-term implications and a Christian vision

The case studies considered earlier reveal specific ways in which Islam has pressured religious liberty in Australia. Yet to grasp the full weight of the issue, we must step back and consider our trajectory.

What do these patterns mean for the future of freedom in Australia? How might cultural submission to Islam reshape our liberties? And what role must the church play in defending and extending religious freedom?

The principle of equal liberty

Religious freedom in Australia has historically been grounded in principle of equal liberty. Each citizen may believe, practise, or reject faith without coercion. The state does not enforce religion but protects right of conscience. This principle has allowed diverse communities to coexist peacefully.

Islam, however, often seeks privilege rather than parity. Demands for prayer rooms, special dietary laws, or exemptions from curriculum are framed as rights but function as claims to dominance. When accommodated without reciprocity, they erode equal liberty. Freedom becomes tilted, privileging one faith at expense of others.

If this trend continues, the very definition of religious freedom will be completely distorted — from liberty for all to privilege for a select few.

The risk of cultural submission

History teaches that freedoms are rarely lost in single moment. More often, they erode gradually through cultural submission.

In Australia, submission takes the form of:

> *Self-censorship:* Christians silenced for fear of offending Muslims.

> *Institutional bias:* Schools, councils, and workplaces privileging Islamic practices while marginalising Christian ones.

> *Legal pressure:* Anti-discrimination laws weaponised to protect Islam while restricting gospel proclamation.

> *Community Intimidation*: Converts threatened, critics ostracised, churches harassed.

Each concession seems minor by itself. But together, they create a culture where Christians hesitate to speak, institutions bend to Islamic norms, and society forgets its heritage. This is slow-motion submission—cultural capitulation to ideology hostile to freedom.

Generational consequences

The consequences will not be felt only today but in generations to come. Children growing up in schools where Christmas is silenced and Eid is celebrated will inherit distorted view of liberty. Young people taught that criticism of Islam is forbidden but mockery of Christianity is permitted will assume inequality is normal.

Over decades, such patterns produce cultural shift. Liberty once rooted in Christian soil is replaced by relativism, where some beliefs are privileged and others suppressed. This trajectory points not to pluralism but to fragmentation.

Lessons from overseas

Europe provides sobering lessons. In Britain, Sharia councils emerged under guise of religious freedom, yet in practice denied women rights available under national law. In France, attempts to accommodate Islamic sensitivities eroded secular freedoms, producing parallel societies. In Sweden, tolerance of Islamic demands bred no-go zones where liberty is absent.

These nations once assumed Islam could coexist peacefully under framework of freedom. Instead, they discovered that Islam, when empowered, reshapes freedom into submission. Australia risks same outcome if it fails to learn.

Long-term implications for Australia

As we have noted in this study already, if unchecked, Islamic influence could reshape religious freedom in several ways:

1. *Restricted evangelism:* Christians may find it increasingly difficult to share faith with Muslims, facing accusations of hate speech or harassment.
2. *Diluted Christian heritage:* Public institutions may continue erasing Christian symbols while promoting Islamic ones, distorting balance of freedom.
3. *Threatened converts:* Muslim-background Christians may live permanently in fear, their legal freedom nullified by social coercion.
4. *Judicial drift:* Courts may interpret anti-discrimination law in ways that privilege Islamic sensitivities, restricting Christian proclamation.
5. *Cultural Silence:* Citizens may internalise self-censorship, avoiding discussion of Islam altogether.

These outcomes would represent not only erosion of freedom but betrayal of heritage.

The Christian vision for defending liberty

How then should Christians respond? Not with despair or hostility, but with clear vision rooted in gospel.

1. Proclaim Christ boldly

Freedom is not preserved by silence but by truth spoken in love. The church must resist intimidation, proclaiming Jesus as Lord openly. As Acts 4:20 records Peter and John saying: *"As for us, we cannot help speaking about what we have seen and heard."*

2. Support vulnerable converts

Muslim-background Christians need practical care—housing, legal aid, fellowship, and discipleship. The church must be family for those abandoned by their own. By protecting converts, believers embody gospel's promise of new community.

3. Advocate for equal liberty

Christians must engage politically to defend one standard for all. Freedom must mean equal treatment, not privilege for Islam. This requires courage to challenge councils, schools, and workplaces when bias emerges.

4. Expose double standards

Wherever institutions silence Christian expression but promote Islamic practices, the church must highlight hypocrisy. Public accountability can restrain drift.

5. Pray and intercede

Ultimately, battle for freedom is spiritual. The church must intercede for leaders, institutions, and Muslim neighbours. In 1 Timothy 2:2 Paul urged Timothy to pray *"for kings and all those in authority, that we may live peaceful and quiet lives in all godliness and holiness."* Prayer is not an escape – it's a weapon.

6. Engage Muslims with love

Defending freedom does not mean hating Muslims. Believers must love neighbours, sharing Christ with compassion. The goal is not only liberty preserved but souls saved.

Theological foundation

Christian defence of freedom rests not on nationalism but theology. Human liberty flows from truth that every person is made in God's image. To deny freedom of conscience is to deny God's design. Islam, by subordinating rights to Sharia, undermines this truth. The church, by contrast, proclaims it. Thus, defending liberty is not political preference but gospel imperative. To protect our freedom is to honour God's image in humanity.

Hope for the future

Though challenges are real, hope remains. History shows God often advances gospel in times of opposition. Early church thrived under Rome's hostility. Modern believers may likewise flourish in adversity. If freedom erodes, church must still witness boldly. Yet prayer and action may preserve liberty, enabling mission.

Revelation 12:11 describes victory of saints: *"They triumphed over him by the blood of the Lamb and by the word of their testimony; they did not love their lives so much as to shrink from death."* The ultimate freedom is not political but eternal. Yet defending earthly liberty serves eternal mission.

Conclusion

Religious freedom in Australia stands at a crossroads. Islam's presence, though comparatively small in numbers, exerts a disproportionate amount of pressure. Schools adjust curricula, councils privilege Islamic festivals, workplaces silence Christian expression, and converts live in fear. Law still affirms freedom, but practice often denies it.

The long-term implications are serious. If unchecked, liberty will erode, heritage will fade, and submission will replace freedom. Yet Christians are not called to despair but to vision. The church must proclaim Christ boldly, support new converts, advocate politically, expose double standards, and engage Muslims with the love of Christ.

For freedom is gift from God, to be defended not only for our sake but for nation's sake. As Galatians 5:1 reminds us: *"It is for freedom that Christ has set us free. Stand firm, then, and do not let yourselves be burdened again by a yoke of slavery."*

Australia must stand firm. The church must rise. And together, with truth and love, we must defend liberty before it is lost.

19. ISLAM AND FREEDOM OF SPEECH

The shrinking space for open debate

Freedom of speech is one of the foundations of our democratic society. It allows truth to be tested, ideas to be refined, and power to be held accountable. Without it, democracy collapses into tyranny. Australia has historically valued this free expression, though never with the absolutism of the United States. Yet in recent decades, this freedom has been placed under increasing pressure. Islam plays a central role in this shift. Where Islam is given influence, calls to restrict speech will follow. Criticism of Islamic belief or practice is labelled 'Islamophobia.' Satire and art that mock Christianity are permitted, but similar treatment of Islam is silenced.

Universities, councils, and media self-censor to avoid offence. Over time, the cumulative effect is chilling: a society where one ideology is now insulated from critique while others remain fair game. We cannot ignore the facts any longer, how freedom of speech in Australia is now shrinking under Islamic pressure. We must see how blasphemy laws are now being reintroduced by stealth, undermining equal liberty.

The charge of 'Islamophobia'

The most common tool for silencing criticism is accusation of Islamophobia.

➢ *Expansive definition:* Originally coined to describe irrational hatred of Muslims, the term has expanded to cover any critique of Islamic doctrine, culture, or politics.
Pointing out treatment of women under Sharia, highlighting radicalisation risks, or questioning halal certification can all be branded Islamophobic.

➢ *Weaponisation:* Islamic organisations, activist groups, and some politicians use the label strategically. By equating criticism of Islam with racism, they place opponents beyond the bounds of civil debate. Accused individuals are then forced to defend character rather than arguments.

> *Cultural Impact:* Fear of being branded Islamophobic silences discussion. Citizens self-censor, institutions avoid sensitive topics, and public discourse narrows. The chilling effect is real: many prefer silence to reputational ruin.

The accusation of Islamophobia thus functions as a new cultural blasphemy law, punishing dissent from orthodoxy.

Legal threats and discrimination law

While Australia lacks such a blasphemy law, anti-discrimination frameworks often serve a similar purpose.

> *State laws:* Victoria's Racial and Religious Tolerance Act (2001) prohibits vilification on grounds of religion. In practice, Muslim groups have used this law to challenge critics.

> *Notable case:* Pastor Danny Nalliah and Daniel Scot were taken to the tribunal after a seminar in which they criticised Islam. Though eventually cleared, they endured years of litigation and significant costs. The process itself punished them, silencing many other Christian voices.

> *Human Rights Commissions:* Complaints to commissions, even if dismissed, impose a burden of defence. Critics of Islam find themselves dragged into bureaucratic proceedings, often intimidated into silence.

These legal tools function less as protection against hatred than as weapons to shield Islam from scrutiny.

Universities and academic freedom

Campuses, once bastions of free inquiry, increasingly enforce speech codes.

> *Cancelled speakers:* Academics or guests critical of Islam are often de-platformed after pressure from student groups. Universities justify cancellations on the grounds of safety, but the effect is suppression of dissent.

> *Curriculum bias:* Courses highlight Islam as the victim of Western prejudice while avoiding examination of its doctrines. Scholars critical of Islam struggle to secure funding or publication.

➤ *Muslim Student Associations* – These groups lobby aggressively against criticism, framing it as hate. Their influence amplifies the climate of self-censorship.

Academic freedom will always erode when ideology is shielded from critique.

Media and cultural intimidation

The media plays a decisive role in shaping debate. Yet coverage of Islam is often skewed.

➤ *Selective reporting:* Crimes involving Muslims are downplayed, details omitted. Headlines avoid naming Islam even when the ideology is central. By contrast, misconduct involving Christians is highlighted.

➤ *Fear of backlash:* Journalists admit reluctance to criticise Islam, fearing lawsuits, boycotts, or threats. Editors pre-emptively silence stories.

➤ *Double standards:* Satire of Christianity, even mocking Jesus, is routine. Satire of Muhammad is unthinkable, after violent reactions globally. Australian media has internalised fear, practising self-censorship without the need of law.

The result is a distorted public discourse where truth is hidden, and citizens are seriously misled.

Artistic and cultural expression

Art has long tested the boundaries of free speech. Yet when Islam is the subject, those boundaries contract significantly.

➤ *Exhibitions:* Galleries avoid works critical of Islam, citing security risks. By contrast, works mocking Christianity are exhibited freely.

➤ *Comedy:* Comedians skewer all religions but tiptoe around Islam. Fear of backlash has created a taboo zone.

➤ *Publishing:* Writers and publishers avoid topics involving Islam critically. Manuscripts exploring sensitive issues struggle to find outlets. I am about to find out how much!

The cultural sphere, once a defender of free expression, has now capitulated to intimidation.

The return of blasphemy by stealth

Together, these various dynamics amount to reintroduction of blasphemy laws by stealth. Though no statute declares it illegal to insult Islam, cultural and legal pressures achieve that effect.

> - Offend Islam, and risk fronting a tribunal.
> - Mock Muhammad, and risk serious backlash.
> - Criticise Sharia, and risk your career.

This asymmetry corrodes our free speech. Christianity, secular ideologies, and politics may be mocked freely, but Islam enjoys a shield. The public square has become unequal.

The consequences for democracy

When speech is curtailed, democracy weakens. Citizens cannot debate policy honestly, institutions avoid accountability, and culture drifts into fear. The very issue which is most urgent—Islam's compatibility with Australia—becomes undiscussable. Silence always benefits ideology that seeks dominance.
Unchecked, this whole dynamic will breed resentment. Citizens sense censorship, lose trust in institutions, and turn to extremes. Polarisation grows, weakening our whole social fabric.

Christian reflection

For Christians, erosion of free speech is not abstract but personal. The gospel itself depends on the freedom to proclaim. If speech about Islam is silenced, speech about Christ will be next.

Paul warned us in 2 Corinthians 4:13: *"It is written: 'I believed; therefore, I have spoken.' Since we have that same spirit of faith, we also believe and therefore speak."* Silence is not an option for church.

Christians must therefore defend free speech not only for themselves but for all. Liberty to speak truth is a gift from God, and stewardship demands courage.

Case studies in censorship and suppression

Principles matter little unless tested in practice. The right to free speech is only proven when those unpopular, offensive, or controversial words are tolerated. It is easy to permit speech that flatters; the challenge comes when speech criticises, exposes, or mocks. In Australia, Islam has become a defining test of whether free expression truly endures.

Across legal systems, universities, media, and culture, patterns emerge: when Islam is the subject, restrictions intensify. Critics face lawsuits, students lose platforms, artists are silenced, and citizens are intimidated. The following case studies reveal how deeply speech has been constrained, often without formal law but through fear, pressure, and cultural submission.

Case Study 1: The Nalliah and Scot Tribunal

Perhaps the most famous example is the case of Pastor Danny Nalliah and Daniel Scot in Victoria. In 2002, they held a seminar critiquing Islamic teaching, drawing on the Quran and Hadith. Several Muslims attended and complained under Victoria's new Racial and Religious Tolerance Act.

➢ *The Tribunal process:* Both pastors were found guilty of vilification, ordered to publish an apology. They appealed, launching a years-long legal battle. Ultimately, their conviction was overturned, but not before immense costs in time, money, and stress.

➢ *The effect:* Though acquitted, they were punished by process. For many pastors, the lesson was clear: avoid criticising Islam publicly. The chilling effect extended beyond Victoria, warning Christians across Australia.

This case illustrates how legal frameworks, even if ultimately defeated, function as blasphemy codes by intimidation.

Case Study 2: Mosque opposition silenced

In various suburbs, residents opposing mosque construction have faced suppression.

- ➤ *Legitimate concerns:* Objections often related to traffic, parking, or noise—normal planning issues. Yet opposition was framed as Islamophobic.

- ➤ *Council responses:* Some councils, fearing accusations of discrimination, pushed approvals through despite resident concerns. Objectors were portrayed as bigots rather than citizens exercising their democratic rights.

- ➤ *Community backlash:* In some cases, residents endured harassment, threats, or media vilification. Ordinary Australians found themselves branded extremists simply for engaging in the normal planning process.

This silencing of community voices demonstrates how freedom to speak on civic issues is curtailed when Islam is involved.

Case Study 3: Universities and de-platforming

Universities, once proud of free inquiry, increasingly restrict debate around Islam.

- ➤ *Cancelled lectures:* Academic conferences considering critique of Islam have been cancelled under pressure from student associations. Speakers raising questions about Sharia or women's rights were deemed unsafe.

- ➤ *Student Associations:* Muslim student groups often pressure administrations to block speakers, labelling them Islamophobic. Universities, anxious about their reputation and the inevitable protests, find it easier to just comply.

- ➤ *Double standards:* By contrast, events mocking Christianity proceed unhindered. Plays ridiculing Jesus or art depicting Christian symbols offensively are defended as free speech. Islam alone is untouchable.

Students graduate unexposed to serious critique, taught that some ideas must never be questioned.

Case Study 4: Artistic self-censorship

Artistic freedom has also contracted significantly in recent times.

➤ *Exhibitions cancelled:* Several galleries declined to show works satirising Islam, citing security concerns. Insurance costs rose, staff feared violence. The lesson for artists: avoid Islam.

➤ *Comedy restrictions:* Comedians, known for lampooning every subject, tread carefully around Muhammad or Islamic practices. Some admit they "don't want a fatwa on their head." Christianity is mocked relentlessly, but Islam remains taboo.

➤ *Publishing fear:* Writers report publishers reluctant to touch manuscripts critical of Islam. The risk of controversy outweighs commitment to expression. Authors self-censor to secure contracts.

Censorship here is not imposed by government but by fear of reprisal. Yet effect is same: Islam shielded from critique.

Case Study 5: Social media intimidation

Digital platforms amplify pressure.

➤ *Coordinated backlash:* – Individuals criticising Islam online often face floods of abuse, threats, and calls for dismissal. Employers, anxious about reputation, sometimes terminate staff.

➤ *Policy bias:* Social media companies remove posts critical of Islam under hate-speech policies, while posts mocking Christianity remain. Algorithms amplify the imbalance.

➤ *Personal risk:* Some users report harassment spilling offline, with families targeted. The cost of speaking out outweighs any perceived benefit.

This digital intimidation silences many voices.

Case Study 6: Media and selective silence

Mainstream media, too, contributes to suppression.

➤ *Avoiding Islam:* When crimes involve Muslims, headlines omit religion. Reports speak of "men" or "youths" without context. By contrast, when perpetrator linked to Christianity, headlines highlight it.

➤ *Fear of lawsuits:* Journalists admit reluctance to name Islamic ideology as factor in extremism, fearing defamation or discrimination claims.

➤ *Taboo in satire:* Programs known for biting humour avoid mocking Islam, while lampooning Christianity every week.

Media thus normalises a double standard, insulating Islam from any real critique.

Case Study 7: The "Respectful Dialogue" illusion

Interfaith events often illustrate subtle suppression.

➤ *Conditions imposed:* Churches invited to interfaith panels are instructed not to claim exclusivity of Christ. Gospel is silenced to maintain social harmony.

➤ *Islamic advantage:* Muslim representatives speak openly of their faith, while Christians self-censor.

➤ *Public narrative:* Media coverage portrays harmony, yet beneath lies coerced silence.

While framed as tolerance, these events erode genuine freedom. Dialogue without truth is propaganda.

Patterns across the cases

These examples, while varied, reveal consistent themes:

1. *Legal intimidation:* Tribunals and commissions punish any critics.
2. *Institutional capitulation:* Universities, councils, and workplaces prioritise Islamic sensitivities.
3. *Cultural fear:* Artists, comedians, and writers self-censor.
4. *Media bias:* Journalists sanitise coverage.
5. *Community pressure:* Citizens face harassment.

Together, they demonstrate a creeping blasphemy code enforced not by statute but by intimidation.

The danger of selective freedom

When freedom applies unequally, it ceases to be freedom. A society that allows mockery of Christianity but forbids critique of Islam has abandoned the principle of free speech. Instead of one law for all, there are privileged zones. This selective freedom erodes democracy. Citizens no longer trust institutions to treat them fairly. Resentment festers, polarisation grows, and liberty diminishes.

Christian reflection

For Christians, this erosion is serious. The gospel depends on freedom to speak. If Islam is insulated from critique, Christianity will soon follow. Already, preaching on controversial topics risks censure. Yet Christians must resist the urge to retreat. Paul urged Timothy: *"Preach the word; be prepared in season and out of season; correct, rebuke and encourage – with great patience and careful instruction."* (2 Timothy 4:2). This clear call is not conditional on cultural approval. Churches must:

➤ Train believers to articulate truth with wisdom and courage.

➤ Support those targeted for speaking against Islam.

➤ Advocate for equal freedom in law and practice.

Speech is a fragile gift. Once surrendered, it is so hard to regain. Free speech is not lost all at once but eroded gradually, through laws, cultural pressures, and fear. Australia is experiencing this erosion right now. Though we are still formally free, the space for debate has narrowed significantly.

Islam, with its demands for protection from offence, accelerates this trend. If left unchecked, Australia risks entering an age of silence, where citizens speak cautiously, truth is muted, and the public square loses its power.

The principle of speech as foundation

Speech is not a luxury but the foundation of democracy. Without the ability to question, expose, and persuade, citizens become subjects, not participants. Truth itself depends on open debate. Suppression of speech is suppression of truth.

Islam's push for censorship strikes at this foundation. By framing critique as Islamophobia, by silencing satire, by intimidating artists and citizens, it undermines the very mechanism by which societies test ideas. Once speech is controlled, truth is lost.

The long-term risks

If current trends persist, Australia faces several risks:

1. *Informal blasphemy laws:* Though no statute forbids criticism of Islam, cultural and legal intimidation creates this effect. Citizens fear the consequences of speaking, effectively reinstating blasphemy law.
2. *Hollow democracy:* Without robust debate, elections become shallow. Policies relating to Islam — immigration, integration, security — cannot be discussed honestly. Voters make choices in ignorance.
3. *Cultural submission:* Citizens internalise silence, censoring themselves without a need of external force. Culture drifts into submission, accepting limits on speech as normal.
4. *Radicalisation of opposition:* When mainstream debate is silenced, frustration drives citizens to extremes. Far-right movements gain traction, polarisation deepens, and violence increases.
5. *Weakening of Christian witness:* If gospel proclamation is curtailed under a charge of hate speech, the church loses the freedom to evangelise. Once silenced, mission suffers.

These risks reveal a worrying trajectory not of pluralism but of authoritarianism.

The cost of silence

Silence may seem safe, but it carries a serious cost.

➤ *Truth suppressed:* Citizens cannot discuss dangers of Sharia, radicalisation, or cultural incompatibility. Problems fester unaddressed.
➤ *Justice denied:* Victims of intimidation, women restricted by Islamic norms, or converts threatened cannot speak. Their stories remain hidden.

> *Faith constrained:* Christians, fearful of offence, dilute the gospel. Evangelism weakens.

The cost of silence is not peace but decay. Freedom withers when truth is unspoken.

The Christian imperative to speak

For Christians, speech is not optional but essential. The gospel itself is message spoken aloud. Romans 10:14 asks: *"How, then, can they call on the one they have not believed in? And how can they believe in the one of whom they have not heard? And how can they hear without someone preaching to them?"* Without speech, salvation cannot be proclaimed. Thus, defence of free expression is not merely political but spiritual. To silence Christians is to silence gospel. Church must therefore champion liberty of speech for all, knowing it safeguards mission.

How Christians must respond

1. *Speak with courage:* Fear tempts silence. Yet believers must resist. Like Peter before the Sanhedrin, we say: *"We must obey God rather than human beings!"* (Acts 5:29). When told not to speak of Christ, the apostles spoke more boldly. Christians today must do same, even if accused of intolerance.

2. *Defend equal freedom:* Christians must advocate one law for all. If Islam is shielded, then the gospel will be a target. Equal freedom ensures truth may be proclaimed without fear.

3. *Expose double standards:* Whenever institutions silence critique of Islam but permit mockery of Christianity, hypocrisy must be exposed. Public accountability can restrain the drift.

4. *Train believers in apologetics:* Courage always requires preparation. Churches must equip members to answer Islamic objections with clarity and grace, able to withstand charges of hate with truth in love.

5. *Support those who are targeted:* When individuals are punished for speaking, the church must rally in support — financially, legally, spiritually. Solidarity strengthens courage.

6. *Engage culture with love:* Defending free speech does not mean hatred of Muslims. Christians must model both truth and love, speaking boldly while serving practically. Free speech is not a licence to insult but the responsibility to proclaim truth with grace.

The spiritual dimension

Suppression of free speech is not merely cultural but spiritual. Scripture describes Satan as the father of lies (John 8:44). Lies flourish when truth is silenced. Suppression of free speech thus serves the enemy's strategy: prevent gospel from being heard. The battle for free expression is therefore part of a larger spiritual war. Christians contend not only for political liberty but for souls. When the gospel is muted, eternity is at stake.

Hope beyond suppression

Even if freedoms erode, the church is never defeated. History shows the gospel thrives in persecution. Underground churches in China, Iran, and North Korea testify to resilience of the Word. If speech is curtailed, God is still at work. Yet while it's possible to endure suppression, it is better to preserve liberty. Freedom amplifies mission, persecution constrains it.

Therefore, believers should both prepare for hardship and work really hard to protect our freedom.

A Christian vision for the public square

The goal is not endless polemics but a redeemed public square where truth may be spoken freely. Christians should envision an Australia where:

➤ Citizens debate Islam without fear of reprisal.

➤ Converts share testimonies openly.

➤ Artists create without intimidation.

➤ Politicians speak honestly about integration.

➤ Churches proclaim Christ boldly in streets and halls.

This vision is not of utopia, but an expression of liberty rooted in biblical truth.

Conclusion

Freedom of speech in Australia is shrinking at an alarming rate. Accusations of Islamophobia, legal intimidation, media bias, de-platforming, artistic censorship, and community harassment all combine to reintroduce blasphemy laws by stealth.

Islam, always demanding insulation from critique, undermines the principle of equal freedom. If unchecked, this trajectory will lead to silence, submission, and hollow democracy. Australia risks repeating Europe's mistakes, where fear stifles truth.

For Christians, the stakes are much higher still. The gospel itself depends on the freedom to speak. To lose freedom of speech is to lose the ground for mission. The church must therefore defend truth boldly, support those targeted, expose double standards, and proclaim Christ regardless of the cost.

As Jesus said in John 8:32: *Then you will know the truth, and the truth will set you free.* Truth liberates — but only if can be spoken. Silence will always enslave. May Australia choose courage over fear, truth over silence, freedom over submission. And may the church rise as a voice of clarity in an age of growing compromise, defending liberty not only for itself but for all.

20. ISLAM AND THE QUESTION OF SECURITY

Terrorism, radicalisation, and Australia's security

Security is the most immediate and visible arena where Islam collides with Western nations. While debates over law, culture, and rights usually unfold gradually, security threats strike suddenly, claiming lives and destabilising societies. Australia, though distant from the Middle East, is not immune. The rise of Islamist terrorism, radicalisation of our youth, and pressure on intelligence services have made Islam and security an urgent national question.

Terrorism as an Islamic strategy

Modern terrorism did not emerge in a vacuum. It draws on ideological roots within Islam. While not all Muslims embrace violence, radical Islamists interpret the Qur'an and Hadith as mandates for jihad. Passages that command fighting against unbelievers (Qur'an 9:29) or promise paradise to all martyrs (Qur'an 9:111) inspire extremists. Groups like al-Qaeda, Islamic State (ISIS), Boko Haram, and al-Shabaab explicitly frame their campaigns as religious. Their aim is not just random chaos but the establishment of Sharia and the restoration of the caliphate. Terrorism becomes both a tactic and theology.

For Western nations, this creates a unique challenge. Unlike separatist movements, Islamist terrorism is not confined to any borders. It is now global, motivated by ideology that transcends nations. For Australia, this means threats can originate abroad yet manifest at home.

Australia and the global Jihadist threat

Australia has long been a target of Islamist networks. Though geographically distant, its Western identity, military alliances, and democratic values place it in jihadist crosshairs.

1. *Bali bombings (2002, 2005):* While occurring in Indonesia, these attacks killed over 200 people, including 88 Australians. They revealed that Australians were seen as legitimate targets simply for being Western and allied with the U.S.A.

2. *Sydney siege (2014):* Man Haron Monis, a self-styled Islamist, took hostages in the Lindt Café. Though a "lone actor," his ideology drew directly from jihadist propaganda. Two Australians were killed.

3. *Foreign fighters (2012–2017):* Over 200 Australians travelled to Syria and Iraq to join ISIS. Some died in combat, others returned radicalised, creating ongoing security risks.

4. *Foiled plots:* Authorities have disrupted numerous planned attacks, including attempts to bomb flights, attack police stations, and stage mass-casualty events.

These incidents prove that Islamist terrorism is not theoretical for Australia. It is an active, ongoing security threat.

Radicalisation of our youth

A key security concern is radicalisation, particularly of young Muslims born in Australia. Second-generation migrants often feel caught between cultures, experiencing alienation from mainstream society while facing pressure from Islamic identity. Radicalisation occurs through several channels:

➤ *Mosques and preachers:* Though most imams in Australia denounce violence, a minority preach radical doctrines. Even when violence is not explicitly endorsed, messages of Muslim victimhood and superiority lay groundwork for extremism.

➤ *Prisons:* Jihadist ideology spreads in prisons, where disaffected youth are recruited by charismatic radicals.

➤ *Online propaganda:* ISIS perfected online recruitment, using slick videos and social media to lure recruits. Even in suburban Sydney or Melbourne, youth encounter radical content on smartphones.

➤ *Peer networks:* Radicalised individuals often influence friends, creating clusters of extremists.

Case studies illustrate this danger. The 15-year-old who shot police accountant Curtis Cheng in Sydney (2015) was radicalised through a local network. Other teenagers have been arrested for plotting attacks inspired by online propaganda.

Radicalisation shows that Islamist terrorism is not just imported but grows domestically when ideology meets alienation.

Lone actors and organised networks

Terrorism in Australia has manifested in two main forms: lone actors and organised networks.

1. *Lone actors:* Individuals inspired by Islamist propaganda act independently, often with minimal planning. The Sydney Siege, the Curtis Cheng murder, and stabbings in Melbourne illustrate this model. These attacks are difficult to predict, as they require little coordination.

2. *Organised networks:* Other plots involve groups with links to overseas organisations. The 2017 plot to bomb an Etihad Airways flight, foiled in Sydney, was coordinated with ISIS operatives abroad. Such networks pose greater potential for mass casualties.

Both forms challenge our security agencies. Lone actors evade detection; organised networks require international intelligence cooperation. Australia must be prepared for both.

Intelligence and counterterrorism

Australia's intelligence agencies—ASIO (Australian Security Intelligence Organisation), AFP (Australian Federal Police), and state police counterterrorism units—have devoted increasing resources to Islamist threats. Key strategies include:

➤ *Surveillance:* Monitoring communications, travel, and associations of suspected extremists.

➤ *Community Engagement:* Working with Muslim communities to identify risks, though this is often met with suspicion.

➤ *Border control:* Preventing foreign fighters from leaving or re-entering.

➤ *Legislation:* Expanding powers for detention, control orders, and passport cancellation.

Australia has had some notable successes, disrupting dozens of planned attacks. Yet challenges remain. Radicalisation can occur quickly, making detection difficult. Encrypted communication hinders monitoring. Civil liberty debates complicate legislation.

Prisons as incubators

Prisons are a growing concern. Radical preachers recruit among inmates, particularly those already disaffected or angry at society. Extremists present Islam as a source of identity and power. Several convicted terrorists in Australia have radicalised others behind bars.

Upon release, they pose ongoing threats. Authorities struggle to manage this cycle, balancing rehabilitation with public safety. Some nations use isolation units for extremists; others attempt deradicalisation programs. Success is mixed. The persistence of ideology makes eradication difficult.

Foreign fighters and returning Jihadists

The Syrian civil war and rise of ISIS created unprecedented flow of foreign fighters. Over 200 Australians travelled to the conflict zone. Some died, others sought to return.

Returning fighters pose unique challenges:

➤ *Combat experience:* They possess training in weapons and tactics.

➤ *Radical networks:* They maintain global jihadist contacts.

➤ *Propaganda roles:* Some seek to inspire others through testimony.

Australia has responded by cancelling passports, prosecuting returnees, and stripping citizenship in extreme cases. Yet the problem persists, especially with women and children seeking repatriation from Syrian camps.

Balancing security with humanitarian concerns is fraught with problems and each side carries its own critics and lobby groups.

Cyber Jihad

The internet has transformed jihad. Groups like ISIS recruit globally through encrypted apps, social media, and videos. Australians have been radicalised entirely online, with little physical contact. Cyber jihad also enables coordination of plots, fundraising, and dissemination of bomb-making instructions. Intelligence agencies face immense challenge in monitoring this domain, especially as technology evolves faster than regulation. Australia, like many other nations, must invest heavily in cyber capabilities. The battle for security is increasingly digital.

Community dynamics and security

Muslim communities in Australia are diverse, yet radicalisation thrives in certain contexts:

➤ *Enclaves* – Concentrated suburbs create echo chambers where radical ideas circulate unchecked.

➤ *Victim narratives* – Some leaders emphasise Muslim victimhood, fostering grievance that extremists exploit.

➤ *Distrust of authorities* – Perceived discrimination discourages cooperation with police, allowing radicals to hide.

Community engagement is absolutely essential, but it is also complicated. Authorities need to work with moderate Muslims while remaining clear-eyed about the deep ideological roots of extremism.

Lessons from abroad

Australia can learn from Europe's failures and America's struggles. Failure to integrate Muslim communities in France created alienated suburbs, fertile ground for jihadists. Repeated terrorist attacks show the cost of neglect. Decades of tolerance for radical preachers in Britain allowed extremist networks to flourish. Attacks in London and Manchester only highlight this risk. Though less affected, cases like the Boston Marathon bombing in the U.S. reveal vulnerability even when borders are strong. The lesson is clear: once radicalisation takes root, it is difficult to uproot. Prevention is key.

Australia's distinct vulnerabilities

While smaller in scale, Australia faces unique vulnerabilities:

➤ *Geographic isolation:* This reduces inflow but creates complacency.

➤ *Small Muslim population:* Easier to monitor, but still significant in urban centres.

➤ *Alliance with the U.S:* Our relationship with America makes Australia a symbolic target for jihadists.

➤ *Prison radicalisation:* A growing concern, as small networks can have outsized impact.

➤ *Online exposure:* Australian youth are just as susceptible to online jihadist propaganda as Europeans.

These vulnerabilities demand vigilance from us. Complacency is the enemy of security.

Christian reflection

For Christians, the security challenge is sobering. It reminds us that ideology always has consequences. Belief shapes behaviour, sometimes violently. Islam's doctrines of jihad inspire terrorism, while the gospel inspires peace.

Jesus said, *"Blessed are the peacemakers, for they will be called children of God"* (Matthew 5:9). Christians are called to embody peace even while acknowledging threats. They must pray for authorities (1 Timothy 2:1–2), support efforts to preserve safety, and proclaim the Prince of Peace. At the same time, Christians must resist fear. Terrorism aims to spread fear disproportionate to its actual power. The church must respond with courage, grounded in Christ's promise: *"In this world you will have trouble. But take heart! I have overcome the world"* (John 16:33).

Organised networks, financing, and counterterrorism

If radicalised individuals pose immediate danger through lone-wolf attacks, organised Islamist networks represent a more sustained and strategic challenge.

These networks provide the infrastructure for radicalisation, financing, propaganda, and coordination. They link the local extremists with global jihadist movements, turning isolated threats into systemic security crises. Understanding these networks, their funding, and Australia's counterterrorism response is essential for assessing the true scale of the challenge.

The nature of Islamist networks

Islamist networks are not random clusters of radicals. They are structured organisations with hierarchy, ideology, and strategy. Some are transnational movements; others are domestic groups aligned with broader causes. Key characteristics include:

➤ *Ideological cohesion*: Networks are bound by radical Islamist ideology, usually Salafi-jihadism.

➤ *Global connectivity:* Even small local groups maintain ties to larger movements (al-Qaeda, ISIS).

➤ *Operational flexibility:* Networks adapt quickly, shifting from large-scale plots to smaller, harder-to-detect operations.

➤ *Community roots:* Networks often grow in enclaves, drawing recruits from mosques, cultural centres, or prisons.

For Australia, these networks are very concerning because they enable relatively small communities to punch above their weight in terms of threat.

Al-Qaeda and ISIS: The global blueprint

These two organisations define global jihad.

➤ *Al-Qaeda:* pioneered spectacular terrorism (9/11), demonstrating how small groups can inflict global shock. Though weakened, it persists in affiliates across Africa and Asia.

➤ *ISIS:* innovated differently. It established a territorial caliphate, drawing tens of thousands of foreign fighters. Its propaganda machine surpassed anything seen before, radicalising youth worldwide, including in Australia.

Even after territorial defeat, ISIS remains potent. Its ideology persists online, and its affiliates thrive in Africa and Southeast Asia. For Australia, ISIS is particularly relevant due to its presence in the Philippines, within striking distance of northern Australia.

Domestic networks in Australia

Within Australia, organised Islamist activity has emerged periodically. While large-scale groups are rare, several networks have been uncovered:

1. *Operation Pendennis (2005):* Authorities disrupted two jihadist cells in Melbourne and Sydney plotting mass-casualty attacks. The groups were inspired by al-Qaeda ideology and sought to wage jihad domestically.
2. *ISIS sympathisers (2014–2017):* Small networks in Sydney and Melbourne recruited fighters, raised funds, and plotted attacks. Several members travelled to Syria; others were arrested at home.
3. *Prison-based networks:* Radical inmates form groups behind bars, spreading ideology and planning future activity.

These networks demonstrate that Islamist infrastructure can form even in a nation with a relatively small Muslim population.

Financing terrorism

Networks require funding. Financing sustains propaganda, recruitment, and operations. Sources include:

➤ *Charities and NGOs:* Some Islamic charities, while legitimate on the surface, divert funds to extremist causes. Investigations have revealed misuse of aid channels for jihadist financing.
➤ *Community donations:* Radical preachers solicit support from sympathetic followers, often disguised as humanitarian appeals.
➤ *Criminal activity:* Fraud, drug trafficking, and petty crime sometimes provide funds for operations.

- ➤ *Foreign funding:* Wealthy donors from the Middle East, particularly from Gulf States, have historically funded radical groups. Mosques and Islamic schools in Australia sometimes receive money from abroad, raising concerns about ideological influence.

While Australia has strict anti-terror financing laws, policing the flow of finance across borders remains difficult. The risk of covert funding persists.

The role of Mosques and community organisations

Most mosques in Australia do not promote violence. However, some will serve as hubs for radicalisation, particularly when leadership aligns with Salafi or Islamist ideology. Radical literature circulates, visiting preachers stir resentment, and young men are recruited.

Community organisations will sometimes act as fronts. Cultural centres will often promote victimhood narratives, reinforcing alienation. Charities may funnel funds overseas. Authorities face a dilemma: how to distinguish between legitimate religious activity and covert extremist networks. Excessive scrutiny risks alienating communities; insufficient scrutiny allows threats to grow.

Prisons as strategic nodes

Prisons are not only incubators of radicalisation (as noted above) but also nodes of organised networks. Charismatic extremists recruit systematically, forming mini-networks behind bars. Upon release, these individuals often reconnect with broader groups.

Australia has witnessed several such cases, where prisoners radicalised inside later plotted attacks. Authorities debate whether to isolate extremists or disperse them, balancing security with rehabilitation. Both strategies carry risks.

Internationally, prisons in France, Britain, and Indonesia have shown how Islamist networks thrive when unchecked. Australia must learn from these lessons.

Recruitment pathways

Networks always recruit systematically, targeting vulnerable individuals. Key methods include:

> *Identity crisis:* Second-generation migrants searching for belonging.

> *Victim narratives:* Propaganda emphasising Muslim suffering globally, creating moral outrage.

> *Adventure and purpose:* Jihad framed as heroic quest, appealing to restless youth.

> *Online grooming:* Recruiters build personal relationships over months, drawing individuals into networks.

These pathways reveal that radicalisation is not just random but cultivated. Networks know their targets and they always exploit vulnerabilities.

International intelligence cooperation

Because networks are global, intelligence cooperation is vital. Australia partners with the *"Five Eyes"* alliance (U.S., UK, Canada, New Zealand) for surveillance and intelligence sharing. Cooperation extends to Southeast Asia, particularly Indonesia, Malaysia, and the Philippines.

Examples:

> *Jemaah Islamiyah (JI):* This Indonesian group responsible for Bali bombings had links to al-Qaeda. Cooperation between Indonesian and Australian agencies has weakened JI but not eliminated it.

> *ISIS in the Philippines:* Australia provides training and support to Philippine forces combating ISIS affiliates in Mindanao. This is crucial, as the Philippines is a regional base for jihad.

Such cooperation will enhance security, but it also highlights vulnerability: Australia cannot act alone. Islamist networks are transnational, requiring constant vigilance.

Counterterrorism legislation

In response to Islamist threats, Australia has enacted extensive counterterrorism laws:

➤ *Control orders:* Restrict movement, communication, or internet use of suspected extremists.

➤ *Preventive detention:* Allows holding of individuals suspected of imminent terrorist activity.

➤ *Passport cancellation:* Prevents travel of potential foreign fighters.

➤ *Citizenship stripping:* Dual nationals convicted of terrorism can lose citizenship.

➤ *Expanded surveillance powers:* Agencies can monitor communications, including metadata.

These laws are among the toughest in the Western world. Critics argue they infringe civil liberties, but supporters insist they are necessary given the scale of the threat.

Community cooperation and its limits

Counterterrorism depends partly on cooperation from Muslim communities. Authorities rely on tips about suspicious activity. Yet cooperation is often limited.

Reasons include:

➤ *Distrust of Police:* Perceptions of discrimination discourage engagement.

➤ *Fear of retaliation:* Informants risk ostracism or harm from within community.

➤ *Ideological sympathy:* While most Muslims reject violence, some sympathise with Islamist grievances, creating reluctance to report.

This gap leaves authorities reliant on surveillance rather than community policing, which significantly increases the costs and reduces effectiveness.

Deradicalisation programs

Australia, like other nations, has attempted deradicalisation. Programs seek to rehabilitate extremists through counselling, education, and mentorship. Results are mixed.

➤ *Successes:* Some individuals disengage from violent networks, especially when given alternative identity and purpose.

➤ *Failures:* Others feign reform, only to reoffend upon release. The persistence of ideology makes transformation difficult.

Internationally, Saudi Arabia's deradicalisation programs have claimed success, though sceptics note many graduates return to jihad. Western efforts, including in Britain and France, show limited results. Australia continues to experiment but faces many challenges: ideology is not easily erased. Without genuine conversion of heart and mind, deradicalisation, more often than not, will fail.

Cyber warfare and propaganda

Networks invest very heavily in online propaganda. ISIS revolutionised this space with professional videos, magazines, and social media campaigns. Even after territorial defeat, its propaganda continues to inspire. Australia faces a rather unique challenge: radicalised individuals consume will this material privately, beyond any community scrutiny. Encryption makes detection difficult. Authorities must develop cyber capabilities equal to the threat.

Counter-narratives are essential. Governments and Muslim leaders attempt to produce content debunking jihadist ideology. Yet such efforts often lack credibility. Only voices perceived as authentic can counter propaganda effectively.

Balancing freedom and security

Australia's counterterrorism response raises ongoing tension between freedom and security. Expansive laws risk eroding civil liberties. Excessive surveillance may alienate communities. Yet failure to act invites catastrophe.

This balance is delicate. In liberal democracies, security agencies operate under public scrutiny. Mistakes fuel distrust; overreach invites backlash. Yet complacency carries deadly cost. Australia must navigate this tension carefully, ensuring that liberty is preserved without leaving doors open to jihadist networks.

Christian reflection

For Christians, the presence of organised Islamist networks is sobering. It reveals the persistence of spiritual warfare.

As Paul wrote, *"Our struggle is not against flesh and blood, but against the rulers, against the authorities, against the powers of this dark world and against the spiritual forces of evil in the heavenly realms."* (Ephesians 6:12).

The battle is not only political but spiritual. Networks are fuelled by ideology that enslaves minds. Counterterrorism is necessary, but only the gospel can transform hearts.

At the same time, Christians must support just action by the state. Romans 13 affirms the role of government to restrain evil. Intelligence, policing, and legislation are legitimate means of protecting society. The church must therefore be praying for authorities, engage communities, and proclaim Christ as the true Prince of Peace. Only the gospel provides freedom that no jihadist network can offer.

Implications for Australia's future

The preceding sections have examined terrorism, radicalisation, networks, and counterterrorism responses. These realities are not temporary. Islamist security threats will remain part of Australia's landscape for the foreseeable future. The challenge, therefore, is not merely to be reacting to individual plots but considering the long-term implications.

How should Australia prepare? What does the balance between liberty and security require? What lessons can Christians and policymakers draw as they seek to safeguard the nation while preserving its democratic identity?

Security as a permanent challenge

One implication is clear: Islamist security threats are not going away. Even if ISIS or al-Qaeda were to vanish tomorrow, the ideology that fuels them endures. The notion of global jihad, rooted in particular interpretations of Islam, continues to inspire individuals and groups.

This means that our security agencies cannot expect a *"post-terrorism"* world. Instead, they must operate on assumption that vigilance will always be required. Just as the Cold War defined an era, the War on Terror defines ours. Australia must accept Islamist extremism as ongoing, not episodic.

Military readiness and regional threats

Security challenges extend beyond domestic policing to military readiness. Australia is geographically close to Southeast Asia, where Islamist groups operate.

1. *Indonesia:* Jemaah Islamiyah and its offshoots remain active. Though weakened since the Bali bombings, they retain capacity.
2. *Philippines:* ISIS affiliates in Mindanao have staged major assaults. In 2017, militants occupied Marawi City, holding it for months. The Philippines remains a base for jihad in the region.
3. *Malaysia:* While more stable, Malaysia faces radicalisation and has arrested hundreds of suspected militants.
4. *Afghanistan and Pakistan:* Though distant, events there ripple globally. The Taliban's return emboldens extremists worldwide.

Australia cannot ignore these developments. Instability in our region directly impacts national security. Military cooperation, training, and deployment may be necessary to prevent Islamist strongholds from emerging nearby.

Border security and immigration controls

Another implication is the need for robust border security. Islamist threats exploit weak borders, whether through foreign fighters, asylum systems, or covert financing.

Australia has long maintained strict border controls, particularly through offshore processing. Critics condemn these policies, but from security perspective, they reduce risk of infiltration by radicals. Immigration screening is essential. Refugee programs must balance compassion with vigilance, ensuring entrants do not carry extremist ideology.

This does not mean rejecting all Muslim migrants, as some are now advocating, but it does mean we must recognise that Islamic extremism poses unique risks. Failure to acknowledge this endangers national security.

Civil liberties under pressure

Counterterrorism will inevitably put pressure on civil liberties. Strong surveillance powers, preventive detention, and passport cancellations expand state authority. Critics fear an erosion of democratic freedoms.

This tension is real. Democracies risk losing their character if they sacrifice too much liberty in pursuit of security. Yet they risk lives if they neglect vigilance. The balance requires our constant evaluation. Laws must always be proportionate, targeted, and accountable. Transparency and oversight help ensure security measures do not become tools of oppression. But naivety is equally dangerous. Islamist threats require strong state capacity.

Social cohesion and integration

Security is not only about police and intelligence. It is also about social cohesion. Alienated communities provide fertile ground for extremism. If Muslims in Australia feel marginalised, radical ideologues exploit resentment. If integration fails, enclaves become security risks.

This means that immigration, education, and cultural policy intersect with security. If multiculturalism tolerates segregation, it undermines safety. Assimilation that affirms shared values strengthens it. Australia must promote unity. Citizenship must mean more than paperwork; it must mean loyalty to the nation and its freedoms. Integration is security policy.

The growing burden on security agencies

ASIO, AFP, and state police already devote enormous resources to counterterrorism. Islamist threats consume a disproportionate share of attention relative to the community size. This strains capacity. Other threats like cybercrime, espionage, organised crime — all compete for resources.

If Islamist threats grow, agencies may be overwhelmed. This underscores importance of prevention. Reducing radicalisation will reduce the burden on security services. Failure to address ideological roots ensures endless policing.

The risk of complacency

Australia's relative success in foiling many plots may breed some complacency. Citizens may assume the threat is exaggerated because major attacks have been rare. Yet this overlooks reality: attacks are rare precisely because agencies remain vigilant.

History warns against complacency. The U.S. felt secure before 9/11. Spain before the Madrid bombings. Britain before the 2005 London attacks. Catastrophe often follows when nations relax. Australia must resist this temptation.

Economic costs of insecurity

Security threats will also carry economic costs. Counterterrorism requires billions in spending. Tourism suffers when threats rise. Communities fractured by fear experience reduced productivity. For example, after the Bali bombings, Australian tourism in Indonesia collapsed. After the Sydney Siege, business confidence wavered. A major attack in Australia could trigger widespread economic disruption. Investing in prevention is therefore not only moral but economic necessity. Safety underpins prosperity.

Implications for the Muslim community

The presence of Islamist threats also impacts ordinary Muslims. They face scrutiny, suspicion, and pressure. While many reject extremism, they are often caught in its shadow.

This dynamic can often fuel resentment, creating a vicious cycle. Extremists then exploit this by claiming Muslims are victims of discrimination, recruiting on that basis. Authorities must balance vigilance with fairness, always avoiding collective blame while still confronting real threats.

Muslim leaders also bear responsibility. They must denounce not only violence but the ideology behind it. Silence enables radicalisation. Genuine cooperation strengthens security.

The church's role in a security context

Christians, though not security agencies, have a part to play. The gospel offers what counterterrorism cannot: transformation of hearts. Deradicalisation programs falter because ideology persists. Only Christ can liberate conscience fully.

The church must therefore:

➤ *Pray* for authorities, as Paul urged (1 Timothy 2:1–2).
➤ *Support* efforts to preserve peace, recognising government's God-given role (Romans 13:4).
➤ *Reach* Muslims with the gospel, offering freedom in Christ.
➤ *Model* courage, refusing to live in fear.

Security threats are sobering, but they should not silence the church. Instead, they should energise mission.

What's on the horizon?

In the long run, Islamist security threats will raise profound questions for Australia's identity. Will the nation defend its freedoms robustly, or compromise them for false peace? Will it integrate communities around shared values, or just tolerate enclaves that breed radicalism? Will it sustain vigilance, or succumb to complacency?

The answers will determine not only safety but also national character. A free, democratic Australia depends on clarity: one law for all, freedom defended, vigilance sustained.

Conclusion

Islam and security are inseparable questions. The ideology of jihad ensures that terrorism, radicalisation, and networks will remain threats. Australia must recognise this as a permanent challenge, not a passing phase.

The implications are vast: military readiness in the region, robust border security, pressure on civil liberties, strain on security agencies, and the need for integration.

Complacency is deadly; vigilance is essential. Christians must respond with courage and truth. They must defend freedom, support justice, and proclaim Christ as the true Prince of Peace. Policymakers must act decisively, balancing liberty with security, compassion with vigilance.

I say it again, Australia stands at a crossroads. To ignore Islamist security threats is to invite disaster. To confront them with clarity is to preserve peace. As the psalmist declares, *"Unless the Lord watches over the city, the guards stand watch in vain."* (Psalm 127:1). Security requires vigilance, but ultimate safety rests in God. Only by recognising both can Australia face the future with hope.

21. ISLAM AND GLOBAL GEOPOLITICS

The global Islamic landscape

When we examine Islam in Australia, we cannot separate it from the global context. Islam is not merely a private religion but a civilisation with serious global ambitions. Its theology, politics, and culture transcend borders.

For Muslims, the *ummah* — which is the worldwide community of believers — takes precedence over national identity every time. What happens in the Middle East, in South Asia, or in Africa inevitably echoes in Australian mosques and suburbs.

Global geopolitics shapes all local realities. To understand the challenge Islam poses to Australia, we must first appreciate the global Islamic landscape.

The Middle East as the heartland

The Middle East remains the epicentre of Islam. It is where Muhammad lived, where the Qur'an was revealed, and where Islamic civilisation first expanded.

Today, the region houses Islam's holiest sites — Mecca, Medina, Jerusalem — and remains the ideological and political heart of the Muslim world.

The Middle East is also riven by conflict. Rivalries between Sunni and Shia, Arabs and Persians, Islamists and secularists dominate its geopolitics. These conflicts are not mere regional squabbles. They shape global energy markets, migration flows, and international security. For Australia, dependent on global trade and part of Western alliances, Middle Eastern instability has direct consequences.

The Sunni–Shia Divide

At the centre of Islamic geopolitics lies the Sunni–Shia divide. This schism, dating back to disputes over succession after Muhammad's death, has become one of the most defining fractures in the Muslim world.

- ➢ *Sunnis:* (about 85–90% of Muslims worldwide) emphasise community consensus and have historically dominated political power.
- ➢ *Shia:* (about 10–15%) emphasise the authority of Muhammad's family, particularly Ali and his descendants.

This theological divide fuels geopolitical rivalry. This is certainly the case between Saudi Arabia (Sunni, Arab) and Iran (Shia, Persian). Their competition plays out in proxy wars across the Middle East.

1. *Iraq:* After the fall of Saddam Hussein, Shia dominance grew, supported by Iran. Sunni groups, feeling marginalised, fuelled insurgency, giving rise to al-Qaeda in Iraq and later ISIS.
2. *Syria:* The Assad regime (Alawite, Shia-aligned) was backed by Iran and Hezbollah, opposed by Sunni rebels, funded by Gulf states.
3. *Yemen:* The Houthi movement (Shia) is supported by Iran, while Saudi Arabia backs the Sunni government.
4. *Lebanon:* Hezbollah (Shia) dominates politics, allied with Iran, opposed by Sunni groups and Israel.

The Sunni–Shia divide ensures perpetual conflict, destabilising the region and spilling over into global politics. For Australia, this means instability in energy supply, refugee crises, and the persistence of global jihadist movements.

Saudi Arabia: The guardian of Sunni Islam

Saudi Arabia occupies unique position. As custodian of Mecca and Medina, it claims leadership of Sunni Islam. It has used its oil wealth to export Wahhabism, an austere form of Islam that has inspired radical movements worldwide.

Saudi-funded mosques, schools, and literature spread Wahhabi doctrine across Africa, Asia, and even Australia. Politically, Saudi Arabia seeks to counter Iran and maintain Western alliances. It relies on U.S. military support while projecting Islamic leadership globally.

Its Vision 2030 reforms suggest modernisation, yet its religious establishment continues to promote conservative Islam. For Australia, Saudi influence is felt through funding of Islamic institutions and the ideological impact of Wahhabi teachings among Muslims at home.

Iran: Shia power and revolutionary Islam

Iran represents the Shia pole of Islamic geopolitics. Since the 1979 Islamic Revolution, it has sought to export revolutionary Islam. Its ideology blends Shia theology with anti-Western politics, presenting itself as defender of the oppressed against Western imperialism. Iran has exerted influence through:

➤ **Hezbollah** in Lebanon, a powerful military and political force.

➤ **Militias** in Iraq, deeply entrenched since the fall of Saddam.

➤ **Support for the regime** in Syria, critical to its survival.

➤ **Houthis** in Yemen, threatening Saudi borders.

Iran's nuclear ambitions add a global dimension. A nuclear-armed Iran would shift regional balance, embolden radicals, and destabilise global security. For Australia, Iran matters not only in geopolitics but also in diaspora communities. Iranian influence extends into Western nations through propaganda, lobbying, and diaspora networks.

>> *A direct attack on Australian soil ...*

Literally whilst this chapter was being written, the shocking news broke of the expulsion of the Iranian Ambassador from Australia. This followed a lengthy investigation into the recent fire-bombing of Jewish properties in Sydney and Melbourne. Prime Minister Anthony Albanese reported that our spy agency ASIO has determined Iran was behind the fires that gutted the Lewis' Continental Kitchen in Sydney on October 20, 2024 and the Adass Israel Synagogue in Melbourne on December 6, 2024. Iran's Ambassador to Australia, Ahmad Sadeghi, together with three other Iranian officials, have been expelled, the Australian embassy in Tehran has been closed, and Iran's Revolutionary Guard Corps (IRGC) will be declared a terrorist organisation.

This development changes everything in terms of Australia's security from radical Islamist threats and now, direct attacks. Before this breaking news, there were probably millions in our nation who did not seriously think we are vulnerable to the kinds of attacks we see overseas. This is a giant wake up call.

Turkey: Neo-Ottoman Ambitions

Turkey, under President Recep Tayyip Erdoğan, has also revived Islamic assertiveness. Once a secular republic, Turkey now positions itself as leader of the Sunni world. Erdoğan invokes Ottoman history, projecting influence into the Balkans, Africa, and the Middle East.

Turkey supports Muslim Brotherhood movements, opposes Western allies on some fronts, and uses diaspora communities in Europe as leverage. While maintaining NATO membership, Turkey increasingly charts independent course.

Its control over migration routes into Europe gives it geopolitical power. For Australia, Turkey's influence is less direct but significant, as Turkish communities within Australia reflect political shifts in Ankara.

Egypt and the Muslim Brotherhood

Egypt, the most populous Arab state, is ideological home of the Muslim Brotherhood. Founded in 1928, the Brotherhood seeks Islamic state through gradual Islamisation. Unlike jihadists who embrace violence immediately, the Brotherhood works through political participation, education, and social services.

Though outlawed in Egypt after the 2013 military coup, the Brotherhood's influence persists globally. It inspires Islamist movements in Europe, North America, and even Australia. Its vision — an Islamic society governed fully by Sharia — remains a powerful alternative to secular democracy.

For Australia, Brotherhood-aligned organisations often appear moderate but subtly promote Islamic identity politics, resisting assimilation and advancing Sharia-based norms.

Pakistan: The nuclear powerhouse of Islam

Pakistan plays pivotal role in global Islamic geopolitics. Created as homeland for Muslims of the Indian subcontinent, it combines nuclear weapons with deep Islamist currents.

Pakistan harbours extremist groups such as Lashkar-e-Taiba (responsible for the 2008 Mumbai attacks) and tolerates Taliban networks. Its intelligence services have often played a double game, supporting jihadists while cooperating with the West.

Pakistan's diaspora is very significant. Pakistani communities in Britain and Australia reflect both entrepreneurial success and radicalisation risks. Australia must pay attention to Pakistan's instability. Nuclear-armed jihadist groups represent a serious existential global threat.

Afghanistan and the Taliban

Afghanistan is another critical arena. The Taliban's return to power in 2021 restored Islamist rule. Women's rights collapsed, minorities face persecution, and al-Qaeda has re-established presence. The country once again provides safe haven for jihadists.

For Australia, which lost soldiers in Afghanistan, the Taliban's resurgence is sobering. It demonstrates resilience of jihadist ideology and the limits of Western intervention. It also emboldens extremists globally, showing that patience can defeat superpowers.

Islamist movements beyond the State

While states like Saudi Arabia, Iran, and Turkey dominate headlines, non-state Islamist movements also shape geopolitics.

1. *Al-Qaeda:* Though diminished, it persists through affiliates in Africa, Yemen, and South Asia.
2. *ISIS:* Despite losing territory, its affiliates thrive in Africa (Nigeria, Mozambique) and Asia (Philippines, Afghanistan). Its propaganda still radicalises globally.

3. *Hezbollah:* Both a political party and military force, tied to Iran, with reach into Latin America and beyond.

4. *Hamas:* Governs Gaza, blending nationalism with Islamist ideology. Its conflict with Israel inflames Muslim opinion worldwide.

These groups demonstrate Islamism's adaptability. Even when defeated militarily, the ideology regenerates elsewhere.

Islam and the West

The global Islamic landscape is defined not only by internal divisions but by relationship with the West. Many Muslims perceive Western dominance as humiliation. From colonialism to the U.S.-led wars in Iraq and Afghanistan, resentment fuels Islamist narratives. Jihadists frame violence as defence against Western aggression. This narrative resonates across the *ummah*, linking Muslims in Australia with global struggles. When Israel and Hamas clash, Australian streets see protests. When U.S. troops act abroad, Australian Muslims feel implicated. Global geopolitics becomes local identity.

Global energy and economics

Islamic geopolitics is also economic. The Middle East controls vast oil and gas reserves. Saudi Arabia, Iran, Iraq, and Qatar influence global markets. Instability in the Gulf impacts prices worldwide. Australia, though resource-rich, depends on global trade. Energy shocks caused by Middle Eastern conflict ripple through its economy. Securing shipping lanes and alliances becomes vital. China's strong dependence on Middle Eastern oil adds another dimension. As China expands influence, Australia, aligned with the West, is drawn into geopolitical competition that intersects with Islamic states.

Migration as a geopolitical weapon

Another dimension is migration. Conflicts in Syria, Iraq, and Afghanistan have produced millions of refugees. Islamist groups and authoritarian regimes will sometimes weaponise migration, pushing flows toward Europe just to destabilise societies.

Australia, though geographically distant, faces similar pressures. Refugee arrivals from Islamic nations raise humanitarian questions and security concerns. Balancing compassion with vigilance is complex.

The global Islamic vision

Underlying all these dynamics is the central Islamic vision of a global *ummah*. For a large number of Muslims, national borders are only temporary; ultimate loyalty belongs to Islam. Islamist movements explicitly seek restoration of the caliphate, whether through gradual Islamisation or violent jihad. This vision ensures Islam's geopolitical impact is never limited to one region. It is transnational by design. For Australia, this means that Islam abroad cannot be separated from Islam at home. What happens in Tehran, Riyadh, Ankara, or Gaza shapes the mindset of Muslims in Sydney or Melbourne.

Christian reflection

From a Christian perspective, global Islamic geopolitics reminds us that nations rise and fall under God's sovereignty. Psalm 2 declares: *"Why do the nations conspire and the peoples plot in vain? The kings of the earth rise up and the rulers band together against the Lord and against his anointed."*

Islam's global ambitions mirror this rebellion. Yet the psalm continues: *"The One enthroned in heaven laughs; the Lord scoffs at them."* God is not threatened. His kingdom advances through the gospel, not the sword. For Christians in Australia, this means two things:

➢ *Do not fear.* Global Islamic movements, however powerful, cannot overturn God's plan.

➢ *Do not disengage.* Understanding global dynamics equips believers to pray, act wisely, and proclaim Christ faithfully.

Islam and the Asia-Pacific

While the Middle East remains the heartland of Islam, the Asia-Pacific region is home to the largest concentration of Muslims in the world.

Indonesia, Pakistan, India, Bangladesh, and Malaysia together account for hundreds of millions of believers — far more than the Arab world. For Australia, located on the edge of this region, developments here are not distant concerns but immediate realities. The geopolitics of Islam in the Asia-Pacific directly impacts Australia's security, economy, and future.

Indonesia: The world's largest Muslim nation

Indonesia is by far the world's most populous Muslim-majority country, with well over 230 million adherents. As Australia's northern neighbour, it is of immense strategic importance. On the surface, Indonesia presents moderate face of Islam. Its national ideology, *Pancasila*, affirms belief in one God while promoting pluralism. Successive governments have sought to balance Islamic identity with secular nationalism.

Yet beneath this surface lies tension. Radical Islamist movements operate openly. Groups like Jemaah Islamiyah (JI) carried out the Bali bombings, killing scores of Australians. Though weakened, JI's networks endure. More recently, Jamaah Ansharut Daulah (JAD), affiliated with ISIS, has staged suicide bombings in Surabaya and Jakarta. Islamist influence also grows politically.

The Indonesian Ulema Council issues fatwas shaping public policy. Islamist parties, while not dominant, exert significant pressure. In 2017, Jakarta's Christian governor was imprisoned for blasphemy after mass Islamist protests.

For Australia, Indonesia represents both opportunity and risk. Cooperation on counterterrorism is essential, yet instability or radicalisation in Indonesia would have immediate consequences for Australian security.

Malaysia: A divided path

Malaysia, though smaller than Indonesia, also plays significant role. About 60% of its population is Muslim, with Islam declared the state religion. While Malaysia has long presented itself as moderate, Islamist influence has steadily increased.

Two dynamics shape Malaysia's trajectory:

1. *State Islamisation:* The government promotes Islamic identity to consolidate power. Sharia courts operate alongside civil courts, increasingly encroaching on family and moral issues.
2. *Political Islam*: The Pan-Malaysian Islamic Party (PAS) advocates full implementation of Sharia. Its influence has grown, especially in rural areas.

Non-Muslims, including significant some Chinese and Indian minorities, face restrictions. Conversion out of Islam is nearly impossible. In some states, hudud punishments have been proposed.

For Australia, Malaysia matters as a trade partner, neighbour in Southeast Asia, and potential source of radicalisation. Its growing Islamist tilt is concerning for regional stability.

Bangladesh and India

Bangladesh, though officially secular, faces growing Islamist pressure. Groups linked to al-Qaeda and ISIS have carried out attacks on foreigners, secular bloggers, and minorities. Islamists also influence politics, challenging the fragile balance of democracy.

India, though majority Hindu, is home to over 200 million Muslims. Islamist groups have operated in Kashmir and beyond. Tensions between Hindus and Muslims regularly erupt into violence. India's rivalry with Pakistan ensures that Islamism remains central to South Asian geopolitics. For Australia, both nations matter through migration. Bangladeshi and Indian Muslim communities contribute to Australia's diversity but also import elements of South Asia's religious tensions.

The Philippines: Southeast Asia's Jihadist front

The Philippines, though majority Catholic, has Muslim minority concentrated in Mindanao. For decades, insurgencies have plagued the region. Groups like Abu Sayyaf and, more recently, ISIS affiliates, have staged kidnappings, bombings, and sieges.

The 2017 siege of Marawi saw Islamist militants occupy city for months, demonstrating their capacity. Though defeated, networks remain. Proximity to Australia makes Mindanao a potential staging ground for jihadists in the region. Australia has cooperated with the Philippines military, providing training and support. Yet threat endures. Instability in the Philippines directly affects Australian security.

Uyghur Muslims in China

China's Xinjiang province is now the home to millions of Uyghur Muslims. Beijing views them as a separatist threat and has implemented harsh repression — detention camps, surveillance, restrictions on worship. Human rights groups decry this as cultural genocide. From Islamic world's perspective, Uyghurs are cause célèbre. Islamist groups cite their plight as justification for jihad. Uyghur fighters have joined ISIS in Syria.

For Australia, the Uyghur issue creates a complex dilemma. On one hand, solidarity with persecuted people aligns with human rights commitments. On the other, radicalised Uyghurs may pose security threats. Australia must navigate balance between condemning repression and preventing jihadist exploitation.

Southeast Asia's radical networks

Beyond individual nations, Islamist networks span Southeast Asia. Jemaah Islamiyah, linked to al-Qaeda, established cells across Indonesia, Malaysia, Singapore, and the Philippines. Though weakened, it remains. ISIS affiliates now dominate headlines, but networks overlap. These groups share training, funding, and ideology. They recruit across borders. Their presence means Australia cannot treat extremism as isolated to one country. The region itself is theatre of jihad.

Maritime security and trade

The Asia-Pacific is not only about populations but also maritime routes. The Strait of Malacca, between Malaysia and Indonesia, is one of world's busiest shipping lanes. Islamist groups have considered targeting maritime trade, which would devastate global economy.

For Australia, reliant on sea trade, maritime security is vital. Cooperation with Indonesia, Malaysia, and Singapore really is essential to protect shipping. Islamist threats to maritime routes are indirect but significant.

Migration and refugees

Conflicts in Afghanistan, Pakistan, and Myanmar (Rohingya crisis) have produced waves of Muslim refugees. Many seek asylum in Southeast Asia, some attempt journeys to Australia. Migration is humanitarian issue, but also security concern. Extremists sometimes exploit refugee flows to infiltrate new nations. Australia's strict border policies reflect recognition of this risk. While compassion remains essential, vigilance is necessary. Migration from Islamic conflict zones will remain feature of geopolitics for decades.

The role of international organisations

Islam in the Asia-Pacific today is also expressing itself through organisations such as the Organisation of Islamic Cooperation (OIC), which includes Indonesia, Malaysia, and Pakistan. The OIC lobbies globally for Islamic causes, from Palestinian statehood to anti-blasphemy measures. These initiatives affect Australia indirectly. When OIC pushes UN resolutions against "defamation of religion," it threatens global free speech. When OIC supports radical positions on Israel, it influences Muslim opinion worldwide.

Australia's strategic environment

The presence of vast Muslim populations so close to Australia ensures that Islam is not distant phenomenon but regional reality. Developments in Jakarta, Kuala Lumpur, or Islamabad reverberate in Sydney and Melbourne. Australia's strategic environment requires constant engagement:

➤ *Counterterrorism cooperation* with Indonesia and the Philippines.
➤ *Diplomatic ties* with Malaysia and Pakistan.

> *Balancing human rights* in China with security concerns over Uyghurs.

> *Managing migration flows* from conflict zones.

The Asia-Pacific is Australia's neighbourhood. Islam is its dominant faith. Geopolitics here directly shapes Australia's future.

Christian reflection

For Christians, the Asia-Pacific landscape is both daunting and full of opportunity. On one hand, radical networks threaten regional security. On the other, vast Muslim populations represent mission field. The gospel is advancing quietly in Indonesia, Malaysia, and beyond, often at great cost. Jesus promised, *"This gospel of the kingdom will be preached in the whole world as a testimony to all nations"* (Matthew 24:14). That includes the Asia-Pacific. Christians must not respond to regional Islam only with fear, but also with faith. They must pray for missionaries, support local believers, and bear witness in their own communities.

Implications for Australia

The survey of Islam's global landscape and the dynamics of the Asia-Pacific makes one truth unavoidable: Australia cannot insulate itself from Islamic geopolitics. What happens in the Middle East and Southeast Asia reverberates across Australian cities, suburbs, and policies. The challenges posed by Islamic ideology, migration, and radicalisation abroad shape national security, trade, diplomacy, and social cohesion at home. The implications are profound, requiring a sober reckoning with how Australia positions itself in a world where Islam remains a force.

Australia's strategic position

Geographically, Australia is an island continent, but it is not isolated. It sits on the southern edge of Asia, the region with the largest Muslim populations in the world. Indonesia alone has more Muslims than the entire Arab world combined.

Pakistan, Bangladesh, Malaysia, and India's Muslims add further weight. This proximity means Australia's immediate neighbourhood is now Islamic by demography. It cannot avoid engagement. Any instability, radicalisation, or conflict in these nations inevitably impacts Australia through migration, trade, and from security spillover. Geography makes disengagement impossible.

Alliances and defence

Australia's security posture is shaped by alliances, particularly with the United States. The ANZUS Treaty and participation in Western coalitions place Australia firmly within the Western camp in global conflicts. This has implications:

➤ *Target for Jihadists:* As a strong ally of the U.S., Australia becomes symbolic enemy for Islamist propaganda. The Bali bombings demonstrated this.

➤ *Military deployments:* Australian troops in Afghanistan and Iraq were targeted not for their own actions but because of alliance commitments.

➤ *Ongoing expectations:* Future conflicts involving Islamist groups will likely see Australia participate alongside Western allies.

Australia must therefore maintain readiness. Defence spending, intelligence cooperation, and regional engagement are not optional luxuries but necessities of alliance.

Diplomacy in the Islamic world

Diplomatically, Australia faces a delicate balance. It must uphold human rights and defend its values yet maintain functional relations with Muslim nations.

➤ *Indonesia* – The most critical relationship. Stability and cooperation are vital. Counterterrorism, trade, and maritime security hinge on healthy ties. Yet diplomatic crises (e.g., executions of Australians for drug offences, or blasphemy cases) show fragility of this partnership.

- ➤ *Malaysia* – Important trade partner but increasingly Islamist in domestic politics. Australia must navigate carefully, balancing commerce with values.
- ➤ *The Middle East* – Relations with Gulf states matter for trade and energy, while Israel–Palestine tensions constantly test diplomacy.
- ➤ *Pakistan* – Nuclear power with diaspora links. Cooperation on counterterrorism is important, but instability is a perpetual risk.

These diplomatic ties require realism. Australia cannot expect Islamic nations to adopt Western values. But it must also avoid compromising its principles to appease Islamist demands.

Trade and economic implications

Global Islamic geopolitics intersects with trade in multiple ways.

1. *Energy markets:* Middle Eastern instability impacts oil and gas prices, affecting Australia's economy indirectly.
2. *Halal certification:* Muslim markets demand halal products. For Australian exporters, compliance creates access, but also controversy domestically, as halal certification sometimes funds Islamic organisations.
3. *Trade with Muslim nations:* Indonesia and Malaysia are key markets. Yet trade is not purely economic; it is tied to political and religious expectations.
4. *Sanctions and conflict:* Global conflicts involving Iran or Afghanistan shape trade patterns. Australia must align with Western sanctions, affecting commerce.

Trade, therefore, is never neutral. It is shaped by Islam's global role, creating both opportunities and vulnerabilities.

Security at home

Global Islamic geopolitics inevitably spills into domestic security. Australian Muslims often view themselves as part of global *ummah*. Events in Gaza, Afghanistan, or Kashmir spark protests in Sydney and Melbourne. Global grievances are imported into domestic politics.

This creates security flashpoints:

➤ *Radicalisation:* Foreign conflicts inspire local youth.

➤ *Community division:* Domestic debates mirror global disputes.

➤ *Protests and violence:* Overseas events sometimes trigger unrest at home.

Authorities need to be monitoring how global events shape local dynamics. Security at home is inseparable from the geopolitics abroad.

Multiculturalism under serious strain

Islam's global dimension challenges Australia's multicultural policy. When migrants arrive from Islamic nations, they often carry grievances from abroad. Instead of leaving conflict behind, they import it into Australia. Examples include:

➤ Lebanese Muslim gangs in Sydney connected to Middle Eastern rivalries.

➤ Protests over Israeli–Palestinian conflict polarising communities.

➤ Pressure for recognition of Sharia-based practices under guise of cultural accommodation.

Multiculturalism assumes that all cultures are compatible. But global Islamic geopolitics demonstrates that some ideologies resist assimilation. For Australia, this demands reassessment of integration policies.

Human rights diplomacy

Australia positions itself as defender of human rights globally. Yet Islamic geopolitics complicates this. Criticising treatment of women, minorities, or apostates in Muslim nations often sparks diplomatic backlash. For example:

➤ Criticism of Saudi Arabia over executions triggered trade threats.

> Advocacy for Uyghur Muslims in China creates complex tensions, as some Uyghurs are radicalised.

> Defending Israel against Islamist hostility generates accusations of bias.

Human rights diplomacy requires courage. Australia must uphold truth even when costly. To compromise is to betray its heritage.

The role of international organisations

Islam exerts influence through international organisations. The Organisation of Islamic Cooperation (OIC), with 57 member states, lobbies at the UN for Islamic causes. It pushes for blasphemy restrictions, recognition of Palestinian statehood, and Islamic perspectives in global policy.

Australia, though not member, is affected. UN resolutions backed by OIC shape international law. Pressure for "anti-Islamophobia" measures threatens free speech worldwide.

Australia must resist attempts to globalise Sharia norms through international institutions.

Australia's Christian heritage in global context

In a world of Islamic geopolitics, Australia's Christian heritage is both liability and strength. Islamists target it as emblem of Western "crusaders." Yet this heritage also anchors Australia in values of freedom, justice, and equality.

Christian foundations distinguish Australia from its neighbours. While Indonesia, Malaysia, and Pakistan drift toward Islamism, Australia's heritage equips it to defend liberty. Abandoning this heritage weakens the nation; embracing it strengthens resilience.

Implications for Policy

The implications of global Islamic geopolitics for Australia can be summarised in policy terms:

1. *Defence Readiness* – Maintain robust military alliances, increase regional engagement, and prepare for Islamist insurgencies in Southeast Asia.

2. *Border Vigilance* – Strengthen screening of migrants and refugees from conflict zones, balancing compassion with security.

3. *Integration Policy* – Abandon naïve multiculturalism. Demand loyalty to Australian law and values from all citizens.

4. *Diplomatic Courage* – Speak truth about human rights abuses in Islamic nations, even at economic cost.

5. *Economic Strategy* – Diversify trade to avoid over-reliance on Muslim-majority markets where political risk is high.

6. *International Resistance* – Oppose UN measures that enshrine blasphemy restrictions or Islamic legal norms globally.

These steps are not optional. They are necessary to preserve Australia's freedom in Islamic century.

Christian responsibility

For Christians, the implications go deeper. Global Islamic geopolitics is not only policy issue but gospel issue. The nations raging against God are mission fields in need of Christ. Australian Christians must:

➤ *Pray for the nations*, recognising that God rules over them.

➤ *Support global mission,* sending workers to Muslim lands and diaspora communities.

➤ *Engage politically*, defending freedom and truth at home.

➤ *Live courageously*, refusing fear in face of Islamic hostility.

The global advance of Islam is sobering, but it cannot stop the gospel. Jesus promised: *"I will build my church, and the gates of Hades will not overcome it"* (Matthew 16:18). That includes the gates of Mecca, Tehran, and Jakarta.

Conclusion

Islam and geopolitics are inseparable. From Middle East conflicts to Asia-Pacific dynamics, Islam shapes global order. For Australia, the implications are simply unavoidable: proximity to Muslim-majority nations, vulnerability to refugee flows, strong dependence on alliances, and exposure to global ideological currents.

Australia must respond with clarity. Defence readiness, border vigilance, diplomatic courage, and integration policy are essential. Christians must respond with faith. They must defend freedom, proclaim Christ, and pray for the nations.

Australia's future will be shaped not only by domestic policy but by global forces. The Islamic world surrounds us geographically, challenges it ideologically, and engages it diplomatically. To survive and flourish, Australia must hold fast to its Christian heritage, defend its freedoms, and trust the God who rules the nations.

As Isaiah declared: *"Nations are like a drop in a bucket; they are regarded as dust on the scales... Before him all the nations are as nothing; they are regarded by him as worthless and less than nothing"* (Isaiah 40:15, 17).

Global Islamic power may loom large, but before God it is dust. Australia must therefore look not to fear, but to faith.

22. ISLAM AND THE FUTURE OF THE CHURCH

The challenge of Islam for evangelism and apologetics

The presence of Islam in Australia presents the church with a profound challenge. It is not simply a demographic or political issue, but a spiritual one. For Christians, the rise of Islam is not only a cause for vigilance but an opportunity for witness. Yet evangelism among Muslims is uniquely difficult. Islam is not secularism, where people are indifferent to God, but a rival faith that denies the central truths of Christianity while offering its own comprehensive worldview.

If the church is to remain faithful in an Islamic age, it must take seriously the challenge of evangelism and apologetics. This will require clarity on the differences between Christianity and Islam, courage to proclaim the gospel in the face of opposition, and compassion to engage with Muslims as people created in God's image.

Why Islam is a unique challenge

The challenge of Islam is distinct from other belief systems for a number of important reasons.

1. *Theological rivalry* – Islam is not neutral toward Christianity. It claims to supersede it. The Qur'an explicitly denies the Trinity, the deity of Christ, and his crucifixion. Muslims are taught that Christians are in error, even if they are "people of the book." This creates immediate theological conflict.

2. *Cultural and communal pressure* – For Muslims, religion is not merely personal but communal. Conversion is often seen as betrayal of family and community. Apostates face rejection, hostility, and even violence. Evangelism therefore threatens deep social bonds.

3. *Identity politics* – Islam provides comprehensive identity. To be Muslim is not only to believe certain doctrines but to belong to a civilisation. This makes evangelism feel like cultural assault.

4. *Defensiveness* – Centuries of conflict between Islam and Christianity, from Crusades to colonialism, have created suspicion. Muslims often assume Christian witness is hostile.

5. *Religious zeal* – Unlike secularists, many Muslims are deeply committed to their faith. They pray, fast, and sacrifice. Their devotion, though misplaced, makes them resistant to conversion.

These five factors combine to make evangelism among Muslims one of the most difficult tasks the church faces.

Core theological contrasts

Apologetics requires clarity on differences. Christianity and Islam are not two parallel paths to the same God. They differ at every fundamental point.

1. **God** – Christianity proclaims God as Father, Son, and Holy Spirit—one God in three persons. Islam insists on absolute oneness (*tawhid*), rejecting the Trinity as blasphemy.

2. **Jesus Christ** – For Christians, Jesus is Son of God, fully divine and fully human, who died for sins and rose again. For Muslims, Jesus (*Isa*) is a prophet, born of a virgin, but not divine. The Qur'an denies his crucifixion, teaching that someone else was substituted.

3. **Salvation** – Christianity proclaims salvation by grace through faith in Christ's atoning death. Islam teaches salvation by works—obedience to Sharia, with hope of Allah's mercy at judgment.

4. **Scripture** – Christians affirm the Bible as God's word. Muslims claim the Bible is corrupted and that the Qur'an is God's final revelation.

5. **Assurance** – Christians can know they have eternal life (1 John 5:13). Muslims live with uncertainty, never knowing if their deeds are sufficient.

These contrasts show that Christianity and Islam are simply not compatible. They proclaim different gods, different saviours and different gospels.

Apologetic engagement with Muslims

Engaging Muslims requires careful apologetics. Christians must be prepared to answer questions, challenge assumptions, and present the gospel clearly.

1. *The Trinity* – Muslims often misunderstand the Trinity as polytheism. Apologists must explain that Christians worship one God in three persons. Analogies (e.g., love requiring lover, beloved, and love) can help, but Scripture itself must be central.

2. *The Deity of Christ* – Muslims respect Jesus but deny his divinity. Christians must show that Jesus himself claimed divine authority: forgiving sins (Mark 2:5–7), accepting worship (John 20:28), declaring oneness with the Father (John 10:30).

3. *The cross* – The Qur'an denies crucifixion. Yet history affirms it. The cross is central to Christianity: *"We preach Christ crucified"* (1 Corinthians 1:23). Apologists must show why atonement is necessary: sin requires sacrifice.

4. *The Bible* – Muslims often claim the Bible is corrupted. Yet manuscript evidence shows remarkable reliability. The Qur'an itself affirms the Torah and Gospel (Surah 3:3), creating internal tension.

5. *Salvation by grace* – Works cannot save. Muslims labour under burden of law, never sure of acceptance. The gospel offers assurance: *"It is by grace you have been saved, through faith"* (Ephesians 2:8).

Apologetics is not about winning arguments, it's only about removing obstacles so the gospel can be heard.

Practical challenges in evangelism

Beyond theology, evangelism among Muslims faces a number of practical barriers.

1. *Fear of rejection* – Many Christians hesitate, fearing hostility or awkwardness. Yet Muslims often respect those who speak openly about faith. Silence communicates indifference.

2. *Cultural sensitivity* – Muslims value hospitality and respect. Evangelists must avoid unnecessarily offensive language while still speaking truth.
3. *Time and patience* – Conversions are rare and often slow. Building trust, answering questions, and living consistently may take years.
4. *Community pressure* – Muslims who show interest in Christ face intense opposition. Evangelism must therefore include long-term support networks.
5. *Risk* – In some cases, evangelism may provoke threats. Churches must be prepared to protect converts and witnesses.

These challenges do not nullify mission but demand courage and wisdom.

Examples of evangelism

Throughout history and today, Christians have shared Christ with Muslims at great cost.

➤ *In the Middle East,* underground churches grow despite persecution. Converts risk death but testify boldly.
➤ *In Africa,* Muslims are coming to Christ through dreams and visions of Jesus. Testimonies abound of supernatural encounters.
➤ *In Europe,* Muslim migrants encounter the gospel in refugee camps and churches, many embracing Christ.
➤ *In Australia,* a small but growing number of Muslims have converted, often through personal friendship with Christians.

These stories remind us: the gospel is powerful. Romans 1:16 declares it is *"the power of God that brings salvation to everyone who believes."* Islam, however entrenched, cannot resist Christ's call.

Strategies for engagement

For Australian Christians, several strategies are essential:

1. *Hospitality* – Invite Muslim neighbours into homes. Share meals, build trust. Hospitality breaks barriers.
2. *Friendship* – Genuine friendships open doors. Listening with respect creates space for honest dialogue.
3. *Scripture engagement* – Encourage Muslims to read the Gospels. Many are surprised by Jesus' words.
4. *Prayer* – Pray for Muslims by name. Only the Holy Spirit opens hearts.
5. *Community support* – Provide safe spaces for seekers and converts. Offer discipleship and protection.
6. *Apologetic training* – Equip Christians to answer Muslim objections confidently.

These strategies require church-wide commitment. Evangelism is not for specialists alone but for all believers.

The opportunity facing the church

While Islam poses threat, it also presents opportunity. Never before have Muslims been so accessible. Migration has brought them to Australia's suburbs. Refugees, international students, and professionals live next door. The church no longer needs to send missionaries overseas to reach Muslims; they are here. This is divine providence. Acts 17:26–27 declares that God determines times and places so people might seek him. Muslims in Australia are here by God's design, that they might encounter the gospel. The question is whether the church will seize this opportunity.

The challenge of Islam tests the church's faithfulness. Will it shrink back in fear, or will it proclaim Christ boldly? Will it compromise truth for peace, or will it contend graciously for the gospel? Will it ignore Muslim neighbours, or will it love them as Christ commands?

Jesus promised that the gospel would reach all nations. Islam is not obstacle but mission field. The church must rise with courage, clarity, and compassion. Only then will it meet the challenge of Islam in Australia and beyond.

Discipleship and resilience in the church

If evangelism is the outward challenge Islam poses, discipleship is the inward one. The rise of Islam in Australia forces the church to consider whether its members are resilient, equipped, and courageous. Islam is not merely a theological competitor but a cultural and social pressure. Christians in workplaces, schools, and universities increasingly encounter Islamic perspectives. Converts from Islam often enter churches seeking refuge, only to find congregations unprepared for the complexities of their situation.

The church must therefore take discipleship seriously. A shallow Christianity cannot withstand Islam's confident claims. A fragile faith cannot support those who risk all to follow Christ out of Islam. If the church in Australia is to thrive in the face of Islamic pressure, it must cultivate resilience, train its people, and become a community of refuge.

Many Australian Christians live in comfort. Faith is treated as private preference, not public conviction. Yet Islam confronts believers with direct challenges. Muslims often question Christians: *"How can Jesus be God?" "Why do you worship three gods?" "How can God die?" "Isn't the Bible corrupted?"*

If Christians cannot answer, their witness falters. Worse, some may feel shaken in their own faith. A generation raised on vague spirituality is always vulnerable to confident Islamic apologetics. Muslims are often trained to be able to debate Christianity; many Christians are not trained to defend their own faith.

Discipleship must therefore include apologetics. Believers must be grounded in Scripture, able to give reason for the hope they have (1 Peter 3:15). This is not optional in an Islamic age. It is essential.

Preparing Christians for public life

The presence of Islam's in schools, universities, and workplaces requires preparation.

1. *Schools* – Muslim students often defend their faith passionately. Christian students must be equipped to respond with clarity and respect. Youth groups must train teenagers not only in Bible stories but in apologetics.

2. *Universities* – Islamic societies on campuses are active, promoting Islam and challenging Christianity. Christian students must be confident to engage, not retreat. Campus ministries must prioritise apologetic training.

3. *Workplaces* – Christians may face pressure to accommodate Islamic practices—halal food, prayer breaks, Ramadan celebrations. Discipleship must prepare them to navigate these pressures without compromising faith.

Preparation involves more than knowledge. It requires courage and conviction. As Paul wrote, *"Do not conform to the pattern of this world, but be transformed by the renewing of your mind"* (Romans 12:2). Christians must resist compromise, stand firm, and engage graciously.

Supporting new converts from Islam

One of the greatest tests for the church is whether it will support converts from Islam. For a Muslim to follow Christ is costly. They risk rejection by family, loss of community, and even violence.

In some cases, converts must leave home, abandon career, or live under threat. The church must be ready to receive such believers.

This requires:

1. *Hospitality* – Providing safe housing, meals, and community. Converts often lose everything; the church must become their new family.

2. *Counselling* – Converts may suffer trauma from rejection or persecution. Professional and pastoral support is essential.

3. *Discipleship* – Former Muslims bring unique questions. They must be taught patiently, grounded in Scripture, and equipped to answer old objections.

4. *Protection* – Some converts face real danger. Churches must consider security — keeping locations discreet, protecting identities when necessary.

5. *Integration* – Converts must not be treated as projects but as brothers and sisters. They need roles, responsibilities, and dignity in the church.

Neglecting new converts is not an option. Jesus said, *"Whoever welcomes one such child in my name welcomes me"* (Matthew 18:5). To fail converts is to fail Christ.

Stories of costly discipleship

Around the world, stories abound of Muslims who come to Christ and pay heavy price.

➤ A young woman in Iran converted after a dream of Jesus. When discovered, her family beat her and confined her. She fled, eventually finding Christian fellowship in secret.

➤ In Pakistan, a man who confessed Christ was accused of blasphemy and imprisoned. Fellow Christians provided legal aid and prayed until he was released.

➤ In Australia, converts testify to losing families but finding church as a true family. Some live quietly, fearing discovery; others speak boldly despite threats.

These stories remind the church of its calling. As Hebrews 13:3 exhorts: *"Continue to remember those in prison as if you were together with them in prison, and those who are mistreated as if you yourselves were suffering."*

Equipping leaders

Resilient discipleship requires equipped leaders. Pastors must teach doctrine with clarity, not vague inspiration. Elders must guide congregations through cultural challenges. Leaders must model courage. Training in Islamic apologetics should be part of all theological education. Seminaries must prepare pastors to engage Islam intelligently. Churches should host seminars on engaging Muslims. Church leaders cannot delegate this task to specialists; they must lead by example.

Building communities of refuge

The church must become community of refuge in Islamic age. For converts, this is literal: they need safety and support. For all believers, it is spiritual: they need encouragement to stand firm. This requires deep fellowship. Shallow Sunday Christianity will not suffice. Believers must share lives, support one another, and carry burdens together. In Acts 2, the early church devoted itself to fellowship, breaking bread, and prayer. Such community is antidote to fear and isolation.

Facing pressure in the public square

As Islam grows in Australia, the pressure increases on public institutions. Schools add Islamic holidays, businesses provide halal certification, politicians court Muslim votes. Christians may feel marginalised if they resist.

Discipleship must prepare believers to face such pressure. Jesus warned: *"If the world hates you, keep in mind that it hated me first"* (John 15:18). Believers must expect opposition. But they must respond with grace, not bitterness. They must speak truth boldly yet love sincerely.

The role of prayer

Resilience is not merely intellectual but spiritual. Christians face not only human arguments but spiritual forces. Paul reminds us Ephesians 6:12: *"Our struggle is not against flesh and blood, but against the rulers, against the authorities, against the powers of this dark world and against the spiritual forces of evil in the heavenly realms."* Prayer is therefore central. Churches need to be praying for courage, wisdom, and protection. They must intercede for Muslims, for new converts, for the authorities. Without prayer, discipleship becomes self-reliance; with prayer, it becomes Spirit-empowered.

Preparing the next generation

Perhaps the greatest challenge is preparing the next generation. Children growing up in Australian schools, encounter Islam as peer religion. They must be taught from early age who Jesus is, why he is unique, and why Islam is false gospel.

Families must disciple children at home. Churches must teach children's and youth ministries with seriousness, not entertainment. If the next generation is not grounded, Islam's confident claims will sweep many away.

Discipleship in Islamic age demands seriousness. It is not enough to produce nominal Christians. The church must produce resilient disciples—believers who know their faith, stand firm under pressure, and love Muslims with compassion.

As Paul exhorted Timothy: *"Guard the good deposit that was entrusted to you — guard it with the help of the Holy Spirit who lives in us"* (2 Timothy 1:14). That is the task before the church in Australia.

The mission of Christ in an Islamic age

The rise of Islam in Australia and across the globe does not only pose significant threats; it also creates unprecedented mission opportunities. For the first time in history, millions of Muslims live in secular democracies where they can freely hear the gospel. Migrants, refugees, and students who once lived behind barriers of culture, language, or law now live next door. Islam may advance socially and politically, but God in His providence has positioned the church to bear witness to Muslims in ways never before possible.

The question is not whether the church will face Islam—it already does. The question is whether the church will retreat in fear or advance in mission.

The Great Commission and the Muslim world

Jesus' command in Matthew 28:19–20 to make disciples of all nations includes Muslims. For centuries, the Muslim world was considered one of the hardest mission fields. Missionaries often struggled to gain access, facing expulsion or death.

Yet in the modern world, migration has brought Muslims into contact with Christians at scale.

The Great Commission compels the church not to see Muslims as threats first, but as people created in God's image and loved by Christ. While Islam denies the gospel, Muslims are not enemies to be hated but neighbours to be loved.

Evangelistic opportunities in Australia

In Australia, Muslim communities are concentrated in suburbs of Sydney and Melbourne, with smaller communities in Perth, Adelaide, and Brisbane.

These communities will include Lebanese, Turkish, Pakistani, Afghan, Bangladeshi, and Somali backgrounds.

Opportunities for mission include:

➤ *Refugees* – many Muslims arrive fleeing war and persecution. They are open to friendship and often disillusioned by violence done in Islam's name.

➤ *International students* – universities host thousands of Muslim students. For many, it is their first experience of living outside Islamic society.

➤ *Neighbourhoods* – everyday interactions at schools, shops, and workplaces provide natural points of contact.

➤ *Digital platforms* – social media and online ministries reach Muslims privately, where they may explore the gospel safely.

Churches that intentionally engage these opportunities discover that Muslims are often curious about Jesus when approached with respect.

Global evangelistic trends

Globally, reports suggest more Muslims are coming to Christ now than at any other point in history. Factors contributing to this include:

➤ *Dreams and Visions* – many testimonies describe Muslims encountering Christ supernaturally, prompting them to seek out Christians.

- ➤ *Disillusionment* – violence by ISIS, Taliban, and Boko Haram causes many Muslims to question Islam.
- ➤ *Migration* – Muslim refugees in Europe encounter the gospel through churches offering aid.
- ➤ *Bible Translations* – Scripture is increasingly available in local languages.
- ➤ *Christian media* – satellite TV and internet ministries reach millions in closed nations

These trends show that God is at work even in Islamic strongholds. The church must join this movement, not ignore it.

The cost of witness

Yet mission to Muslims is costly. Converts face persecution from families and communities. Evangelists may face hostility, harassment, or worse. In some contexts, churches are attacked for their witness.

In Australia, the cost is less severe but still real. Believers who share the gospel with Muslims may face accusations of "Islamophobia." Converts may lose family ties and live under threat. Churches that welcome them may become targets of suspicion.

The New Testament prepares believers for this. Jesus said: *"You will be hated by everyone because of me, but the one who stands firm to the end will be saved"* (Matthew 10:22). Cost is not accident but expectation of mission.

Building mission-minded churches

For the church to embrace its mission in Islamic age, it must cultivate mission-minded culture. This means:

1. *Preaching mission* – Pastors must teach congregation that reaching Muslims is part of Great Commission.
2. *Training members* – Equip believers to share faith with confidence and respect.

3. *Partnering with ministries* – Support organisations focused on Muslim evangelism, both locally and globally.

4. *Welcoming converts* – Prepare for the reality that evangelism will bring Muslims into church family.

5. *Prioritising prayer* – Mission to Muslims is spiritual battle. Churches must intercede faithfully.

Mission-minded churches see Islam not only as challenge but as opportunity for gospel advance.

Discipling Muslim background believers

When Muslims come to Christ, discipleship must be intentional. Many have deep questions about Trinity, incarnation, and cross. They must be taught patiently, grounded in Scripture, and integrated into community. Challenges may include:

➤ *Family opposition* – Many converts face rejection or violence from relatives. Church must become new family.

➤ *Cultural adjustment* – Converts often struggle with identity, navigating between old and new worlds.

➤ *Ongoing threats* – Some live under fear of exposure. Churches must protect them wisely.

Discipleship must be long-term. The parable of the sower warns against shallow roots. Muslim-background believers need depth to withstand storms.

Mission beyond Australia

Australia's church also has role globally. It can send missionaries, support workers, and partner with churches in Islamic nations. The Asia-Pacific alone holds hundreds of millions of Muslims within reach of Australia's mission agencies. Australian Christians can contribute through:

• *Bible Translation* – Supporting translation into Muslim-majority languages.

• *Refugee Aid* – Providing humanitarian relief in Christ's name.

- *Media Ministry* – Producing digital content that reaches Muslims worldwide.
- *Training Leaders* – Equipping pastors in Muslim-majority contexts.

Global mission must remain a high priority. The gospel is for all nations, including Muslim ones.

Hope for the future

While Islam appears strong, the gospel is stronger. Church history proves this. Roman Empire persecuted Christians, yet gospel triumphed. Communism sought to eradicate faith, yet church grew. Islam may resist, but it cannot stop Christ.

Jesus promised: *"This gospel of the kingdom will be preached in the whole world as a testimony to all nations, and then the end will come"* (Matthew 24:14). That includes Muslims. The future of the church is not retreat but advance.

Conclusion

Islam poses one of the greatest challenges of our time. It denies gospel, pressures society, and seeks dominance. Yet for the church, Islam is not merely a threat but a mission field. The future of the church in Australia will be shaped by how it responds. If the church retreats, it will lose influence. If it compromises, it will lose truth. But if it advances with courage, clarity, and compassion, it will see Muslims come to Christ and disciples grow strong.

The mission of the church is clear: preach Christ crucified and risen, make disciples of all nations, and trust God with the harvest. Islam cannot prevail against the gospel of Christ. As Jesus declared, *"I will build my church, and the gates of Hades will not overcome it"* (Matthew 16:18).

This is the church's future—not fear, but faith; not defeat, but victory; not silence, but proclamation. The mission is costly, but the reward is eternal. The gospel will advance, and Christ will be glorified.

23. AUSTRALIA AT THE CROSSROADS

Nations rarely change overnight. They drift. Gradual shifts in culture, politics, and demographics accumulate until one day a society awakens to find itself transformed. Australia is at such a moment. Though most citizens carry on with their daily routines unaware, the trajectory of our freedoms, values, and identity is being shaped by decisions made today.

The challenge of Islam is not simply a question of immigration policy or community relations; it is a test of whether Australia will even remember its foundations or just surrender them under pressure.

In this chapter I want us to all lift our eyes to the horizon and ask: What future awaits if present trends continue? What alternative future could emerge if the nation stands firm? And what must Christians do in this decisive hour? The answers will determine whether Australia remains free, cohesive, and confident in its heritage — or fragments into a society fearful of its own shadow. Australia faces two possible futures, each shaped by the way it responds to Islam's growing influence.

Future one: cultural submission

If current trends persist, Australia may slowly surrender freedoms in name of tolerance. Speech about Islam will be further restricted, schools will dilute Christian heritage, councils will privilege Islamic festivals and converts will live in fear. Citizens will learn to self-censor, institutions will capitulate, and democracy will be hollow. In such a future, Australia remains prosperous but loses its soul. Liberty becomes a memory, not reality.

Future two: confident freedom

Alternatively, Australia could reaffirm its foundations. It could insist on equal liberty for all, resist pressure to silence debate, and protect rights of converts and critics. It could preserve Christian heritage as source of national values, while extending hospitality without surrender.

In such a future, Muslims would still live here — but under a framework of liberty that prevents domination. Christians would proclaim gospel openly, citizens would speak without fear, and institutions would stand firm.

The choice between these futures is urgent. History shows nations that delay often discover the decision has been made for them by demographic momentum or cultural capitulation.

What is at stake?

The stakes are higher than mere politics. At issue are:

1. *National identity:* What does it mean to be Australian? Is it shared history rooted in Christian heritage, or is it endless accommodation of competing identities until nothing distinct remains?

2. *Freedom of conscience:* Will citizens continue to believe, worship, and speak without fear? Or will some ideas be privileged and others suppressed?

3. *Security and cohesion:* Can Australia maintain unity amid diversity? Or will enclaves grow, polarisation intensify, and violence threaten stability?

4. *Gospel mission:* Most profoundly, will the church be free to proclaim Christ without intimidation? Or will Christians be silenced, converts threatened, and mission curtailed?

These questions are not theoretical. Already, signs of drift are evident. The trajectory must be corrected if liberty is to endure.

The drift toward silence

The greatest danger is not open persecution but gradual silence. As noted in earlier chapters, criticism of Islam is already labelled Islamophobia, satire avoided, and public institutions cautious. Citizens learn instinctively which topics to avoid. This cultural censorship is more effective than law, because it colonises the mind. The drift toward silence also erodes courage.

Over time, people forget what it felt like to speak freely. They adapt to limits, believing them normal. Generations grow up assuming some beliefs cannot be questioned. By then, freedom is lost not by decree but by consent. Australia is not yet there — but the direction is clear. Without correction, silence will deepen.

The role of leadership

Leadership is decisive. Nations drift when leaders lack courage to confront uncomfortable truths. Many politicians today avoid discussion of Islam, fearing backlash. Some actively suppress debate, framing critics as divisive. Yet history shows cowardice never secures peace. Appeasement only emboldens those who demand more.

Australia desperately needs leaders who are willing to:

➤ Speak honestly about Islam's challenge.

➤ Defend equal liberty for all citizens.

➤ Resist intimidation by activist groups.

➤ Uphold Christian heritage as source of national values.

Such leadership will be unpopular with elites but essential for future.

The vital role of the church

Even more decisive is role of the church. Political courage matters, but spiritual clarity is greater. The church must reject temptation to retreat into private faith. Freedom of speech, worship, and conscience are not luxuries but conditions for mission. The church's role includes:

➤ *Proclamation:* Continue preaching gospel openly, regardless of cultural pressure.

➤ *Discipleship:* Equip believers to engage Islam with truth and grace.

➤ *Advocacy:* Defend rights of converts, critics, and communities under pressure.

➤ *Hospitality:* Welcome Muslims with love, showing Christ's character while resisting Islam's ideology.

Why hope remains

Despite dangers, hope remains. Australia has not yet lost its freedoms. Citizens still debate, churches still gather, Christians still preach. The drift is real but not irreversible. With courage, trajectory can be changed.

History reminds us that small groups of determined people often redirect nations. Reformers in England defended liberty of conscience against monarchy. Civil rights leaders in America overturned unjust laws. Early Christians, though minority, transformed Rome with gospel witness. Australia, too, can be redirected if church rises and leaders speak.

A Biblical perspective

Scripture reminds us that freedom is gift but also responsibility. Paul wrote to Galatians: *"You, my brothers and sisters, were called to be free. But do not use your freedom to indulge the flesh; rather, serve one another humbly in love"* (Galatians 5:13). Freedom is not licence but stewardship.

Australia has been entrusted with liberty. To squander it through cowardice is sin of negligence. To defend it courageously is act of faithfulness. The future of nation may depend on whether church remembers this truth.

Looking ahead

This first part of the final chapter has set stage. Australia is at crossroads, facing choice between cultural submission and confident freedom. At stake are identity, liberty, security, and mission. Drift toward silence is real, but hope remains if leaders and church act.

The cost of cultural submission

Freedom is fragile. History shows it is rarely surrendered in a single dramatic collapse but lost step by step, concession by concession, until people discover their liberties gone. Australia today stands at risk of such drift. If current trajectory continues unchecked, the nation of Australia will slowly move into cultural submission.

Liberty lost

The first casualty of submission is liberty.

➤ *Speech* – Already constrained by accusations of Islamophobia, freedom of speech would narrow further. Citizens will avoid criticism of Islam altogether, journalists will self-censor, universities will silence debate. Law may not formally forbid critique, but culture will make it unthinkable.

➤ *Christian faith* – Christian proclamation will be branded intolerance. Evangelism among Muslims will be discouraged or penalised. Converts will live in fear, supported only by underground networks. Churches will hesitate to speak truth, diluting gospel to avoid offence.

➤ *Expression* – Artists, comedians, and writers will internalise taboo. Islam will become off-limits, while Christianity remains mocked freely. Cultural production will narrow, creativity suffocated by fear.

Thus, liberty survives in name but dies in practice. Freedom lost is not only personal but national. Identity itself will shift:

➤ *Heritage Forgotten:* Christian foundations of law, education, and culture will be airbrushed. Christmas, ANZAC Day, and Easter will be rebranded or downplayed to avoid offence. Schools will emphasise multiculturalism while erasing Christian narrative.

➤ *New Norms:* Public institutions will adjust to Islamic sensitivities. Prayer rooms multiply, halal becomes default, gender segregation is tolerated. What was once distinctively Australian becomes bland accommodation.

➤ *Fragmentation:* Rather than shared national story, Australia becomes patchwork of enclaves. Western Sydney or northern Melbourne become culturally Islamic, shaping local councils, schools, and businesses. Unity dissolves into parallel societies.

The cost of submission is identity hollowed until *"Australian"* means little beyond geography.

Security undermined

Submission also weakens security.

> *Intelligence Constraints:* Agencies will hesitate to investigate radicalisation, fearing accusations of profiling. Extremists exploit leniency.

> *Community Shielding:* Radical preachers or organisations will be defended as victims of Islamophobia. Police investigations stall, councils appease, and security gaps widen.

> *Domestic Polarisation:* As mainstream Australians perceive concessions, resentment grows. Far-right groups expand, fuelling tension. Violence becomes more likely, not less.

Submission therefore does not produce peace but instability.

The church is silenced

Perhaps greatest cost falls on the church.

> *Fear of Offence:* Pastors will avoid preaching texts that contradict Islam. Sermons on Christ as only way, or critiques of false religion, will be softened. Evangelism will decline, gospel muted.

> *Persecuted Converts:* Muslim-background Christians will worship in secret, fearing families or communities. Churches offering them fellowship will face intimidation. The cost of discipleship will rise.

> *Institutional Marginalisation:* Chaplaincy programs will cut Christian presence while expanding Islamic services. Christian schools will be pressured to dilute doctrine. Christian voices in public debate will be sidelined.

Silence in church means loss for the whole nation. Without a clear gospel witness, moral clarity vanishes, and culture drifts unchecked.

Generational impact

Cultural submission shapes not only present but generations to come:

- ➤ *Children:* Young Australians raised in schools where Christian heritage is hidden, and Islam celebrated will grow up ignorant of our nation's roots. They will assume equality means privileging Islam. Courage to resist will be absent.
- ➤ *Universities:* Graduates trained in climate of self-censorship will enter professions as journalists, lawyers, and teachers unwilling to question Islam. Institutions will entrench submission.
- ➤ *Political class:* Parties courting Muslim votes will craft policies favourable to Islamic communities. Leaders will avoid any critique of Islam, fearing electoral backlash. Over decades, political courage will atrophy.

Once embedded in a generation, submission becomes normal. Liberty lost may never return.

The illusion of peace

Submission often masquerades as peace. Leaders may argue that concessions will keep harmony. Councils approving mosques, schools cancelling Christmas, media silencing critics — all justified as preserving unity. But peace built on silence is illusion.

- ➤ *Resentment is hidden:* Citizens who feel silenced simmer with anger. Frustration grows, sometimes exploding in extremism.
- ➤ *Communities are divided:* Rather than integrating, Islamic enclaves retreat further, emboldened by concessions.
- ➤ *Truth is buried:* Real issues — women's rights, radical preaching, community intimidation — remain unresolved. Problems deepen, hidden under veil of peace.

True peace is built on truth and justice. Cultural submission will offer our nation neither.

The spiritual dimension of cultural submission

Beyond politics, cultural submission has spiritual cost. Silence about Islam often leads to silence about Christ. When Christians hesitate to proclaim exclusivity of gospel, mission suffers.

When churches downplay doctrine to avoid offence, discipleship weakens. Submission is not neutral. It is a spiritual battle. The enemy delights when truth is muted, when fear triumphs, when gospel hidden. As Paul warned in 2 Corinthians 4:4: *"The god of this age has blinded the minds of unbelievers, so that they cannot see the light of the gospel."* Submission blinds society to truth.

A sobering vision of tomorrow

If this drift continues, Australia in 2050 could look like this:

➤ Cities with Islamic-majority suburbs, functioning as parallel societies.

➤ Councils dominated by Islamic representation, privileging community demands.

➤ Schools minimising Christian heritage, emphasising Islamic festivals.

➤ Media avoiding any critique of Islam.

➤ Converts to Christianity worshipping in secret.

➤ Churches intimidated into silence.

➤ Citizens cautious in speech, fearing accusations.

The nation may remain economically strong, but spiritually and culturally, impoverished. Liberty, which was once a defining foundation, becomes just a memory.

Why this must be faced head-on

Some may argue that such a vision is just alarmist. But ignoring the trajectory ensures it becomes reality. Australia must face cost of submission honestly. Only by confronting consequences can experience the courage to resist. Silence is complicity; clarity is necessity.

Christian reflection

For Christians, this vision is sobering but also clarifying. It reveals the pressing urgency of mission. If submission continues, opportunities to proclaim Christ will narrow. Gospel must be shared while freedom endures.

It also reveals the urgency of discipleship. Believers must be equipped to stand firm when culture drifts. Faith must be resilient, not dependent on approval. Finally, it reveals necessity of prayer. Only God can turn hearts, redirect culture, and preserve liberty. The church must intercede for our leaders, communities, and nation.

A hopeful alternative and the call to action

The vision of cultural submission is sobering, yet it is not inevitable. Nations are not helpless before destiny. They are shaped by choices, values, and courage of people who refuse to drift. Australia still has time to change direction. Freedom can be defended, heritage reaffirmed, and gospel advanced. But this requires clear vision of alternative future — one marked not by fear and silence but by confidence and truth.

A different future

Imagine an Australia that stands firm:

➤ *Freedom of Speech Preserved:* Citizens debate Islam openly without fear. Journalists investigate honestly, comedians satirise fairly, universities permit critique. No idea is insulated from scrutiny.

➤ *Religious Liberty Protected:* Christians proclaim Christ without intimidation. Converts from Islam testify openly, supported by communities and safeguarded by law. Churches grow in confidence rather than retreat.

➤ *National Identity Strengthened:* Australia embraces Christian heritage not with triumphalism but with gratitude. Schools teach truth about foundations, public rituals honour history, and diversity is welcomed within a framework of unity.

➤ *Integration Encouraged:* Muslims living in Australia are invited to participate fully in civic life but without special privilege. They are equal citizens under one law, not enclaves demanding exception.

➤ *Church Courageous:* The church preaches the gospel boldly, disciples converts faithfully and engages culture lovingly.

What is required

This alternative future does not emerge by accident. It requires deliberate action in four key areas:

1. *Political courage:* Leaders must defend liberty even at cost of criticism. They must reform laws that chill speech, resist activist intimidation, and insist on equal treatment for all.

2. *Institutional integrity:* Universities, schools, and councils must resist pressure to privilege Islam. They must preserve neutrality, ensuring freedom for all faiths equally.

3. *Cultural confidence:* Citizens must reject self-censorship, speaking truth with civility. Artists, writers, and comedians must refuse taboos. Media must rediscover commitment to honesty.

4. *Christian witness:* Above all, church must rise. Without spiritual clarity, political courage falters. The church must proclaim gospel, defend freedom, and model love.

This combination of political, cultural, and spiritual courage could secure future of liberty.

The Christian call

Christians in particular carry responsibility. Scripture affirms both value of truth and cost of silence.

➤ *Proclaim boldly:* Paul wrote in Romans 1:16: *"For I am not ashamed of the gospel, because it is the power of God that brings salvation to everyone who believes."* Shame silences, but gospel demands boldness.

➤ *Defend liberty:* Galatians 5:1 commands: *"It is for freedom that Christ has set us free. Stand firm, then, and do not let yourselves be burdened again by a yoke of slavery."* Freedom must be defended actively, not assumed passively.

➤ *Love Muslims as neighbours:* Defending against Islam does not mean hating Muslims. On the contrary, Christians must embody love of Christ, offering friendship and gospel. The church's greatest weapon is not hostility but truth in love.

➤ *Prepare for a cost:* Even if liberty preserved, speaking truth will bring opposition. Jesus warned in John 15:20: *"If they persecuted me, they will persecute you also."* Courage is costly but necessary.

Practical steps for the church

What steps might churches take to ensure they are a beacon of hope in a time of confusion?

➤ *Support Converts:* Create safe spaces, offer discipleship, provide material help.

➤ *Educate Congregations:* Teach truth about Islam's ideology, avoiding both naivety and hatred.

➤ *Engage Politically:* Encourage believers in public service, advocate for policies defending freedom.

➤ *Model Hospitality:* Welcome Muslim neighbours, embodying love while resisting ideology.

➤ *Pray Faithfully:* Intercede for your nation, leaders, and communities.

The cost of courage

Courage will not be easy. Those who speak will be maligned as intolerant. Those who defend liberty will be accused of hate. Those who evangelise Muslims will be criticised as divisive. Yet cost of silence is greater.

The church must decide whether to endure temporary reproach or accept the permanent loss of our freedom. As Hebrews 13:13 urges: *"Let us, then, go to him outside the camp, bearing the disgrace he bore."* Better to bear reproach with Christ than enjoy comfort in silence.

Hope for transformation

While Islam challenges liberty, it also presents mission opportunity. Thousands of Muslims in Australia are hearing gospel for first time. Many disillusioned by Sharia's failures are open to Christ. Converts testify to joy of freedom in Him.

If the church proclaims the gospel boldly, our future may not be one of submission but revival. Muslims turning to Christ could transform communities, creating testimonies of grace. What the enemy intends for oppression, God can use for salvation.

Conclusion

The nation therefore stands at crossroads. One path leads to silence, submission, and hollow freedom. The other leads to courage, liberty, and gospel witness. Decision will not be made in single moment but through countless small choices by leaders, citizens, and church.

If the majority remain silent, submission will certainly advance. If the minority rise with courage, liberty can be preserved. The question is not whether challenge exists but whether Australia will meet it. Australia's future hangs in the balance. Islam poses challenge not only of integration but of freedom itself. Speech, religion, and identity are at stake. The nation may drift into cultural submission or stand firm in confident liberty.

For Christians, the call is clear. Defend our freedom, proclaim the gospel, love Muslims, prepare for a cost. The alternative future of courage is not guaranteed but possible. Hope rests not in politics alone but in God who directs history.

As Jesus promised in Matthew 16:18: *"I will build my church, and the gates of Hades will not overcome it."* Church cannot be silenced, for Christ reigns. Yet whether Australia remains free is question of courage.

May this nation choose liberty over submission, truth over silence, Christ over compromise. And may the church rise as voice of clarity in age of fear, declaring that true freedom is found not in Sharia, not in silence, but in Son of God who sets captives free.

24. EPILOGUE: A CALL FOR COURAGEOUS FAITH

Every generation faces its test. For some, it is war. For others, economic collapse. For others still, political upheaval. For our generation in Australia, the test is quieter, more subtle — yet no less serious. It is whether we will defend the freedoms we have inherited, rooted in Christian truth, against ideologies that seek to erode them. Chief among these threats is Islam.

Throughout this book, we have unveiled Islam's incompatibility with Christianity, its collision with Western freedoms, and its growing influence within Australia. We have examined law, culture, security, politics, and the church itself. The evidence is overwhelming. But evidence alone will never change a nation - decisions will. The crossroads lies before us. The question is urgent: what will we do?

The danger of forgetfulness

History teaches that nations often lose freedom not through invasion but through forgetfulness. They forget what made them strong, what gave them liberty, what bound them together. They assume democracy is permanent when it is fragile. They neglect the moral foundations of society until the house collapses.

Australia risks this very fate. We enjoy freedoms purchased by generations past, yet many have forgotten the Christian soil from which they grew. Secularism tells us values are relative, religion is private, and truth is only subjective. In such confusion, Islam advances — not because it is strong, but because we are weak.

The first need in renewal is memory. We must remember that Australia's freedoms were built on gospel foundations. Our laws, schools, and civic life were shaped by a Christian vision of dignity, justice, and liberty. Without Christ, there is no true freedom.

As Psalm 11:3 asks: *"When the foundations are being destroyed, what can the righteous do?"* The answer is: remember the foundations and rebuild them.

The need for courage

Memory alone is not enough. Courage must follow. Freedom is never preserved by cowards. It requires men and women willing to stand when others fall silent. Courage means speaking truth about Islam, even when unpopular. It means defending one law for all, resisting Sharia's encroachment. It means refusing to sanitise history or silence criticism in the name of tolerance.

Courage is also spiritual. It will mean sharing the gospel with Muslims, even when risky. It means supporting converts, even when costly. It means proclaiming Christ's uniqueness, even when branded intolerant. Such courage does not come naturally. It comes from faith. Paul reminded Timothy: *"For the Spirit God gave us does not make us timid, but gives us power, love and self-discipline."* (2 Timothy 1:7). The Spirit of God equips His people to stand boldly.

A call to the church

The Australian church must wake up! For too long it has been complacent, content with a private faith while our culture drifts. Islam's advance exposes this weakness. A timid church cannot withstand a bold ideology. The church must reclaim confidence in the gospel. It must train believers in apologetics, ground them in Scripture, and call them to holiness. It must welcome converts from Islam, not as projects but as brothers and sisters. It must recover its missionary zeal, seeing Muslim communities not as threats to avoid but as mission fields at our doorstep. Above all, the church must refuse compromise. Interfaith dialogues that blur gospel truth are betrayal. Silence in the face of falsehood is sin. The church must declare boldly with the apostle Peter in Acts 4:12 that, *"Salvation is found in no one else, for there is no other name under heaven given to mankind by which we must be saved."*

A call to leaders

Political and cultural leaders carry weighty responsibility. They cannot protect our freedom through appeasement. They must defend free speech, secure borders, and uphold equality before the law. They must also reform multiculturalism into genuine integration, not relativism.

They must always remember that their authority is given by God to restrain evil and promote good (Romans 13:4). History will not be very kind to leaders who surrendered liberty for convenience. But it will honour those who stood firm, even when mocked. The test of statesmanship is not whether one avoids controversy but whether one tells the truth.

A call to citizens

Yet the future of the nation does not rest in Canberra alone. Every Australian citizen must choose. Freedom is not preserved only in parliaments but also in homes, in schools, in workplaces, and in communities. Citizens must value their heritage, teach their children truth, and refuse silence. They must vote with wisdom, speak with courage, and engage with their neighbours with love and honesty. Freedom is never kept by apathy. Edmund Burke's warning remains true: *"The only thing necessary for the triumph of evil is for good men to do nothing."*

Hope in the gospel

Though the challenge is great, hope is greater. The gospel is not in retreat. Around the world, Muslims are turning to Christ in unprecedented numbers. They are encountering the risen Lord in dreams, in refugee camps, and in underground churches. No ideology, no law, no government can stop Jesus Christ. The same gospel is power for Australia. Islam may advance, but Christ still reigns. As Jesus declared (Matthew 28:18–19): *"All authority in heaven and on earth has been given to me. Therefore, go and make disciples of all nations."* That command includes Muslims. That authority guarantees victory. The final hope is not in politics or policy but in the cross and the resurrection. Christ triumphed over sin and death; He can also triumph over submission and fear. The church must not act from despair but from confidence that His kingdom cannot be shaken.

Which way will Australia turn?

Australia is certainly at a crossroads. One path is compromise — appeasing Islam, silencing Christianity, losing freedom. The other is renewal — recovering our Christian heritage, defending truth, proclaiming Christ.

The choice will not be an easy one. It requires sacrifice. It may cost popularity, comfort, even safety. But it is worth it. For what is at stake is nothing less than the soul of the nation. Moses once placed Israel at similar crossroads: *"This day I call the heavens and the earth as witnesses against you that I have set before you life and death, blessings and curses. Now choose life, so that you and your children may live."*(Deuteronomy 30:19). Australia must hear the same call. Choose life — not submission. Choose truth — not compromise. Choose Christ — not silence.

A final word

This book has been long and heavy. The issues are sobering. Yet the final word is not despair – it is always hope. For Australia is not abandoned. God still rules. The gospel still saves. The church still stands. What is needed is great faith and courage. Faith to trust God's sovereignty. Courage to act boldly. Together, they can shape a future where Australia resists Islam's incompatible demands, preserves its freedoms, and shines as a nation renewed in Christ.

In every generation the church must face its moment of testing. For Christians in Australia, that moment has come in the rise of Islam and the growing drift from our Christian foundations.

I pray that we will not falter at the crossroads. I pray that we will choose truth over lies, courage over fear, faith over compromise. I pray that history will eventually record that in our day, Australia remembered its foundations, resisted Islam's advance, and proclaimed the name of Jesus with clarity and love.

For His kingdom is eternal, His truth is unshakable, His victory is certain. And it is in that confidence, we go forward — not shrinking back but pressing on with the cry of the early church still ringing in our ears: *"We cannot help speaking about what we have seen and heard."* (Acts 4:20).

www.ingramcontent.com/pod-product-compliance
Lightning Source LLC
Chambersburg PA
CBHW051710020426
42333CB00014B/925